DEDICATION

To the three women in my life: Eleanor, Catherine, and Charlotte,
and also to Matt, my son-in-law, who takes care of the last two.

First published in 2015 by Zenith Press, an imprint of Quarto Publishing Group USA Inc., 400 First Avenue North, Suite 400, Minneapolis, MN 55401 USA

The information in this book is true and complete to the best of our knowledge. All recommendations are made without any guarantee on the part of the author or Publisher, who also disclaims any liability incurred in connection with the use of this data or specific details.

We recognize, further, that some words, model names, and designations mentioned herein are the property of the trademark holder. We use them for identification purposes only.

This is not an official publication.

Zenith Press titles are also available at discounts in bulk quantity for industrial or sales-promotional use. For details write to Special Sales Manager at Quarto Publishing Group USA Inc., 400 First Avenue North, Suite 400, Minneapolis, MN 55401 USA.

To find out more about our books, visit us online at www.ZenithPress.com.

ISBN: 978-0-7603-4757-7

Library of Congress Control Number: 2015932618

Editor: Jordan Wiklund
Design Manager: James Kegley
Designer: Simon Larkin

On the front cover: American AR-15 assault rifle. *Shutterstock*

Printed in China

10 9 8 7 6 5 4 3 2 1

365 GUNS
YOU MUST SHOOT

THE MOST SUBLIME, WEIRD, AND OUTRAGEOUS GUNS EVER

T. J. MULLIN

ZENITH
PRESS

CONTENTS

Abu Dabi 8

Chile 39

France 81

Argentina 8

China 41

Germany 94

Australia 10

Czechoslovakia 43

Greece 138

Austria 12

Denmark 53

Hungary 140

Belgium 25

England 55

Israel 141

Canada 38

Finland 77

Italy 144

KEY TO WEAPONS

handgun

shotgun

rifle

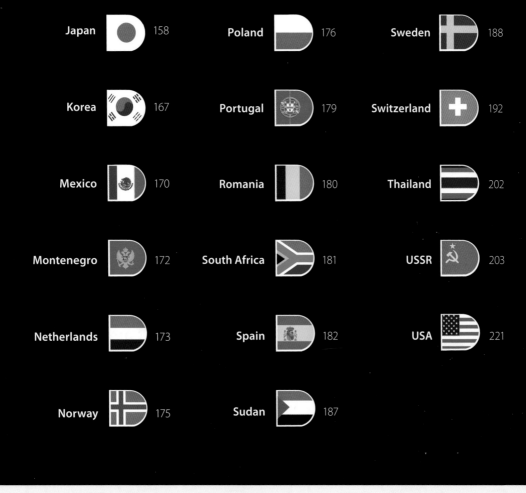

Japan 158	Poland 176	Sweden 188
Korea 167	Portugal 179	Switzerland 192
Mexico 170	Romania 180	Thailand 202
Montenegro 172	South Africa 181	USSR 203
Netherlands 173	Spain 182	USA 221
Norway 175	Sudan 187	

small machine gun

heavy machine gun

large machine gun

INTRODUCTION

When faced with the challenge of picking 365 weapons to shoot, many people may wonder: are there that many firearms to even choose from? Indeed there are, and many more after that. My criteria for picking firearms for this volume were to select the most interesting and useful ones. They also had to be weapons that I have personally shot enough to make intelligent comments about. Unlike many books of this type, each of these weapons has been shot by me, or carried in the field or on the streets for an extended time. Accordingly, I have mainly included weapons that are military, law enforcement, or self-defense-oriented, as that is my field of interest, and only weapons that take cartridges. I do not use cap-and-ball nor flintlock firearms. I do little hunting and have no interest in shotgun field sports. Someone else will need to do the book where those weapons are tested. But if you want the real-deal low-down on serious weapons (in a few hundred words, at least), this is the book for you.

– T. J. Mullin, 2015

CARACAL 9MM MODEL F

Caliber: 9x19mm   **Manufacturer:** Caracal Manufacturing   **Typical Use:** Military, police, and self-defense

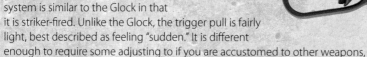

The Caracal is a Glock competitor. Made in Abu Dabi and designed by people who have worked on the Glock, the Caracal seeks to equal the Glock in all aspects and improve in some areas. The trigger system is similar to the Glock in that it is striker-fired. Unlike the Glock, the trigger pull is fairly light, best described as feeling "sudden." It is different enough to require some adjusting to if you are accustomed to other weapons, and I'm not sure it's worth the effort. The angle of the grip is a bit more extreme than the Glock, but good and allows you to hold the weapon deep in your hand, helping control muzzle whip, which results in fast follow-up shots. Accuracy is not as good as I had hoped, as sight adjustment is based on the front sight only—the rear sight is an integral part of the slide. Without different heights of front sights available, proper zeroing is difficult. You are forced to file them down or add material to them to lower the point of impact. I don't believe this weapon will ever displace the Glock, but it is an interesting alternative.

MANNLICHER M1900/M1901

Caliber: 7.63x27.5mm   **Manufacturer:** Steyr   **Typical Use:** Military and self-defense

The Mannlicher M1901 was one of the first auto loading pistols used by modern armies. It reflects a period when pistol designers were unclear about how a pistol should be loaded and what caliber worked best. The pistol is well made and its grip allows the knuckles to line up rather than be staggered across it. The barleycorn front sight makes it difficult to shoot easily. The rear sight is lower with a narrow notch and hard to pick up rapidly. The weapon does shoot accurately, however. The safety is very slow to disengage and requires you to break your grip or carry it hammer-down. If you do that, you need to break your grip to cock it. The recoil causes the safety to flip on, preventing you from firing a second shot. The hammer drops but the gun does not fire because the safety blocks the hammer. The cartridge has very little stopping power, always a flaw in a military handgun. Because of the stripper-clip reloading feature, the weapon must be shot out before it can be reloaded. Frankly, there are better choices.

M91 MAUSER 7.65MM

Caliber: 7.65mm   **Manufacturer:** Mauser   **Typical Use:** Military

Argentina develops and uses excellent military weapons. They adopted the M91 Mauser in 1891. The M91 has a very long barrel, which makes it unwieldy, but the barrel is light enough so the weapon is not muzzle-heavy. The long barrel limits the report of the weapon and minimizes the flash. Recoil is moderate. The front sight is an unprotected typical pyramid front, and the rear sight is a V-shaped notch. This sight is graduated from four hundred to two thousand meters so the rifle's point of aim is too high for typical engagement distances. The sights are hard to see and use even in good light. This hampers accuracy, which is fair. The bolt handle sticks straight out and is smooth, so it can be worked quickly with the palm of the hand. The magazine is a single column, which is awkward to carry. The rifle lacks a bolt-hold-open device. The trigger is a typical two-stage, but is crisp once pulled to the second stage. Although long, the M91 is not unbalanced for either kneeling or off-hand work. In good condition, Argentine M91 Mausers are beautiful examples of pre-1900 German engineering.

At the start of World War II, the Australia Army did not have, and saw no need for, an submachine gun. Events soon changed their minds. A native Australian design, the Owen Gun is odd looking, with unusual characteristics. The Owen uses a top-fed magazine, which looks ungainly but makes shooting from a prone position easy, allowing the shooter to change magazines rapidly. This double-feed magazine, aided by gravity, helps make the Owen reliable. The sights are offset, which seems awkward, but when you raise the weapon to your shoulder, they work perfectly, but only for right-handed shooters. The barrels come out rapidly with a quick-change button which allows for easy cleaning. The cocking handle on the Owen is non-reciprocating. You are not distracted by watching the handle go back and forth as you shoot. The sealing system design on the bolt prevents dirt and debris from getting into the system. The rear sight is a fixed peep, which is very fast to use. It lacks adjustment, but you can adjust the point of aim off the front sight. The front and back pistol grips are handy and give the shooter greater stability. It is preferable to leave the bolt closed and pull it to the rear when you need to shoot instead of using the safety because the bolt may slip forward past the safety, firing the weapon. The Owen is much longer than most modern weapons and almost twice the weight of the MP5. It looks ungainly and odd, but it is easy to handle and very reliable. I rate it as the best SMG in the world made prior to 1946, and it holds up well even compared with more recent weapons.

The Austen can best be
described as combining
the main body of a
Sten, the folding stock
of the German MP40, and the front
grip design of an early Thompson. It was
not produced until towards the end of World War
II. The folding stock on the Austen has a tendency to
wobble, and the metal struts on the stock hit your cheek,
reducing accuracy. The stock lock is difficult, making it hard
to fold and unfold the stock. Because of the front pistol grip,
you risk pinched fingers when folding the butt plate down.
As on the Sten, the safety consists of turning the bolt handle on a slot on the stock, which
is slow. If the weapon is dropped, the bolt can easily jump out of the slot and fire. Generally,
you can retract the bolt and fire faster than you can remove the safety. Wet or cold hands tend to
slip off of the handle. Fine, time-consuming motor skills are needed to pull the bolt back then twist
it down and out of the safety slot. The cyclic rate on the Austen equals the Sten, and both are easy
to fire. Single shots are easy, although a selector does exist. The Austen has a vertical foregrip, which
makes it easier to hold because the side-mounted magazine projects out into the normal grip area,
but its protrusions may present problems in the field, especially when prone.

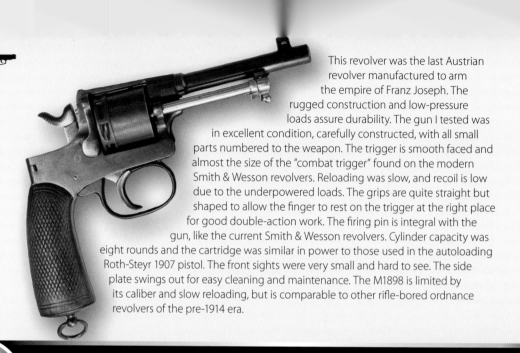

This revolver was the last Austrian revolver manufactured to arm the empire of Franz Joseph. The rugged construction and low-pressure loads assure durability. The gun I tested was in excellent condition, carefully constructed, with all small parts numbered to the weapon. The trigger is smooth faced and almost the size of the "combat trigger" found on the modern Smith & Wesson revolvers. Reloading was slow, and recoil is low due to the underpowered loads. The grips are quite straight but shaped to allow the finger to rest on the trigger at the right place for good double-action work. The firing pin is integral with the gun, like the current Smith & Wesson revolvers. Cylinder capacity was eight rounds and the cartridge was similar in power to those used in the autoloading Roth-Steyr 1907 pistol. The front sights were very small and hard to see. The side plate swings out for easy cleaning and maintenance. The M1898 is limited by its caliber and slow reloading, but is comparable to other rifle-bored ordnance revolvers of the pre-1914 era.

ROTH-STEYR M1907

Caliber: 8mm   **Manufacturer:** Steyr   **Typical Use:** Military and self-defense

Invented by Czech arms designer Karel Krnka, the "Roth"-Steyr was the first auto-loading handgun officially adopted by Austria-Hungary. It is beautifully made and finished. Mine was made in 1910 at the Steyr factory in Austria and is superior to anything you find today, except a SIG P210-1. The trigger system is difficult for target shooting, but an asset in the real world. It uses 8mm Steyr ammo and has a locked breach. This weapon has some unusual qualities. It uses a stripper-clip system to load which, prior to detachable magazines, was attractive. The handgun is difficult to load without the stripper clips, but with practice it is as fast as using a detachable magazine, precluding tactical reload. The stripper clip avoids most malfunctions in autoloaders, which are primarily due to faulty or dirty magazines. On the formal range, the trigger pull and sights were not helpful. On the cinema range, the trigger system worked well. Rapid repeat shots were possible and felt like a typical DA-revolver rather than a self-loader. Recoil is quite light. Grip angle is good and assists rapid indexing and instinctive firing. All in all, this is an impressive pistol. This is one of the most surprising pistols I tested. It seems heavy, bulky, and awkward until actually used where it belongs—in combat situations.

STEYR "HAHN" M1911/M1912

Caliber: 9mm Steyr   **Manufacturer:** Steyr   **Typical Use:** Military, police and self-defense

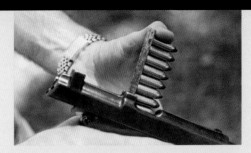

The Austro-Hungarian government adopted this pistol in 1912. "Hahn" refers to the hammer, distinguishing it from the M1907 Steyr. During World War II, the Germans re-barreled many M1912 Steyrs for 9x19mm. It was primarily issued to German troops in Austria. As was common at that time, the Hahn uses stripper clips to load the magazine. This limits the ability to top off a magazine during a lull in combat, but avoids the problem of damaged magazine lips. The pistol uses a rotating barrel lock instead of a Browning-style lock. The front sight is typical barleycorn, small and dark. The rear sight is a shallow V-notch, which makes holding the proper elevation difficult. On the cinema range, the front sight was difficult to pick up, although the shiny metal rear sight block aided triangulation and indexing. The trigger pull is quite abrupt, and it takes discretion to avoid unintentional shots. The trigger is SA-type only with a side-mounted safety on the left. This pistol has an unacceptable and dangerous design flaw: when you push the safety off and pull the trigger, the weapon fires. After firing a few more shots, your thumb tends to bump the safety upward, but not enough to fully engage. The weapon will fire without pulling the trigger when pushed down.

GLOCK 17

Caliber: 9mm Parabellum   **Manufacturer:** Glock GmbH   **Typical Use:** Military and self-defense

The Glock 17, first used by the Austrian Army, has spread throughout the world. There was an initial controversy because it has a synthetic frame. The Glock 17 is probably the best 9mm military handgun on the market today. The sights are quite big for target shooting and the trigger pull is gritty. The trigger system uses a self-cocking mechanism similar to the Roth-Steyr M1907: you pull up on the trigger part way, the firing pin retracts, then you continue the trigger pull to fire. The pull is light and fires readily. The pistol does not recoil as much as many other 9mm pistols, although the Glock 17 weighs approximately one-third less than many others. The sturdy plastic frame has the benefit of having a double-column magazine without the drawback of a wide butt. The Glock, despite its seventeen round magazine, is not any wider than many other conventional single-column 9mm pistols. The Glock 17 has to be rated the number one military handgun today. It is rapidly stripped, efficient to manufacture, low in cost, holds seventeen rounds, has light recoil, and has an ideal safety system. This is clearly one of the waves of the future in handgun design. I recommend it highly for military application, although I do not think it as good for civilian law enforcement due to their concern over the weapon-snatch issues.

GLOCK 18

Caliber: 9mm Parabellum   **Manufacturer:** Glock   **Typical Use:** Military and self-defense

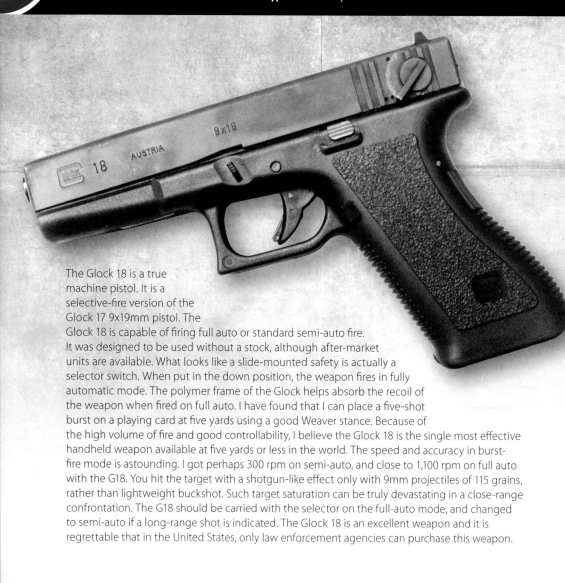

The Glock 18 is a true machine pistol. It is a selective-fire version of the Glock 17 9x19mm pistol. The Glock 18 is capable of firing full auto or standard semi-auto fire. It was designed to be used without a stock, although after-market units are available. What looks like a slide-mounted safety is actually a selector switch. When put in the down position, the weapon fires in fully automatic mode. The polymer frame of the Glock helps absorb the recoil of the weapon when fired on full auto. I have found that I can place a five-shot burst on a playing card at five yards using a good Weaver stance. Because of the high volume of fire and good controllability, I believe the Glock 18 is the single most effective handheld weapon available at five yards or less in the world. The speed and accuracy in burst-fire mode is astounding. I got perhaps 300 rpm on semi-auto, and close to 1,100 rpm on full auto with the G18. You hit the target with a shotgun-like effect only with 9mm projectiles of 115 grains, rather than lightweight buckshot. Such target saturation can be truly devastating in a close-range confrontation. The G18 should be carried with the selector on the full-auto mode, and changed to semi-auto if a long-range shot is indicated. The Glock 18 is an excellent weapon and it is regrettable that in the United States, only law enforcement agencies can purchase this weapon.

GLOCK M20/21

Caliber: 10mm (.45 ACP)   **Manufacturer:** Glock   **Typical Use:** Military, police, and self-defense

These Glocks are big in caliber and size. They aren't heavy, but their grip size makes them difficult if you have small hands. As with all Glocks, they feature the polymer frame and trigger system that has made the weapon famous. Their weather-resistant finish, ease of parts interchange, high durability, light weight, and power levels make the Glock 20/21 great explorers' weapons. The polymer frame in all chamberings seems to soak up the recoil, which is moderate. The trigger system has a lot of creep and stack in it, so fine work is difficult. This is fine when used as a combat weapon, but the ability to place rounds on target is hindered by the trigger, limiting its use as a long-range, outdoor gun. The Glocks are handy to carry even fully loaded, as they weigh less than the equivalent steel-framed Smith & Wessons and Colts. The slide width makes carrying the weapon inside the waistband awkward. It carries well on a belt. If the large grips make handling the weapon difficult, you can get a Robar Grip reduction, which makes the weapon feel much livelier. The big Glocks have not sold well compared to their smaller brothers. They are fine weapons, just too big in the grip.

GLOCK M22

Caliber: 9x19mm   **Manufacturer:** Glock   **Typical Use:** Police and self-defense

Smith & Wesson developed the .40 S&W cartridge in the early 1990s, and Glock quickly modified their 9x19mm pistols for it, making the Glock M22 a common police and self-defense weapon in the United States. Many doubt the efficiency of the .38 Special, and a 9x19mm pistol is just a slightly more powerful auto-loading version. Better ammo and greater round capacity, however, have made people comfortable with a 9x19mm pistol such as the Glock 17/19. Many people still wanted a .45 ACP weapon, but .45 ACP pistols are big for small-handed individuals, and many agencies would not use a "cocked and locked"-style autoloader as a duty weapon. The Glock M22 in .40 S&W offered a modern design in auto-loading pistols, improving on the caliber and capacity. This was an acceptable compromise for many who disliked small bores, but wanted a modern design. The M22 Glock unites everything good about the Glock with a good, effective cartridge. It is deservedly popular.

BLUE GLOCK G17T

Caliber: 9mm simulation   **Manufacturer:** Glock   **Typical Use:** Training for military, police, and self-defense

The Glock G17T is designed to shoot Canadian simulation ammo. It looks and feels exactly like a Glock G17/22, but has many subtle (and not so subtle) changes to permit use of this training ammo only. The pistol has no locking system because the pressure of the training ammo is very low, but relies on slide weight alone to keep it closed when fired. The front sight is shorter than on a standard Glock to insure the projectile hits point of aim, but is otherwise identical in design. The barrel bore is off-set. The pistol, when fired, has a distinctive two-jump recoil feel to it. The bullets, which come in red/pink or blue color, hit at about four hundred fps and definitely can be felt, but will not penetrate the body. They could destroy an eye and cause big welts, so you must wear goggles, a neck guard, a face mask, and heavy clothing. The paint pellets, unlike paintballs, release a small amount of paint. Practice with simulation weapons obviously does not create the same level of stress that real-life situations will bring.. Thankfully, most people have no real-life experience in gun-fighting. But practice will certainly improve ability and confidence, giving you a better chance if faced with a serious confrontation. The Blue Glock, the G17T, is a good training tool.

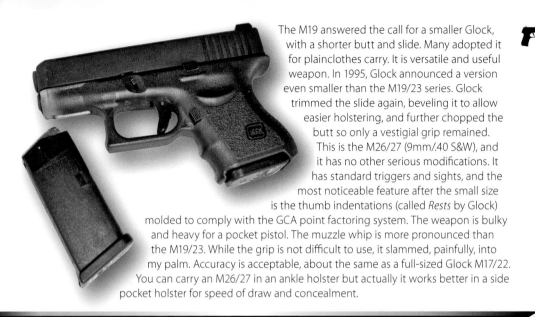

The M19 answered the call for a smaller Glock, with a shorter butt and slide. Many adopted it for plainclothes carry. It is versatile and useful weapon. In 1995, Glock announced a version even smaller than the M19/23 series. Glock trimmed the slide again, beveling it to allow easier holstering, and further chopped the butt so only a vestigial grip remained. This is the M26/27 (9mm/.40 S&W), and it has no other serious modifications. It has standard triggers and sights, and the most noticeable feature after the small size is the thumb indentations (called *Rests* by Glock) molded to comply with the GCA point factoring system. The weapon is bulky and heavy for a pocket pistol. The muzzle whip is more pronounced than the M19/23. While the grip is not difficult to use, it slammed, painfully, into my palm. Accuracy is acceptable, about the same as a full-sized Glock M17/22. You can carry an M26/27 in an ankle holster but actually it works better in a side pocket holster for speed of draw and concealment.

GLOCK M29 10MMMA IN

Caliber: 10mm Auto   **Manufacturer:** Glock   **Typical Use:** Police and self-defense

The M29 is a mini-sized 10mm pistol. The 10mm is not a weak cartridge if you use the full-power loading, which turns most 10mm pistols into real 125-yard weapons. But the M29 has such a short barrel that a full-power 10mm cartridge produces excessive muzzle flip, substantially slowing down repeat shots. The short sight radius coupled with the visually-thick front sight limits your ability to place rounds on target at long distances. The typically spongy Glock trigger greatly impacts performance, particularly for the distances that the 10mm allows. This is not an easy weapon to shoot well. My off-hand test at 50 feet using the defense-10mm loading of choice—135 grain JHP Corbon at 1,240

fps—yielded 98 percent performance with good groups. I was barely able to keep shots on a twelve-inch target from the sitting position at fifty yards, yet I easily achieved two-inch groups with other weapons, such as an M686 4-inch Smith & Wesson, or a Colt National Match pre-war .45 ACP pistol fired the same day. The grip on the M29 is quite short but I can get all three fingers in the weapon. My little finger, however, slides over the bottom of the weapon, hitting the magazine's floor plate, pinching it with each shot. This is not an effective weapon for good groups.

The Glock M37 is chambered for the newly-developed .45 GAP cartridge. It is a blend of the M17-size frame, and M21-size slide. Like all Glocks, the trigger action is a challenge to master, with lots of overtravel. The sights are wide but easily seen, and the frame absorbs much of the recoil impulse. The .45 GAP cartridge uses a shorter case than the 23mm .45 ACP. As a consequence, it can be fitted to the grip size of a pistol that typically fires 9x19mm, yielding the same bullet weight and velocity that comes with a standard .45 ACP round thanks to powder development. The pressure is higher and recoil is sharper, but performance is the same. If you are an agency or person considering this weapon, in light of improved ammo in a cartridge such as 9x19mm, you are better off not selecting the ten-shot .45 GAP pistol instead of the seventeen-shot 9x19mm pistol M17. If you want a .45-caliber weapon, are you better with a thirteen-shot M21 short frame or a ten-shot M37? The power level is the same, slide width identical, and grip sizes are so close that most find the differences inconsequential. Had the .45 GAP had been available in 1911, the .45 ACP would likely not have lived to see its wide popularity today. But since it is in many different weapons, the M37 offers little other than being unique and expensive to shoot.

GLOCK M42

Caliber: .380   **Manufacturer:** Glock   **Typical Use:** Police and self-defense

Pistols chambered for the .380 cartridge are popular with people who have recently obtained concealed-carry licenses. They offer a reasonable degree of stopping power in conveniently-sized packages. Many .380 pistols are easier to shoot than short-barrel .38 Special revolvers, and they hold more rounds. This demand has brought many new .380-chambered pistols into the market. The Glock M42 is perhaps the best of the lot. Recoil is mild as it is a locked-breech weapon. The sights are excellent as on all Glock pistols, and the slide and receiver are quite slim so the pistol fits into the pocket quite nicely. The Glock M42 uses the standard Roth-Steyr/Glock firing system, which has proven successful by many different levels of shooters. There is no manual safety to be disengaged, so it is fast to use. A proper pocket holster will keep the trigger from snagging, and perhaps firing, when placed in the pocket. All told, the M42 is an excellent .380-chambered weapon. However, you must carefully consider whether the cartridge is powerful enough for your purposes. The first duty of a weapon is to perform as you need it to.

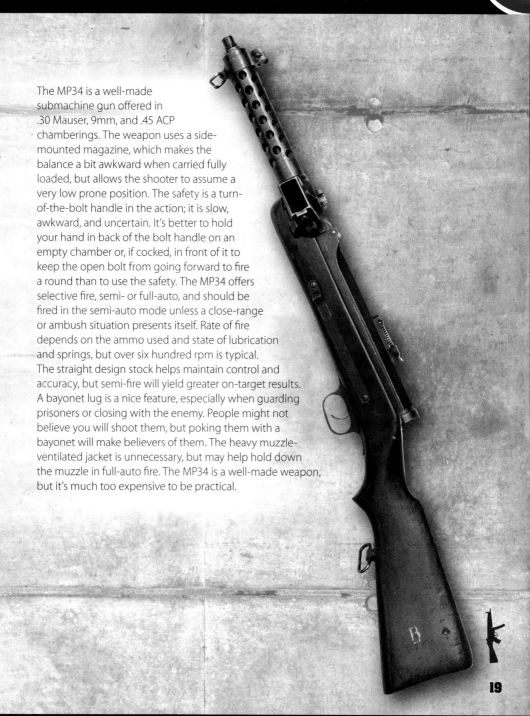

MP34

Caliber: 9mm (.30 Mauser, .45ACP)   **Manufacturer:** Steyr   **Typical Use:** Military and police

The MP34 is a well-made submachine gun offered in .30 Mauser, 9mm, and .45 ACP chamberings. The weapon uses a side-mounted magazine, which makes the balance a bit awkward when carried fully loaded, but allows the shooter to assume a very low prone position. The safety is a turn-of-the-bolt handle in the action; it is slow, awkward, and uncertain. It's better to hold your hand in back of the bolt handle on an empty chamber or, if cocked, in front of it to keep the open bolt from going forward to fire a round than to use the safety. The MP34 offers selective fire, semi- or full-auto, and should be fired in the semi-auto mode unless a close-range or ambush situation presents itself. Rate of fire depends on the ammo used and state of lubrication and springs, but over six hundred rpm is typical. The straight design stock helps maintain control and accuracy, but semi-fire will yield greater on-target results. A bayonet lug is a nice feature, especially when guarding prisoners or closing with the enemy. People might not believe you will shoot them, but poking them with a bayonet will make believers of them. The heavy muzzle-ventilated jacket is unnecessary, but may help hold down the muzzle in full-auto fire. The MP34 is a well-made weapon, but it's much too expensive to be practical.

The AUG rifle system lends itself to a conversion to 9x19mm chambering. All the features of the AUG rifle are found with the AUG 9x19mm SMG in bullpup length: good optical sights, poor trigger pull, and a magazine release system which is fairly slow to operate. Still, it feels quite nimble in comparison to its major competitor, the MP5. The AUG 9x19mm SMG may be easier to maintain in the field than the MP5, which has many nooks and crannies to keep clean. But since both weapons are typically used for light-duty police-type operations, it may not matter much. The real issue is whether an AUG 9x19mm is better than a fourteen-inch 5.56x45mm AUG. The power level of the 9mm is lower, as is the blast. Felt recoil and length are much the same. With the advent of good 5.56x45mm ammunition such as the Blitz 40 gr. load, the issue of over-penetration (always a major police concern) is effectively gone. Police organizations might well want to standardize one ammo chambering, so the 9x19mm AUG gets the nod there. The low muzzle blast is an excellent feature for most shooters' purposes.

STEYR M81

Caliber: 9mm   **Manufacturer:** Steyr   **Typical Use:** Military and police

The Steyr M81 developed from the M69. The M69 was a simple, blowback SMG designed to compete against the Uzi for countries that did not want to buy an Israeli weapon. The M81 used many of the M69's good features. It changed the way the bolt was retracted, going back to a traditional design. The M81's cyclic rate is low enough to allow firing single shots while in burst mode, and the trigger action made firing semi quite easy. The trigger action is well designed; a partial pull results in semi-fire, a full pull gives full-auto fire. In an emergency, this trigger system is fast and offers ease of switching firing modes. The M81 is built on a stamped, square-size frame. Magazine release is adequate. The magazine is in the grip, which makes changing it easy, but makes the grip too wide for many people's hands. Sights are a good peep rear and a black front post. The safety is a thumb-operated push button easily manipulated by right-handed shooters. The weapon feels lively in the hands, but the wire butt stock is hard on the cheekbones. The stock can be placed in two positions to permit either smaller shooters or those wearing ballistic vests or winter clothing to effectively utilize the weapon. While it is a decent weapon, there are many weapons that surpass the M81, such as the Beretta and Star SMG if you prefer open-bolt, HK MP5 if you prefer closed-bolt.

STEYR SPP/TMP

Caliber: 9mm   **Manufacturer:** Steyr   **Typical Use:** Military, police, and self-defense

The Steyr SPP (Special Purpose Pistol) is the semi-automatic version of the TMP (Tactical Machine Pistol). As such, it lacks the selective-fire feature as well as the forward grip. I was disappointed at how it shot in the instinctive style and when placing the rear of the receiver against the stomach. The magazine, safety, and bolt release are well placed, but I was not satisfied with the actual performance, even at fifty feet. Still, all of those noted controls were far superior to those found on the Micro Uzi or SP89. Using a standard Weaver-style, two-hand hold produced much better results. Sights are a bit rough and too dark for quick pick up in dim light, but they are fine in good light. The Steyr SPP offers a hold-open device so you know when the last shot is fired. The magazine in the grip makes it fast to reload in the dark. The Steyr's polymer frame is less bulky and has a better grip feel to it than the metal Micro Uzi frame. Equipping the Steyr SSP/TMP with a small dot-style optical sight makes for a very nice, deadly package. The Steyr SPP fits a few closely-defined market niches. It allows US consumers to get a weapon that otherwise they could not freely own which is similar, if not identical, to the machine pistol version. For the collector, this is important. It is also an effective self-defense weapon.

STEYR M95 8X50R

Caliber: 8x50R   **Manufacturer:** Steyr   **Typical Use:** Military, police, and self-defense

The M95 Steyr was the standard Austrian service rifle during both World Wars, and was re-chambered by the Germans to 8x57mm during World War II. It is a straight pull bolt-action rifle, fast to operate. The standard rear sights are calibrated from 600 to 2,600 meters with two battle sights. The basic one is set for five hundred meters, but raising the slide to three hundred meters exposes a V-notch. These raised, projecting slides tend to catch on things, so many soldiers only used the five hundred-meter sight. When you wrap your hand around the rear of the action, the safety operates quickly. The trigger guard on this rifle is small, and would not accommodate a gloved or mittened hand. The barrel is quite long but light weight, and it will get hot after a few quick shots. This long barrel adversely affects balance but it does help reduce muzzle blast. If the sights were more practically regulated, the straight-pull action, coupled with a decent trigger pull, would make for a nice shooting rifle.

AUG

Caliber: 5.56mm   **Manufacturer:** Steyr   **Typical Use:** Military and self-defense

The Austrian AUG (Army Universal Gun) is a modern bullpup in 5.56x45mm. Adopted in 1977, it had a groundbreaking plastic design, had a rapidly-detachable barrel, and unlike anything else at the time, came standard with an optical sight. Standard barrel length is twenty inches, but fourteen-, sixteen-, and twenty four-inch lengths also exist and can be easily installed. The weapon utilized a front forward grip, a feature now copied by many military rifles. Steyr claims the scope/mount are nearly indestructible. The rifle offers a short overall length. The drawback is a poor trigger pull due to the linkage involved. Parts for a left-handed shooter are available, but not likely to be found in the field. If you shoot it off the opposite shoulder, you must use great care not to put your face where a fired case will strike it. The large trigger guard allows me to shoot it with winter mittens in place, and the safety is fast to operate. On selective-fire AUG rifles, pulling partially back yields semi-fire, while a full pull to rear results in full-auto fire. Rate of fire is around 900 rpm in my test but, thanks to the straight line stock, is quite controllable. The cleaning kit in the butt of the rifle is nice, and current versions have all the typical rails on them for all the fashionable lights and sights to be installed.

STEYR STG 77 AUG LMG

Caliber: 5.56x45mm   **Manufacturer:** Steyr   **Typical Use:** Military

The Steyr STG 77 LMG is a variant of the standard Steyr infantry rifle chambered for the 5.56x45mm cartridge. It is not really a light machine gun, but more of a squad automatic weapon.
It uses the same AUG-style stock but has a longer and heavier barrel than the infantry rifle. A heavy, multiple-position bipod is affixed to the muzzle area. The LMG variant uses a forty two-round magazine, although it can use the standard thirty-round magazine. This longer magazine can be problematic when shooting prone without the bipod, or if shooting uphill. The cyclic rate on the AUG is high, and it takes effort to get two-shot groups. The trigger system of halfway back on the trigger to semi, all the way back to full-auto is also likely to result in inadvertent bursts of fire. The muzzle-heavy bearing of the STG 77 LMG allows better groups at all ranges than that found with a standard infantry rifle when fired prone on full-auto. The safety is a cross-bolt flipper style that falls readily under the thumb. The easily-replaced barrel is handy on this LMG variant. The magazines are translucent and easily loaded without tools. The optical sights on the weapon are one of its best points. The STG 77 LMG uses an optical sight with a crosshair in it rather than a simple circle like those on the standard infantry rifle version.

BROWNING M1910/22

Caliber: 7.65mm (.32 ACP; .380 ACP) **Manufacturer:** Fabrique Nationale, Herstal SA
Typical Use: Military, police, and self-defense

The Browning M1910 was designed to be a pocket pistol, but the military only accepted it once the M1910/22 version came out. The models are identical except that the M1910/22 has a longer barrel and butt, and the firearm is available in 9x17mm (.380) as well as 7.62x17mmSR (.32 ACP) calibers. The Dutch and Yugoslav armies adopted it before World War II, and more than one million M1910 pistols and a large quantity of M1910/22s were produced. The front sight is small, shallow, and thin, and the rear sight is small, making it difficult to properly index on the cinema range. The safety is well placed and with practice could be rapidly flipped on and off. As with most steel-framed .32 ACP pistols, recoil is low, and heavier in .380 caliber. This pistol weighs almost as much as a Glock 17 or Colt Commander .45, making the weight-to-power ratio bad. The pistol lacks a hold-open device to indicate when the pistol is empty. This pistol would seem to be a poor military choice, given its sights, caliber, safety, and weight-to-power ratio. But when it appeared in 1922, there was a dearth of semi-automatic pistols being produced for the military. The M1910/22 looked good to those seeking a new weapon; it does not hold up against what is available today.

BROWNING P35

Caliber: 9mm Parabellum **Typical Use:** Military, police, and self-defense
Manufacturer: Fabrique Nationale, Herstal SA or John Inglis Co. Also made in Argentina, Indonesia, Israel, and Hungary.

The P35 is considered John Browning's crowning achievement. The Belgian Army adopted it prior to World War II to replace the M1903 9x20mmSR long pistols. The German Army used it during World War II. For many years, it was the only double-column 9mm handgun in production. Its fourteen rounds were the highest capacity of any pistol. The P35 Hi-Power has some shortcomings. The safety on all the factory guns is much too flat and difficult to push off rapidly. To compensate, most people either carry the weapon with the hammer down and a round in the chamber, and then try to cock the hammer, which is always slow and inefficient, or they fit larger non-standard safeties, which allow a bigger platform from which to push off. Although it is reliable, the P35 is typically heavy for its caliber. The grips are thick and the safety is difficult. Despite its design shortcomings, people love these pistols. The FBI "Super SWAT" National Hostage Response Team (HRT) carried them, as did the British Special Air Service (SAS) units. There is no better recommendation.

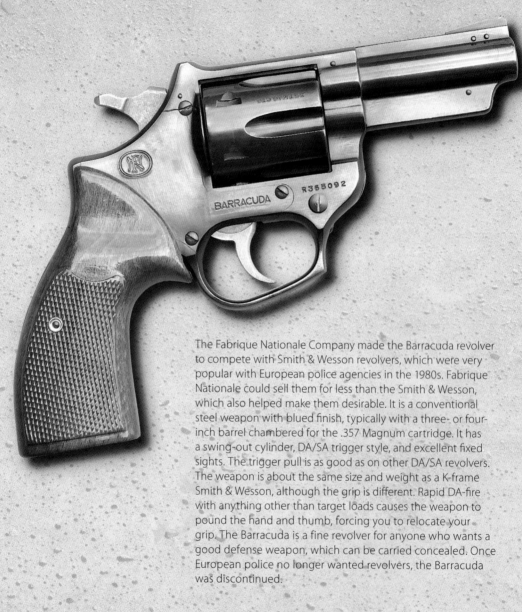

The Fabrique Nationale Company made the Barracuda revolver to compete with Smith & Wesson revolvers, which were very popular with European police agencies in the 1980s. Fabrique Nationale could sell them for less than the Smith & Wesson, which also helped make them desirable. It is a conventional steel weapon with blued finish, typically with a three- or four-inch barrel chambered for the .357 Magnum cartridge. It has a swing-out cylinder, DA/SA trigger style, and excellent fixed sights. The trigger pull is as good as on other DA/SA revolvers. The weapon is about the same size and weight as a K-frame Smith & Wesson, although the grip is different. Rapid DA-fire with anything other than target loads causes the weapon to pound the hand and thumb, forcing you to relocate your grip. The Barracuda is a fine revolver for anyone who wants a good defense weapon, which can be carried concealed. Once European police no longer wanted revolvers, the Barracuda was discontinued.

FN FIVE-SEVEN

Caliber: 5.7x28mm   **Manufacturer:** Fabrique Nationale, Herstal SA   **Typical Use:** Military, police, self-defense, and hunting

The FN57 is a polymer-framed weapon of concealed hammer construction. It weighs 1.36 pounds (22 ounces) with a loaded weight of 27 ounces. Though the FN is long through the grip, it is not thick, and is comfortable to hold. The FN57 comes in two versions: a DAO-style, on which you must pull the trigger through a long arc to fire, and the tactical version, on which the trigger works through a much shorter arc. There is no jolt at the end, so the pull is better than most of today's autoloaders. The DAO model lacks a safety. The tactical model has a safety located immediately above the trigger. It is awkwardly placed and difficult to remove or apply with any certainty or speed. It's best to ignore it and keep your finger off the trigger until ready to fire. The sights are nicely shaped and offer a good sight picture. They come with a night sight and standard three-dot sights. Fixed and adjustable styles are available. The plastic magazines have double-feed lips, not a double-column going to a single-feed system, so they are quite easy to load. The pistol lacks a magazine safety. A variety of ammo are available, which yield excellent penetration on armored subjects, and still give fine stopping power on a non-armored target. The FN's ability to use these varieties of ammo with their excellent performance makes it a star.

FNP .45

Caliber: .45 ACP   **Manufacturer:** Fabrique Nationale, Herstal SA   **Typical Use:** Military, police, and self-defense

When the Special Operations Command (SOCOM) of the US Army announced it wanted a new issue pistol, many manufacturers were interested. It was Fabrique Nationale who developed the FNP .45. Due to SOCOM's requirements, this is a very fine, reliable military weapon, but less effective as a civilian defense or police handgun. The pistol is big. The slide is thick and the butt is wide so it can accept the .45 ACP cartridges in a twelve-or-more shot capacity. The grip panels are replaceable to allow for bigger or smaller hands. They are checkered, which is hard on bare hands but fine if wearing gloves. The weapon is a selective DA/SA style but the safety lever (located on both sides) is thin, making it hard to disengage rapidly. The DA pull is heavy and long, and the SA pull has a lot of overtravel to it. Sights are nice and visible, and certain models can be equipped with an optical red dot sight. Accuracy is acceptable and, due to the size and weight, felt recoil is low. Conventional rifling is used, so lead bullet reloads can be utilized.

Fabrique Nationale developed the FN P90, then promoted it as a military weapon for those who didn't want a rifle, but needed a weapon they could shoot from the shoulder. The P90 can easily be shot off either shoulder. The top-mounted magazine is difficult to replace quickly, so the fifty-shot capacity is smart. The safety is conveniently located. You must not push down on it as you slide it into the fire position or it will bind. Your non-shooting hand goes through the trigger guard with your thumb wrapping around it to make certain your hand does not migrate in front of the muzzle. Recoil is very light. Fast semi-fire is easy, as are good bursts. The standard ammo offers a penetrator so that the bullets penetrate ballistic vests and helmets commonly used today. Good tracer rounds exist, as well as subsonic rounds to be used with a suppressor. You must be careful when you select optical sights. If they are too big, the weapon is awkward. A small dot-sight like an RMR allows you to use it on man-size targets at two hundred yards, and makes for a nimble package on close-range targets.

This was the first post–World War II semi-auto rifle made in quantity by Fabrique Nationale. You typically find it in 7x57mm, 8x57mm, and .30-06, as it came out before the 7.52x51mm NATO round became dominant, although some were made in that chambering. The ABL is much like the FAL rifle. It is stocked like a conventional rifle with no separate pistol grip, and it contains a ten-shot magazine that is slow to detach, but the sights and the way it shoots are similar to the FAL. You load the stripper clips through the top of the ABL's receiver. The rifle cannot be loaded with a round in the chamber. The stock feels thick in the hand. The safety lever, which pivots on the trigger guard, is slow to remove. You must push it firmly with your trigger finger to disengage it. The trigger guard is also small, hindering operation with mittened hands. The sights are scaled from one hundred to one thousand meters, and are similar in appearance to those on the FAL, improving on Fabrique Nationale's prior efforts. The weapon fieldstrips easily. Because the weapon uses a gas-operated system, recoil is lighter than expected. The ABL does not have a chromed barrel, so you must exercise care when using corrosive ammo to make certain that all residue is out of the system to avoid clogging it up. The ABL is a good rifle, although its wood stock, weight, and limited magazine capacity are drawbacks.

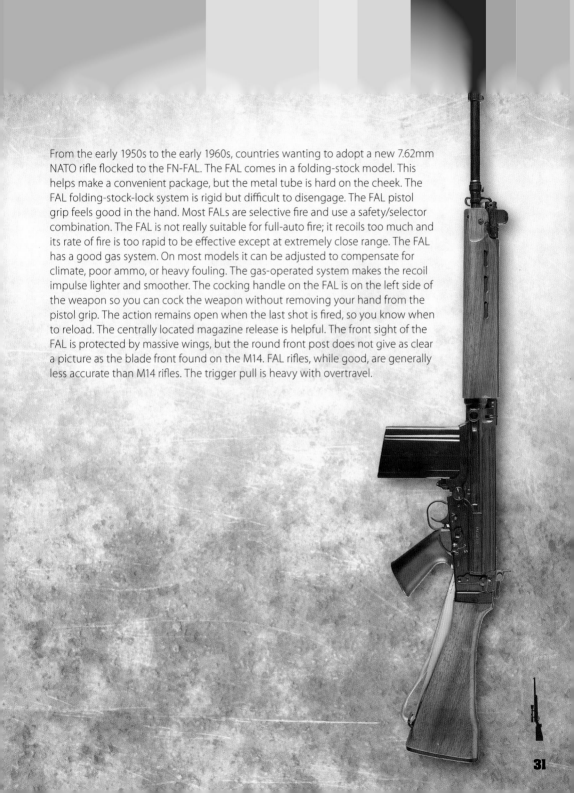

From the early 1950s to the early 1960s, countries wanting to adopt a new 7.62mm NATO rifle flocked to the FN-FAL. The FAL comes in a folding-stock model. This helps make a convenient package, but the metal tube is hard on the cheek. The FAL folding-stock-lock system is rigid but difficult to disengage. The FAL pistol grip feels good in the hand. Most FALs are selective fire and use a safety/selector combination. The FAL is not really suitable for full-auto fire; it recoils too much and its rate of fire is too rapid to be effective except at extremely close range. The FAL has a good gas system. On most models it can be adjusted to compensate for climate, poor ammo, or heavy fouling. The gas-operated system makes the recoil impulse lighter and smoother. The cocking handle on the FAL is on the left side of the weapon so you can cock the weapon without removing your hand from the pistol grip. The action remains open when the last shot is fired, so you know when to reload. The centrally located magazine release is helpful. The front sight of the FAL is protected by massive wings, but the round front post does not give as clear a picture as the blade front found on the M14. FAL rifles, while good, are generally less accurate than M14 rifles. The trigger pull is heavy with overtravel.

When the United States convinced its NATO allies to use the 5.56x45mm cartridge as the new standard, weapons were needed for it. The FNC became the new Belgian service rifle. The rifle has an involved muzzle-braking flash hider and grenade launcher combination. The flash hider works. I had no grenades to test. The sights are a typical cylindrical post which adjusts tor elevation by screw threads. The front and rear sights are protected by wings. The rear sight is adjustable for windage only. It has two peeps for 250 and 400 meters. The bolt handle is on the right side and curves upward; you can easily cock it with either hand. The FNC's dust cover is attached to a spring. As the bolt travels to the rear, the cover flips down, allowing the bolt to clear it; as the bolt goes forward, the cover returns to its original position. This helps protect the weapon from dirt and water. The FNC uses M16 magazines which are widely available. The magazine release is set up for right-handed shooters, but you can release it with the left hand by wrapping your fingers around the front of the magazine. The selector/safety and pistol grip are similar to the FAL. Trigger pull on the FNC is spongy and has creep and overtravel. The rifle has a three-shot burst system.. The FNC comes with a fixed fiberglass stock or a folder. The folder is tube-like and comfortable on the cheek because of the low recoil energy of the caliber. The lock on the stock is excessively involved. You must push the button in and push down on the stock while you swing it open. Doing these things simultaneously is difficult, and you tend to pinch your fingers. The forearm of the FNC is better protected from heat than many and not as bulky as others. You can grasp it easily, and even one hundred rounds fired rapidly will not get it too hot. It does not cover the gas tube. If you grasp the weapon around the top, the gas tube will burn you. The FNC is a well-made, reliable weapon, as easy to use as an AR15 or M16A2 rifle.

FN FS 2000

Caliber: 5.56x.45mm   **Manufacturer:** Fabrique Nationale, Herstal SA   **Typical Use:** Military, police, and self-defense

Bullpup rifles give you full-length barrel while retaining a short overall length. The drawbacks are a trigger which, due to linkage, is not very crisp, magazines which are hard to change, and the fact that you can't fire it off your left shoulder. The FN FS2000 rifle resolves this last issue. Empties are pushed through a centrally-located tube, and once five have been fired, they are pushed out the front at the shooter's feet. Thus, the shooter can use the weapon off either shoulder without restriction or having to hold the weapon in some odd way. It is difficult to tell if the rifle is empty. You must lift the back hatch, peer into the action, then insert a finger to "feel empty." While not difficult, if you have fired a lot of cartridges, you risk being burned on a hot chamber. Trigger pull on the FS2000 is not great. Changing the magazine is slow and hardly instinctive. The weapon is fairly short but not especially light. The compact size is not a big enough plus to overcome the other negatives, but if you want a bullpup-type rifle, this is clearly superior to others available, such as the FAMAS, AUG, and L85A1.

SCAR 16/17, SCAR 16 SBR

Caliber: 7.62 x81, 5.56x45mm   **Manufacturer:** Fabrique Nationale, Herstal SA   **Typical Use:** Military, police, and self-defense

When the US Military announced it was considering replacing the Colt M4 rifle, manufacturers saw an opportunity to make big bucks and prepared a number of alternatives to meet the military's criteria. Fabrique Nationale submitted the SCAR rifle. It is a reliable weapon with many good features. The SCAR comes in two chamberings (5.56x45mm and 7.62x57 NATO) and many barrel lengths. The rifle can alternate chamberings so one receiver can be used with either 5.56 or 7.62 parts. I have shot many versions of the SCAR rifle. Accuracy is not match-grade due to the poor trigger pull rather than to an inherent design flaw. The pull is heavy, gritty, and has much overtravel. The safety is well located, although the lever is short and difficult to flip with the thumb without breaking your grip. There is no winter trigger guard, so you cannot shoot the weapons wearing mittens. The rifle has rails on all sides, which make mounting optics easy. You may want to add a pistol grip in the summer to the bottom forward rail, as firing several quick magazines will make the weapon too hot to hold. The fold-down front and back sights are excellent. The sliding butt stock allows the reach to be greatly adjusted. The cheek comb rest allows you to place your head on exactly the right position to use your optical sights so a proper cheek weld can be maintained. Sling swivels are conveniently located. The bolt handle can be shifted from one side to the other, and it is also big and strong enough so you can kick it with your boot to open the bolt if needed. These are good weapons, although somewhat heavy and difficult to get good results with. They are not as nimble as other weapons that compete with them.

FN-D
Caliber: 7.62x51mm, 30.06, 8x57, 7x57, 7.65 Argentine   **Manufacturer:** Fabrique Nationale, Herstal SA   **Typical Use:** Military

The FN-D model is the ultimate BAR, with all the good points of a BAR plus two improvements: the quickly-detachable barrel and the variable cyclic rate. To detach the FN-D's barrel, push the button on the forearm and pull the carrying handle up. Using the same handle, pull the barrel forward and it will come out of the receiver. Insert a new barrel by the handle, push down on the handle once the barrel is fully seated. The barrel has cooling fins on 40 percent of its length, helping to dissipate heat. The D Model uses the standard BAR gas system, which is a nuisance to clean when fired with corrosive ammo, but a reliable way to get a weapon to function. An integral bipod is pinned to the weapon. Sights are typical pyramid-front V-notch rear graduated out to 1,500 meters, which may be unrealistic. The receiver has a dust cover permanently attached. If you put it on with the bolt closed, racking the bolt will disconnect it, which is handy. The action is full-auto only but with two cyclic rates. The trigger system uses a mousetrap device to create a rate reducer. On slow fire, with a cyclic rate of 300 rpm, single shots are easy. On regular fire, with a cyclic rate of 650 rpm, firing single shots is difficult. The weapon does not have a semi-auto-only setting. The butt stock is solid wood and stable. The pistol grip and forearm are also wood. I find the grip on the FN-D uncomfortable: the wood overlaps the metal pistol grip and the trigger guard is not large. The weapon can be quickly disassembled without tools for full cleaning and repairs, but repairs are rarely needed.

FAL HEAVY BARREL

Caliber: .308   **Manufacturer:** Fabrique Nationale, Herstal SA   **Typical Use:** Military

The FAL rifle is the standard by which all other .308 battle rifles are measured. Only the advent of the 5.56x45mm cartridge caused it to pass from the scene. Shortly after the infantry rifle FAL was released, the heavy-barrel variant appeared. The only difference is a longer, heavier barrel and a steel bipod. Converting an infantry rifle into a squad automatic weapon has never been totally successful. The heavy barrel and steel bipod at the front make for a heavy, poorly balanced rifle. The bipod on the weapon swings back and forth, which makes it noisy and constantly ill balanced, catching everything you pass. If you tip the weapon upside down, the legs spring out and can hurt your hands or face. The heavy-barrel variant of the FAL is often equipped with a thirty-round magazine to make it appear more like SAW. Unfortunately this magazine is so long it hits the ground when firing prone. While the heavy-barrel FAL with bipod in use will be more accurate firing on full-auto than the standard rifle, the cyclic rate is too high, and even the heavy-barrel variant is too light for good, full-auto results past three hundred yards.

The FN MAG 58 is one of the three major machine guns of the post–World War II era in the West. It has been used worldwide and has never been found wanting. The MAG 58 is heavy and ill balanced. It is almost impossible to shoot off-hand from the shoulder, although kneeling makes it possible for short periods. It is best fired from the prone position from its bipod or, better yet, tripod. The MAG is a gas-operated gun but has adjustments to compensate for fouled conditions or weather. The barrel can be quickly removed without touching it and just as easily installed by using its sturdy handle. It is a durable and well-built gun. My friend, the late Kent Lomont, put 250,000 rounds through one without breaking a part. The sights on the MAG are good, offering a peep rear sight on the tangent. Taking time to carefully sight in the weapon with its various barrels will pay off. The weapon uses either German MG3 belts or M60 links. The cyclic rate is low enough to fire single shots easily, and 3-to-5 shot bursts are easy to maintain. The MAG fires its rounds smoothly. The pistol grip is comfortable. There is a push-through safety that can be operated with the thumb. It is not convenient and I do not trust safeties on open-bolt guns. Ignore it, except in ambush positions, and rely on cocking the weapon when ready to fire. The MAG is really too heavy to be used at the squad level, but a couple of them at the platoon level can be valuable.

ROSS MK III (M-10) .303

Caliber: .303 British   **Manufacturer:** Ross Firearm Co.   **Typical Use:** Military

The Canadian Army stopped using this weapon during World War I, as the bolt tended to blow out, hitting the shooter's eye. Respected Canadian author and Army World War I veteran Herbert McBride, however, thought it a wonderful, accurate rifle. The bolt stayed in during my testing, although accuracy was not great. This may have been due to the sights, which were well worn and wobbled. The MK III has a long sight radius, a peep rear sight located close to the eye, and a front sight that is square on its face and flat-topped. The trigger pull is excellent. The weapon's weight and long barrel length make both recoil and report light, so it was pleasant to shoot. The weapon balanced well, making off-hand shooting easy. Perhaps the major problem with the Ross—except the bolt difficulty—is the peep sight; when it's up, there is a gap between the sight and the mounting site. The gap is almost the same size as the peep. My eye kept catching the gap, using it as the peep sight. The problem worsened when shooting rapidly, and would be difficult in the dark. Having no experience with Ross straight-pull rifles prior to my tests, I was surprised to find this weapon very fast. With a straight-pull rifle, you avoid two steps needed with a standard bolt action: lifting the handle at the beginning and pushing it down at the end. I have read that straight-pull rifles have trouble when dirty, but improved uniformity of cartridges would solve most of these issues. These straight-pull rifles are so much faster than even the slickest bolt actions, and are well worth trying.

The FAMAE 9mm SMG is based on a shortened STG 90 (SIG 550) action modified to accept 9x19mm ammo, and is meant to compete with the HK closed-bolt SMG. It is as good as an HK MP5 but much less expensive, yet it has not found a market among military or police organizations. The stock folds readily and does not feel painful on the cheek as the HK MP5 unit can. The bolt and receiver are exactly like the STG 90 and the cocking handle is pleasant to use and a good size. The sights are like those found on the MP5, but the open notch is for fifty yards with peeps at 100 and 150 meters, which are realistic ranges for a 9x19mm SMG. Access to the magazine release was a bit tight between the trigger guard, but acceptable. The weapon lacks a swing-away trigger guard for winter use. The test weapon had a four-position safety. To use it, you must break your grip. This is too complicated to be efficient. The cyclic rate of the weapon and the short receiver length (thus short bolt movement) was quite high. Attempts at two-shot bursts too easily went to three. The weapon does not lock open on the last shot fired. The magazines are double-column feed-type, easily loaded, and made out of translucent plastic. They interlock so the shooter can put two or more together. The FAMAE SMG shoots well. At sixty yards firing single shots, whether from off-hand or any other position, it delivers everything its higher-priced German cousin does.

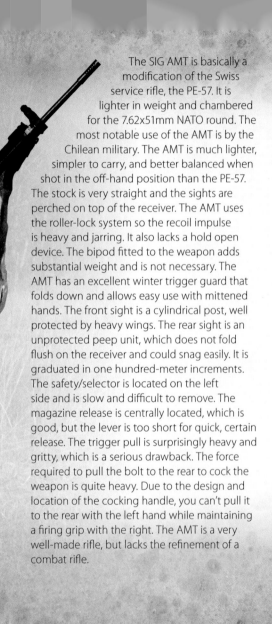

The SIG AMT is basically a modification of the Swiss service rifle, the PE-57. It is lighter in weight and chambered for the 7.62x51mm NATO round. The most notable use of the AMT is by the Chilean military. The AMT is much lighter, simpler to carry, and better balanced when shot in the off-hand position than the PE-57. The stock is very straight and the sights are perched on top of the receiver. The AMT uses the roller-lock system so the recoil impulse is heavy and jarring. It also lacks a hold open device. The bipod fitted to the weapon adds substantial weight and is not necessary. The AMT has an excellent winter trigger guard that folds down and allows easy use with mittened hands. The front sight is a cylindrical post, well protected by heavy wings. The rear sight is an unprotected peep unit, which does not fold flush on the receiver and could snag easily. It is graduated in one hundred-meter increments. The safety/selector is located on the left side and is slow and difficult to remove. The magazine release is centrally located, which is good, but the lever is too short for quick, certain release. The trigger pull is surprisingly heavy and gritty, which is a serious drawback. The force required to pull the bolt to the rear to cock the weapon is quite heavy. Due to the design and location of the cocking handle, you can't pull it to the rear with the left hand while maintaining a firing grip with the right. The AMT is a very well-made rifle, but lacks the refinement of a combat rifle.

TYPE 85 W SILENCED SMG

Caliber: 7.62x25mm   **Manufacturer:** Chinese state factories   **Typical Use:** Military and police

All military and most police forces need a suppressed SMG, and the Chinese knew there were many clients to sell it to. The test example was lightweight, unlike many suppressed SMGs. The Chinese offer a heavy-ball subsonic load, but we only had standard military surplus 7.62x25mm ammo. While not nearly as quiet as a good 9mm suppressor on an SMG, it reduced the noise level to a remarkable degree. I could shoot it without hearing protection. There was a lot of powder blowback and after firing a round, the next two up for chambering were covered with a sooty residue. It uses standard iron sights and has a mount on top of the tube for other options. The weapon lacks a bolt lock and this, coupled with the light-pressure recoil spring, could result in a round being picked up and fired if dropped. The safety lever is convenient to use, with safe in the middle, top single shot, and the bottom full-auto. As it is meant to be fired in the semi- mode, the reverse would be a better approach for rapidly disengaging the safety to shoot. The suppressor grows very hot after thirty rounds. The weapon has a fast cyclic rate, but I could get off two-shot bursts readily. The suppressor works well on full-auto. The pistol grip feels good in the hand and the weapon is comfortable to carry, balanced well, and was lively. I could easily hit a ten-inch plate at sixty yards firing on semi; at ten yards, head shots on a man-target were easy. Even with heavy ball ammo, the noise level is quiet enough to not be noticed in a normal urban setting. This was a very impressive piece of kit. It is reliable and works perfectly to achieve its intended purpose.

China got the machinery to build the Russian-designed SKS rifle in the 1950s and has since built millions of them. The SKS rifle is a fine semi-automatic rifle but is limited by its integral box magazine, which holds ten rounds that must be fed with a stripper clip. Because of the available manufacturing capability and the desire to improve the SKS rifle, the Type 63 and 68 were developed. These rifles are modified to accept the AK47 magazine and are capable of selective fire. The addition of the box magazine was a real improvement; the selective fire capability is less useful, as experience shows that shoulder-fired, full-auto weapons are generally useless. Testing using the full-auto feature made it clear the weapon is difficult to control; second, third, and subsequent shots typically went high and over the shoulder of man-targets. The weapon became too hot to hold after rapidly firing two magazines.

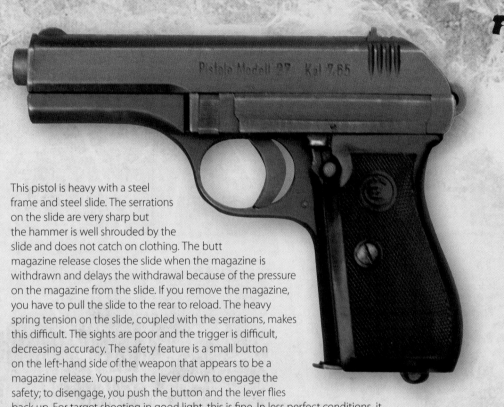

This pistol is heavy with a steel frame and steel slide. The serrations on the slide are very sharp but the hammer is well shrouded by the slide and does not catch on clothing. The butt magazine release closes the slide when the magazine is withdrawn and delays the withdrawal because of the pressure on the magazine from the slide. If you remove the magazine, you have to pull the slide to the rear to reload. The heavy spring tension on the slide, coupled with the serrations, makes this difficult. The sights are poor and the trigger is difficult, decreasing accuracy. The safety feature is a small button on the left-hand side of the weapon that appears to be a magazine release. You push the lever down to engage the safety; to disengage, you push the button and the lever flies back up. For target shooting in good light, this is fine. In less perfect conditions, it is difficult. This safety feature creates problems for carrying. If you carry hammer down, chamber empty, it's too slow going into action. If you carry hammer down, chamber loaded, it is difficult to cock. Carrying this firearm cocked and locked is dangerous, as even light pressure will flip the safety off. The CZ 27 is made from good materials, but the weapon itself is heavy and slow to operate. It has an ergonomically problematic safety, a difficult trigger, and poor sights.

This pistol is better in practical use than on a target range. The CZ 38 was originally developed to Czech Air Force specifications as a defensive weapon, resulting in clean, snag-free lines. The CZ 38 is a DA-only pistol (actually self-cocking), making target groups very difficult to fire. Aside from the caliber, this is a great military weapon. The self-cocking-only trigger makes it safe. It is a flat weapon with no projection to catch on clothing and no safety to worry about; it will not go off unless you pull the trigger. All this adds up to a good combat gun. The weapon has a few undesirable features. The slide closes when you pull the magazine out, but it functioned perfectly in all firing tests. The sights are difficult to see and index on the range; painting them white solves this problem. It is a superior .380 caliber pistol, somewhat large for the caliber, but easily stripped and put into operation. I would rate it as my favorite of the .380s. I like the self-cocking-only feature, the convenient oversized trigger guard that is easy to use with your gloved hand, the easy stripping, and the fact that it is flat and safe to use without any safety worries. With good .380 ammo, it is a much better pistol for military use than the common Walther series of pistols.

SINGLE-SHOT .22

Caliber: .22mm   **Manufacturer:** Gunmaker's Cooperative LOV   **Typical Use:** Target shooting, hunting

Czechoslovakia made this single-shot pistol in the immediate post-war period. While it doesn't look like much, it is quite a nice pistol. The sights are good and the trigger pull is great. These pistols were created due to various laws in Europe and elsewhere, as .22 rimfire single-shot weapons were not subject to restrictive legislation. They were not viewed as weapons, as a single-shot handgun seems pretty innocent. Some are still made today for this reason in 4mm or .22 smooth bore. These are excellent weapons for training people just learning to shoot. Many people resist using them because of the single-shot functionality. They should not discount this weapon. It has good sights and trigger, inherent accuracy coupled with low noise, light recoil, and low-cost ammunition. Such a weapon can be comfortably left at a second home as they are inexpensive and not likely to be used in a crime. Many do not have serial numbers, which is also a nice point. To me, they reflect a leisurely time period when shooting .22 shots without ear muffs at pine cones or walnuts was a pleasant way to spend an afternoon with a companion, away from the distractions of modern life.

VZ52

Caliber: 7.62mm (7.63; .30 Mauser)   **Manufacturer:** Ceska Zbrojovka, Uhersky Brod   **Typical Use:** Military and self-defense

When the Soviet Union compelled its former puppet states to adopt Soviet calibers, the Czechs, instead of adopting the Tokarev, designed the VZ52 as their service pistol. When they later adopted the CZ 82 in 9mm Makarov, the Czechs sold off the VZ52 pistols. They are common throughout Africa, South America, and with European terrorist organizations. The caliber lacks stopping power despite its projectile speed. It is small, lightweight, full-jacketed, and round-nosed. The .30 Mauser cartridge in the hot Czech loading does offer some prospects for vest penetration. Using Fiocchi ammo on the cinema range, I encountered a great deal of flash. The trigger pull is hard and the sights are small and difficult to pick up. The weapon points extremely low. The grip is too long because of the long cartridge. The safety is small, stiff, and difficult to disengage. Worse, it tends to hit your thumb when in the shooting position and gets bumped back into the safe, making the weapon inoperable. The design suggests carrying in the cocked-and-locked position, but the small safety is hard to disengage and can be accidentally bumped to the "off" position. Cocking the burr hammer is difficult, forcing you to break your grip, slowing response time. Although this pistol looks like a DA pistol, it is SA. The weapon can be rapidly field stripped for cleaning, but the roller locking system requires a screwdriver to disassemble. Overall, the VZ52 is not a great combat pistol but it is as good as, if not better than, the Tokarev TT33 7.62x23mm. This is the strongest production handgun ever chambered for this caliber.

Designed in Czechoslovakia for export, the CZ 75 is an intriguing weapon. Many military organizations and counter-terrorist police agencies use it. It has been purchased in quantity in India, is carried by many Latin American military officers, and is common in Lebanon, Africa, and Europe. It was rare in the United States because of the prohibitive tariffs on arms from Warsaw Pact countries, but that is now changing. The CZ 75 is the most copied design since John Browning's pocket pistols. Design spin-offs are produced all over the world. View this pistol as a combination of a Browning P35 and a SIG P210. It has the double-column magazine of the P35 but uses the slide-receiver system of the P210. It offers a DA trigger but unlike most others, you can also carry the weapon in condition one. You can carry it loaded with the hammer down, pull the trigger for the first shot, and then reapply the safety if you anticipate shooting again but don't want to restart from the self-cocking position. This solves the problem of running around after firing a shot with a cocked auto and no safety. The CZ 75 does have some drawbacks. The DA trigger system is more complex than the P35 SA trigger system. Because the Czech government arsenals load all of their ammo hot, the bore is frequently a little larger than is desirable. After about five thousand rounds, the edge is frequently off. The front sight is fine on the CZ 75 although it could be improved by painting it white. The rear sight is too narrow and hinders rapid indexing. The trigger pull on both DA and SA is good, and the recoil is quite light.

CZ 82/83

Caliber: 380 ACP (9mm Makarov) **Manufacturer:** Ceska Zbrojovka, Uhersky Brod **Typical Use:** Military and self-defense

The CZ 82 was the standard duty weapon in the Czech Army in 9mm Makarov caliber, and is available for commercial sale in .380. The trigger pull is quite good and the weapon feels good in my hand. The white front and rear sights allowed quick pick-up in the dark and rapid indexing. Recoil was light due to the caliber and the steel frame. One of the best features of this pistol, as well as the CZ 75, is that the shooter can put the weapon in the loaded-chamber, hammer-down mode and fire the first shot by merely pulling the trigger guard. With most DA autoloaders, to re-fire you must lower the hammer and start all over from the DA mode, or you have a loaded, cocked pistol in your hand. With the CZ 83 (and CZ 75/85), you can simply flip the safety on, then flip it off to fire again from the easier-to-control SA trigger mode. The thirteen-shot magazine made the grip somewhat thick, forcing me to shift my grip to hit the magazine release button with my thumb. This may not matter due to the number of rounds the magazine holds. I like this pistol and prefer it in 9mm Makarov to .380, especially with Czech loads because that gives me a borderline 9x19mm equivalent.

CZ P07

Caliber: 9x19mm, .40 S&W **Manufacturer:** Ceska Zbrojovka , Czech Republic **Typical Use:** Military, police, self-defense

The Czech factory developed the P07 once polymer pistols were the new standard. It is a service-size pistol chambered for 9x19mm and .40 S&W, suitable for military, police, and self-defense use. The polymer receiver creates a thin frame, which feels good in the hand. It is long but holds seventeen rounds in 9x19mm. The P07 is a DA/SA pistol but can be carried in condition one, which allows the weapon to be carried with the hammer back, safety applied when moving after initial shots are fired. Many people are comfortable carrying the pistol "cocked and locked" due to the heavy DA pull, and will like the P07 for that reason. Accuracy is acceptable and the weapon is reliable. Sights are good. Models with extended suppressor-ready barrels have higher sights, which are visible over the suppressor.

ZK 383

Caliber: 9x19mm Parabellum   **Manufacturer:** Ceska Zbrojovka, Uhersky Brod   **Typical Use:** Military

The ZK 383 was the standard-issue SMG during World War II in Bulgaria, and was widely used by German SS units. It shoots well and is similar to a heavy self-loading carbine. The sights on the ZK 383 are typical of Central European guns: a pyramid-front type protected by sturdy wings and a tangent V-shaped rear, which is graduated out to eight hundred meters. I find these difficult on SMGs; they become a total blur after the first shot. The cocking handle is on the left, which makes it convenient for either hand, and the magazine is similar to the Sten gun in that it feeds from the left. The magazine release is a large button on the left side. The weapon has a selector on the left marked "1" and "30" to allow for selective fire, and is slow to change given the location. The barrel is covered by a thick jacket, which keeps the ZK 383 from getting warm. The weapon has a very straight fixed wood stock. The butt plate is standard metal-plate type. The weapon has an integral bipod, permanently affixed to the weapon, but one would rarely, if ever, use a bipod with a 9x19mm open-bolt SMG. The ZK-383 has the multiple cyclic rate. By removing the weight in the bolt, you can make the cyclic rate higher. Reference books state the rate without the weight is seven hundred rpm; with the weight, it is five hundred rpm. I did not have access to a timer, so cannot confirm that, and noticed only a slight difference in rates when fired.

SKORPIAN M61

Caliber: .32 ACP, .380, 9x19mm   **Manufacturer:** Czech state factory   **Typical Use:** Military, police, and self-defense

The Czech M61 Skorpian is a selective-fire weapon designed to be fired from the shoulder using its wire stock. This weapon is quite small, and has light recoil. I believe it was designed for Czech military and police personnel who found better results with it than a standard pistol, but could not carry the M58 rifle. Sadly, most of the M61 use has been by terrorists who appreciated its qualities. Technically it can be viewed as a submachine gun, machine pistol, or both. As an SMG, the M61 it is not nearly as effective as an Uzi, MP5, Owen, or Star Z-63. Its .32 ACP cartridge seems feeble compared to a 9mm Luger round. Compared to a Glock 18, it lacks power and is big and bulky. Firing one without the stock in place is not as effective as a Glock 18 or a Beretta M93. View the M61 as a six- to eight-inch single-barrel, twelve-gauge shotgun; with the stock in place and the weapon on semi-auto, one can easily hit a man target at two hundred yards off hand. While a .32 ACP bullet is not the stopper of all time, it is fine. The M61 really shines at close range and on full auto. It is like a shotgun loaded with 000 buckshot. Thanks to its light recoil, when fired on full auto the M61 will deliver a magazine full of seventy one grain .32 caliber bullets into the target, and they are more effective than buckshot. The M61 can be rapidly reloaded to permit additional doses of .32 ACP as desired. Viewed in this fashion, the M61 is really quite a weapon.

SHE M23/25 9MM

Caliber: 7.62x39mm   **Manufacturer:** Czech state factory   **Typical Use:** Military and police

The Czech SHE M23/25 9mm SMG began as a 7.62x25mm version and was later modified to accept the nearly-universal 9x19mm cartridge. Some of the features needed for an SMG chambered for the 7.62x25 mm cartridge—which is a high-pressure number—exceeds the needs of a 9x19mm-chambered weapon. The weapon fired from an open bolt. It does not have a selector. But the cyclic rate is low enough that single shots by trigger manipulation only are easily achieved. There is a small flipper-type safety in the trigger guard which is convenient to use. The bolt contains a bolt lock feature so when you are carrying a loaded magazine and jumping from trucks or helicopters, you will not get an inertia slam-fire. The weapon comes in two versions: a fixed stock of either wood or plastic, or a folding unit. The rear sight is an interesting four-position rear that betrays its origin in 7.62x25mm with four positions at one hundred/two hundred/three hundred/four hundred meters. The front sight is a typical pyramid with a large front-sight guard on it. The pistol grip feels slightly big. While a little wide and deep, it is not terrible. The magazines are of the double-column type and load easily without tools. The hollowed-out bolt does a number of things. The barrel is enclosed in steel, so if a cartridge explodes or ruptures, it will not harm the shooter. It provides a heavy weight forward which aids balance. Lastly, even with a long barrel, the overall length is short. The longer barrel gives you better velocity in a given cartridge. But this system makes it difficult to check if the weapon is clear. The whole weapon handles nicely and cycles smoothly, allowing good two-shot bursts at ten yards. The bolt on the M23/5 9x19mm floats back, never hitting the end of the receiver. This prevents jarring, so you easily maintain your sight picture for better shooting.

VZ58

Caliber: 7.62 x25mm (9x19mm) **Manufacturer:** Czech state factory **Typical Use:** Military and police

The VZ58 rifle was the Czech service rifle during the Cold War era used in lieu of the AK47, the standard service rifle of the Eastern Bloc. Czech arms makers could design as they pleased as long as the weapon took the standard cartridge. Although it looks like an AK47 rifle, the VZ58 has a different design. It has a locking-block system like a P38 pistol, a convenient flipper-style safety, and a sturdier folding stock. Magazines hold the same number of rounds as the AK47, though they aren't interchangeable. Sights are the open-rear and post-style front sights. The forearm does not have a heat deflector in it and will get hot within three quick magazines. It is a man-made material unlikely to catch fire, as the wood handguards of the AK47 can. The VZ58 is lighter than the AK47, so seems livelier in the hands. Fast semi-auto fire gets good results, but the full-auto cyclic rate is quite fast. Coupled with the weapon's stock design and light weight, this results in bullets hitting high/left; anything over two shots is likely to miss a man-target at ten yards or more. Many VZ58 rifles appeared in Vietnam. They were reliable, although many thought they were not as dependable as the AK47. But with less weight and a much faster safety system, the VZ58 is a practical alternative and a better choice for a combat rifle.

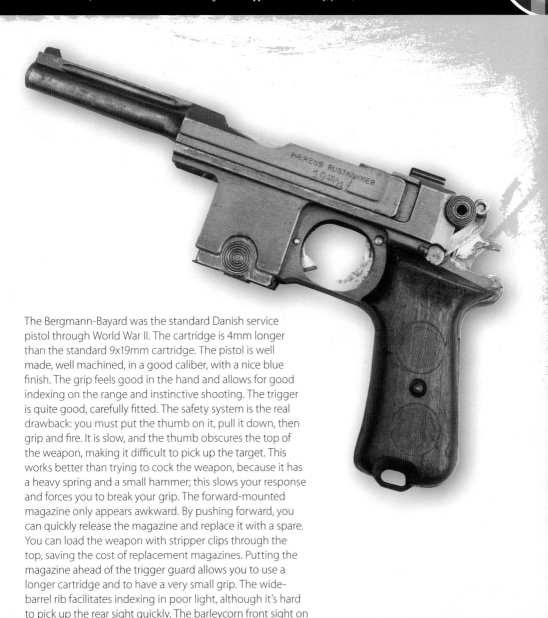

The Bergmann-Bayard was the standard Danish service pistol through World War II. The cartridge is 4mm longer than the standard 9x19mm cartridge. The pistol is well made, well machined, in a good caliber, with a nice blue finish. The grip feels good in the hand and allows for good indexing on the range and instinctive shooting. The trigger is quite good, carefully fitted. The safety system is the real drawback: you must put the thumb on it, pull it down, then grip and fire. It is slow, and the thumb obscures the top of the weapon, making it difficult to pick up the target. This works better than trying to cock the weapon, because it has a heavy spring and a small hammer; this slows your response and forces you to break your grip. The forward-mounted magazine only appears awkward. By pushing forward, you can quickly release the magazine and replace it with a spare. You can load the weapon with stripper clips through the top, saving the cost of replacement magazines. Putting the magazine ahead of the trigger guard allows you to use a longer cartridge and to have a very small grip. The wide-barrel rib facilitates indexing in poor light, although it's hard to pick up the rear sight quickly. The barleycorn front sight on a skinny barrel did pick up well in the dim light.

M1889 ENGINER CARBINE (INGENIOR KARBIN M1889)

Caliber: 8x58mm (.30-40 Krag, 6.5x55 Rimless)   **Manufacturer:** Kongsberg Våpenfabrikk   **Typical Use:** Military

European armies of the pre-1914 era commonly issued their engineers a rifle longer than the carbine issued to horseback or bicycle troops, yet shorter than infantry rifles. This rifle has the typical V-shaped rear sight graduated from two hundred to two thousand meters, so at least some practical sighting distances are provided. The front sight is pyramid-type modified by having a flat top on it, which allows a much better sight picture than the thin, sharp top of typical pyramid sights. The V-notch is still too narrow, making it slow to get a sight picture, and difficult in poor light. As with the standard rifle, a magazine cutoff is supplied, and the Krag loading system precludes clip loading. The trigger pull is typical two-stage and quite heavy. Such trigger pulls, while helpful in avoiding accidental shootings, are particularly troublesome in the off-hand or kneeling position, although even the best work cannot be done from prone with such excessively heavy pulls. A good trigger pull is the key to good shooting with either a rifle or pistol. Although fairly heavy for its length, the rifle felt fairly lively in my hands, and it was only slightly muzzle-heavy when used in the off-hand position. This *liveliness* characteristic is hard to define: some rifles have it, while others do not. I suppose it is the distribution of the weight that is critical. In any event, the Ingeniør Karbin M1898 has it, and the infantry model does not.

BLAND 20-GAUGE HOWDAH

Caliber: 20-gauge   **Manufacturer:** Bland   **Typical Use:** Military and self-defense

In the mid- to late-nineteenth century when quality control over cartridges was spotty and the revolver was fairly new, many British officers preferred the double-barrel pistol. As with double rifles, the shooter knew he had two weapons in his hand, and it was unlikely both would break. English officers thought highly of the Bland 20-bores. The Bland 20-bore is neither a lightweight nor small weapon. But with two hands using a Weaver-style stance, it works fine. That stance allows the shooter to pull the weapon out of recoil, quickly cocking the next barrel for a shot. You should not cock both barrels simultaneously lest the weapon double fires, leaving you faced with an assailant and an empty weapon. If possible, you should reload after firing one shot, keeping the spare barrel in reserve, much as you use a double rifle. The Bland 20-bore can be used to fire shot or slugs. The slugs are good for stopping at very close range, but you limit yourself to one projectile. The better course of action is large-size shot. By the time the Webley MK I, a reliable big bore revolver, came out during the Boer War, very few Bland 20-bores were used except by very, very conservative shooters.

WEBLEY RIC M83

Caliber: .455   **Manufacturer:** Webley   **Typical Use:** Military and police

Although never an official military revolver, many officers and NCOs carried the M83 Webley as their personal weapon. It was shown in catalogues from 1884 until 1939. Many British police and colonial agencies used the weapon, so they are found worldwide. The Webley M83 has a solid frame construction, .455 caliber chambering five-shot capacity, and weighs twenty one-ounces. It lacks the rapid ejection system of the swing-out cylinder or break-top revolver, but this is not very important. On the negative side, the sights are hard to see because they're dark with a shallow, narrow back sight. The SA pull is quite good, but the DA trigger is stiff and has a lot of slack. The hammer spur would be troublesome in pulling the weapon from a pocket. Many Webley M83s have lanyard rings which add bulk. The recoil is heavier than a standard Webley since the RIC is lighter to carry. Because of its construction, reloading is slow. Solve this by carrying two revolvers—one in your pants pocket, one in your coat. Nickel finish insures maximum rust resistance. Use Webley MKIII man-stopper loads. Paint your sights white to allow rapid pickup.

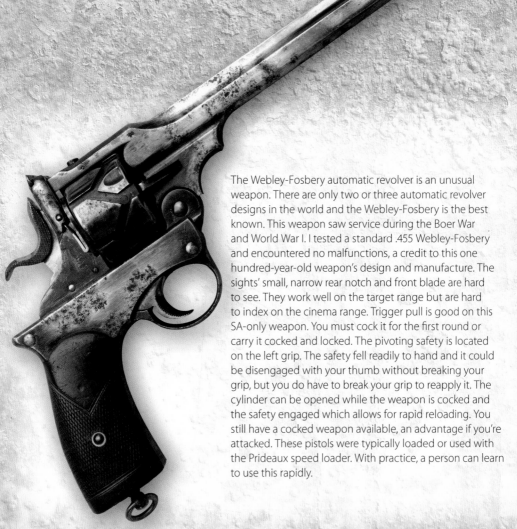

The Webley-Fosbery automatic revolver is an unusual weapon. There are only two or three automatic revolver designs in the world and the Webley-Fosbery is the best known. This weapon saw service during the Boer War and World War I. I tested a standard .455 Webley-Fosbery and encountered no malfunctions, a credit to this one hundred-year-old weapon's design and manufacture. The sights' small, narrow rear notch and front blade are hard to see. They work well on the target range but are hard to index on the cinema range. Trigger pull is good on this SA-only weapon. You must cock it for the first round or carry it cocked and locked. The pivoting safety is located on the left grip. The safety fell readily to hand and it could be disengaged with your thumb without breaking your grip, but you do have to break your grip to reapply it. The cylinder can be opened while the weapon is cocked and the safety engaged which allows for rapid reloading. You still have a cocked weapon available, an advantage if you're attacked. These pistols were typically loaded or used with the Prideaux speed loader. With practice, a person can learn to use this rapidly.

WEBLEY SELF-LOADING MK I

Caliber: .455 SL   **Manufacturer:** Webley   **Typical Use:** Military and self-defense

The Webley self-loading Mark 1 pistol chambered for the .455 SL cartridge was an early rival of the Colt Government Model. Many officers during World War I purchased it privately. One hundred were issued to the Royal Horse Artillery (fifty with a shoulder stock) and to the Royal Flying Corps, where they were used for shooting at enemy airplanes in the initial stages of the war. As the ".455 Pistol, Self-Loading Mark 1, 1912," it was adopted as supplemental issue in the navy. Although less rugged than the Colt and subject to mud clogging it, due to the action opening at the top, exposing the entire interior to the elements, it was easily stripped and well made. The example tested was manufactured in 1913. It was marked with British government acceptance stamps. Despite its age, its condition was still quite good and I encountered no malfunctions.

WEBLEY MK VI

Caliber: .455 Webley   **Manufacturer:** Webley-Scott   **Typical Use:** Military and self-defense

The Webley Mk VI was the standard British handgun in World Wars I and II. It differs from the earlier MkIV in that it has a front sight that can be replaced, its six-inch barrel is two inches longer, and it uses the grip-style from the commercial Webley revolver series. The rear sight on the Mk VI was the same as on the MkIV, too shallow and dark. The front sight is better since it is more distinct and also easier to hold elevation and windage. The longer barrel balances well and, except as a concealment piece, the six-inch barrel is not a major weakness. The grip is what really makes the Webley Mk VI the best .455 Webley ever made. It is wonderful. You can use a Webley Mk VI without any adapter. It will not shift in your hand while firing rapid DA strings. The ejection system is quite good. By using the Prideaux speed loaders in conjunction with the rapid ejection system, you can almost equal the rate of fire of the M1911. During World War I, the British also adopted a bayonet and stock for the Webley Mk VI. For a less experienced shooter or when one is tired and out of breath, the stock can be truly useful. At first, the bayonet seems worthless, but when you put it on the pistol with the stock, you get a dandy little carbine, a stocked Webley Mk VI with bayonet seems just the ticket for trench clearing. It is light, easy to shoot, and quick to reload.

SMITH & WESSON NEW CENTURY TRIPLE LOCK

Caliber: .455   **Manufacturer:** Smith & Wesson   **Typical Use:** Military and self-defense

The famous Smith & Wesson Triple Lock revolver was designed to be a target shooter and hunter's weapon. Between September 1914 and September 1916, the British bought 5,000 Smith & Wesson Ejector First Models and 69,755 Second Model revolvers chambered for the MK II .455 cartridges. The mud of France was the undoing of the design and no doubt a fitter's nightmare. However, anyone who really likes revolvers and sees a Triple Lock wants one. I looked forward to testing this revolver and thus was disappointed at the poor group I fired. A 3⅛-inch group really is too big, but I think it was because of the sights not the weapon. The sights are hard to see on the cinema range because they are dark and the rear notch is low and small. The sights would be better if white and broader. The trigger in the DA mode is quite good and allows rapid follow-up shots. With the low recoil of the .455 cartridge, the non-Magna grip design is not much of a problem, unlike the heavier-recoiling loads of the .44 Special. Only with rapid repeat shots does the .455 rounds drive the weapon into the web of the hand enough to cause shifting. Interestingly enough, the face of the trigger is smooth, like that of the modern combat revolver, unlike the grooved triggers that you would expect with a revolver for target shooting. Smooth triggers are better for fast DA-shooting. This is a large pistol with an N frame and 6½-inch barrel, but the skinny barrel and large holes in the barrel and cylinder prevent the weight from being excessive. Although the New Century is a very well-made and designed revolver, better combat revolvers exist for the 1914 period. Its grip design is not as good as that found on a Webley Mk VI which, in my estimation, is a better military revolver for an officer or NCO.

OLD PATTERN 5-INCH NO. 2 MK I

Caliber: .455 (10mm Italian, .44-40 W.C.F.)   **Manufacturer:** Garate, Trocaola, Aranzabal y Cia   **Typical Use:** Military

During World War I, Britain was in desperate need of small arms and ranged far and wide buying weapons, including from the United States and Spain. The Old Pattern No. 1 and No. 2 Mk I revolvers were made by Garate in 1915 as a substitute standard. These revolvers are serviceable if in good condition. They were a hybrid design that incorporated a Webley-style top-break action, an Smith & Wesson-type action lock, and had a semi-bird's-head grip common to neither. Though thousands were produced, they are hard to find today. This weapon, also known as the "Hermanos Ovbea," was made in 10mm Italian for Italy and .44-40 W.C.F. for the South American market. The weapon functioned without a hitch. On the cinema range, the front sight is thin and hard to see; the thin rear sight is impossible to see. Accuracy suffers due to this. The design allows very fast reloading. Flipping the latch and breaking the frame down will flip out all the empties. The smooth finish of the trigger allows rapid repeat shots, and the grip feels good when used for instinctive cinema range shooting. The trigger pull is heavy but acceptable. The low recoil of the .455 makes repeat shots easy.

After World War I, British Army leaders decided the powerful, reliable Webley Mk VI .455 was too heavy and had too much recoil. So the Webley firm offered its Webley Mk IV model. It had all the good features of the Webley Mk VI, as it was basically a scaled-down Mk VI. Even so, the British eventually chose Enfield-designed revolvers. Webley then offered the model to British police forces. Many agencies, including overseas police forces, used the Webley Mk IV .38. Enfield could not produce enough handguns once World War II began, so the British called on Webley, who provided high-quality weapons for the then-service cartridge of .38 S&W. The Webley Mk IV .38/200 has a very good grip and needs no adapter. The trigger pull on the DA is heavy in comparison to a Smith & Wesson but generally quite smooth. SA pull is very satisfactory. The sights are easy to use on the darkened range and allow quick indexing. The top-break feature allows you to reload rapidly and easily. The drawback is the cartridge. The .38 S&W is really the same power as a .380 ACP—not great. It lacks penetration, a drawback for the military, although fine for individual civilian defense work. Using two hundred-grain bullets, as they tend to tumble, will give better stopping power.

I tested two Enfield Revolver models: No. 2 Mk I, the original model with a hammer spur with both SA and DA trigger mechanisms, and No. 2 Mk II, known as the Commando Model, introduced for tankers who found that the hammer spur would catch on things inside the tank. The hammer spur was deleted, the SA notch left off the hammer, and the mainspring lightened. Quality varies tremendously with these weapons depending on where they were made. The Enfield Revolver was developed in the 1920s as a replacement for the Webley Mk VI revolver when the British military wanted a lighter, smaller, easier-to-handle weapon with less recoil. To comply with the Hague Convention, they went to a full-metal-jacketed 167- 178-grain bullet. The weapons are sighted for those loads. When you use commercial ammo that has 148-grain lead bullets, it shoots to a different point of impact. Front sights are easily replaced, and you can raise the point of impact by changing the front sight. The pistol's load is the problem: .38 caliber, 178-grain, full-metal-jacketed loads at 650-odd fps are not reliable man-stoppers. These loads are slightly less powerful than .380 automatic loads. On both of these models, the grips feel very good. Recoil is low, much like a .22. The DA pull is heavy, tends to stick, and is harder than a Smith & Wesson DA pull. The SA pull on the hammer model is adequate. The report of the .38/200 round is also quite low and not much greater than that of a .22. The notch of the rear sight is too narrow, although the sight picture is quite good. The front sight is also narrow and tends to reduce accuracy. The cylinder latch breaks with some difficulty; one tends to hit the latch with your thumb and tie up the weapon. Once opened, it ejects the empty cases vigorously, allowing you to reload rapidly. The groups with the No. 2 Mk I Enfield ran about 2³⁄₈ inches at fifty feet; the No. 2 Mk I model, groups were about three inches. On the No. 2 Mk I, the DA pull is heavy and stacks at the end. The sights are hard to see. The hammerless model has thumb indentations that were designed to align the weapon for rapid DA work. The weapon can be fired rapidly in bursts of two because of the light recoil and low report. The heavy DA pull makes it difficult to stay on the target because of the weapon's lightness and the trigger's stacking. The grips are plastic and feel bulky. They taper the wrong way; they get wider at the bottom so you tend to spread out your hand, which weakens your grasp.

SMITH & WESSON VICTORY MODEL MILITARY & POLICE .38

Caliber: British Service .380 (.38 S&W/.38 Special)   **Manufacturer:** Smith & Wesson
Typical Use: Military, police, and self-defense

This Military & Police (M&P) Model is the most successful revolver ever made. During World War II, the British and Commonwealth countries ordered more than 568,000 them in .38 S&W caliber. The British M&P revolvers had four-, five-, and six-inch barrels with blue and sandblasted finish. To comply with The Hague Convention, the British stopped using the original two hundred-grain lead bullet and adopted a 178-grain full-metal-jacketed projectile and thus got a .380 ACP equivalent, which was not sufficient. US forces bought over 542,000 of them to use during World War II. They were chambered in .38 Special with 130-grain full-metal-jacket loads. US guns are either 2- or 4-inch guns and are typically found with a parkerized finish and a lanyard ring in the butt. During the war, navy and marine pilots, intelligence units, and guards carried them. The M&P revolver is an excellent weapon with a few shortcomings. Without an adapter, the grips do not feel good. The parts are good-sized and durable. Because of the cartridge and the all-steel construction, recoil is low and rapid DA fire is easy. SA pulls are good, and the DA pull is good with little stacking. Sights are distinctive in the front and can be rapidly indexed, but the rear sight is low and narrow, making formal target work difficult. The four-inch weapons are handy and can be easily carried concealed. The two-inch model is easier to shoot than a J frame two-inch because of the width of the sights and the trigger pull, but is bigger so harder to conceal.

WALTHER PP22

Caliber: 22RF long rifle   **Manufacturer:** Walther   **Typical Use:** Police, self-defense, hunting, and plinking

The Royal Irish Police used the Walther PP22 as their concealed-carry pistol in the 1980s, when off-duty officers were frequently attacked by members of the Irish Republican Army. The Walther PP in .22 Rimfire is not usually highly regarded as a self-defense weapon, but the British found it effective. The light recoil, low noise level, and DA/SA trigger system, and small size made it a handy, easy-to-shoot weapon. It can be deadly when using .22 Rimfire hollow points, and is inexpensive to shoot. But rimfire ammo can be unreliable, failing to fire far more frequently than center-fire ammunition. The Walther PP sights are small but visible and the weapon can be properly zeroed. The DA trigger pull is heavy and the SA, while smooth, has a lot of overtravel. Accuracy is face-size patterns at twenty five yards, and eye-socket at seven yards. With some practice, magazine capacity burst fire is achievable, helpful for self-defense.

When British officers first encountered the SMG, they rejected it, declaring they had no use for such "gangster guns." When the British realized the SMG was a very important weapon, they were stuck. Britain purchased every Thompson SMG it could get, but they were expensive ($two hundred each in 1939), across an Atlantic Ocean infested by German U-boats, and not the best SMG available. The British took the German MP28 and attempted to reproduce it but didn't understand it was expensive to make. Starting in 1941, the Sterling Engineering Company made about one hundred thousand of its version of the MP28, the Lanchester. Because of the advent of the Sten gun, they were earmarked for the British Navy. The Lanchester is built solidly. It it is a heavy weapon, more than 9½ pounds unloaded. The stock is solid wood, fitted with a brass butt plate, which makes it very stable. The Lanchester uses the bolt-handle safety mechanism; you pull the bolt to the rear and twist it to engage the safety. That method is certainly cheap and simple, but it is faster to keep the bolt closed and rack the weapon when ready to fire. The bolt has no lock on it, which could cause the weapon to fire if dropped. The weapon has a selector, allowing you to fire semi-auto as well as full-auto. Later models omitted this. The cyclic rate is low enough at six hundred rpm to permit firing of single shots by trigger manipulation. The sights are a protected blade front with tangent U-notch rear. They are adjustable out to six hundred yards, well beyond the range of an SMG's use. The barrel jacket is massive and holds the lug that accepts the long Enfield bayonet. The magazine is a single-column-feed fifty-round magazine and demands a loader to fill it. The side mount allows them to work well. The Lanchester is not well balanced with so much weight to the front and a loaded fifty-shot magazine pulling it to the side. The forearm is short and tends to force a slightly unnatural grip.

The Sten gun was created in 1941. The British, who captured vast quantities of 9x19mm ammo from the Italians, wisely designed the Sten for that caliber. The first Sten was the MK I. It had a wooden forearm, a downward projection stud for grasping with the non-shooting hand, and a flash hider on the barrel. Next came the MK II Sten, which is the more familiar version. Canadian producers got costs down to a little more than $ten, compared with the $two hundred Thompson. The Sten's magazine projects from the side. While odd at first, it allows you to get very low prone position, something not feasible with normal long-magazine submachine guns. This helps to eliminate the most common malfunction in a Sten: the magazine. You must use a loader to fill this magazine as it is a single-feed style. The Sten magazine housing can be rotated down, sealing the weapon from dirt. The Sten barrel comes out quickly for cleaning or replacement. The rest of the parts on the weapon are large and solid, so there are few that are likely to be lost or broken. The sights on the Sten are a fixed peep and a front pyramid sight in a slot, which may be drifted for windage. I find it too big and dark for good work at long range, say two hundreds yards, but at close range, it picks up quickly. The Sten safety is very elemental. Pull the bolt back to the notch, rotate, and put into the safety notch. Take it out by pulling to the rear and rotating downward. It takes more time to pull it off safe than to pull the bolt to the rearward cocked position, and the noise involved is only marginally lower. Stocks on Sten guns come in many patterns, including the simple tube and the wire frame. The cyclic rate on the Sten, depending on ammo, runs about 550 rpm. You can easily fire single shots even in full-auto, and control is good. The weapon is light for a World War II-era SMG, less than seven pounds. The MK IV and V were intended to be an upgrade to the Sten. Originally available only to elite airborne units, the MK V became the standard post-war British SMG until replaced by the Sterling.

The Sten MK III was simpler to make than the earlier MK II. The MK III used a lightweight sheet of steel that was wrapped around a cylinder and then spot-welded on top to hold it together. At the front, the barrel was pinned in place so you cannot unscrew the barrel for either cleaning or concealment. The tube also made a handguard to hold the weapon. Shooting three fast magazines through the weapon on a hot day makes the weapon too hot to hold. The slight sheet metal lip riveted to the side by the ejection port keeps your hand from getting into the port to either be injured or tie up the weapon. The MK III has a fixed peep rear on a front blade-type sight. It sighted in acceptably for short-range work, which is what it's intended for. The cyclic rate on the MK III is the same as on the MK II and quite controllable. The push-button selector switch is handy. The bolt safety system is slow. If the gun is carried with the bolt closed, you need to push the handle in to avoid inertia slam if the weapon is dropped. That substantially slows drawing the bolt to the rear to fire the weapon. The magazine release on the MK III is the same as the on MK II, but the magazine housing will not swing around to act as a dust cover, which it does on the MKII. Both models will accept the two variations of butt stocks: The T-type and the loop type. Both butt stocks lock up tightly and provide a stable platform. The MK III, is lightweight for an open-bolt SMG and feels very lively in the hands. This and its cyclic rate promote quick and accurate shooting. Unfortunately, the safety is slow and awkward, and the sights are marginal for anything beyond shotgun ranges. That said, the Sten remains a benchmark in the field.

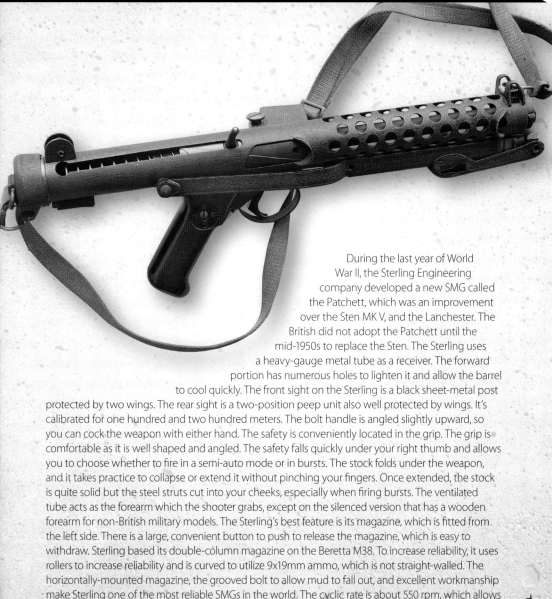

During the last year of World War II, the Sterling Engineering company developed a new SMG called the Patchett, which was an improvement over the Sten MK V, and the Lanchester. The British did not adopt the Patchett until the mid-1950s to replace the Sten. The Sterling uses a heavy-gauge metal tube as a receiver. The forward portion has numerous holes to lighten it and allow the barrel to cool quickly. The front sight on the Sterling is a black sheet-metal post protected by two wings. The rear sight is a two-position peep unit also well protected by wings. It's calibrated for one hundred and two hundred meters. The bolt handle is angled slightly upward, so you can cock the weapon with either hand. The safety is conveniently located in the grip. The grip is comfortable as it is well shaped and angled. The safety falls quickly under your right thumb and allows you to choose whether to fire in a semi-auto mode or in bursts. The stock folds under the weapon, and it takes practice to collapse or extend it without pinching your fingers. Once extended, the stock is quite solid but the steel struts cut into your cheeks, especially when firing bursts. The ventilated tube acts as the forearm which the shooter grabs, except on the silenced version that has a wooden forearm for non-British military models. The Sterling's best feature is its magazine, which is fitted from the left side. There is a large, convenient button to push to release the magazine, which is easy to withdraw. Sterling based its double-column magazine on the Beretta M38. To increase reliability, it uses rollers to increase reliability and is curved to utilize 9x19mm ammo, which is not straight-walled. The horizontally-mounted magazine, the grooved bolt to allow mud to fall out, and excellent workmanship make Sterling one of the most reliable SMGs in the world. The cyclic rate is about 550 rpm, which allows good control. Single shots can be fired even in the full-auto mode, and firing is smooth. An excellent suppressed version is available. It fires from an open bolt, unlike some suppressed designs, but the bolt noise is minimized.

NO. 1 MK III ENFIELD .303

Caliber: .303   **Manufacturer:** Enfield   **Typical Use:** Military

This rifle was the workhorse of British and Imperial forces in World War I and was much used in World War II. It is probably the finest bolt-action battle rifle ever made. The No. 1 Mk III has a twenty five-inch barrel, making it handy and well balanced yet giving it good practical accuracy and power. It could be used in lieu of a short carbine. The front sight is well protected by the massive wings on the front that give the No. 1 Mk III its distinctive appearance. I find the front sight rather narrow and difficult to pick up rapidly, but its size helps make accurate shooting at long ranges possible. The sights on the Enfield go up to 2,200 yards and farther with the side-mounted long-range unit. The rear sight is very well machined with enough subtle adjustments to please everyone. The has one of the smoothest and most reliable bolt-action rifle actions made. The No.1 Mk III can be reloaded rapidly by stripper clips, or you can use extra box magazines. No other bolt-action rifle used in World Wars I or II can claim that feature. The stock is a two-piece design, which allows the weapon to use different butt lengths to suit different size soldiers. During World War I, there were four stocks available: regular, long, short, and bantam. The trigger is the typical two-stage military pull unit that is not very crisp and is often heavy. The pistol grip of the stock is not full size but it is adequate. The forearm is well rounded and comfortable. The stock is wood and the action cannot be removed from the stock for cleaning, but the fit is close enough to keep out most mud. There is no heat deflector in the stock, and the rifle barrel is quite thin. The muzzle of the rifle is protected by a heavy fitting that both protects the sight and the muzzle area of the stock and serves as a fitting for the long bayonet used with the No. 1 Mk III. With the long bayonet, the No. 1 Mk III makes quite the spear. The British soldier who carried the No. 1 Mk III had a great combat rifle.

ENFIELD M1914/17

Caliber: .303/.30-06 **Manufacturer:** Winchester/Remington **Typical Use:** Military

The British Military adopted the Lee-Enfield rifle in the 1880s but by 1910, the troops realized that it was not as strong as they desired. The Pattern 1913 was created to replace the Short Magazine Lee Enfield (SMLE), but World War I intervened and you don't change rifles mid-war. However, it was an excellent design and was quickly re-chambered to fire the .303 British cartridge, and the British forces soon found it was a very accurate rifle. When the United States entered the war, the M1903 Springfield rifles were in short supply. The Pattern 14 was available and the action was long enough to accept the .30-06 cartridge. The weapons were re-chambered to that caliber and produced. The rifles lacked the long-range indirect-fire sight on the M1917, but the military realized machine guns and mortars would handle that distance. The M1917 was the main battle rifle of American Expeditionary Forces in World War I. Sergeant Alvin York won his fame in part because of his skill with an M1917. The twenty six-inch barrel gives a reduced report. The safety is excellent, quick to flip off and on. Trigger pull is acceptable. The sights are the stars of this weapon. The good blade front, well protected by wings, and the adjustable peep rear sight are the best to be found on any World War I combat rifle.

P14 SNIPER

Caliber: .303   **Manufacturer:** Winchester   **Typical Use:** Military and police

This was the rifle that allowed the British to seize the initiative in the sniper war during World War I, turning the tables on the Germans. When testing many military weapons, two things become apparent: First, World War I's soldier was as well armed as many soldiers today; and, second, the development of optic technology advanced steadily. The field of view on a 1918 scope is narrow and the eye relief critical. It is dark, and therefore useless at night. Today's scopes can gain a shooter an extra forty five minutes of shooting as dusk falls. The scope is mounted very high on the P14, which permits the shooter to use iron sights at the same time. The stock should be designed to be used with the scope, the iron sights are a bonus. The P14 sniper rifle was standard in all aspects except that only Winchester-made models were used as sniper rifles. The trigger was standard P14 as were the action and sights. As with all P14 rifles, a bolt hold-open exists. When tested, the rifle grouped into 1⅝ inches at one hundred yards with Greek surplus ammo; decent for a ninety five-plus-year-old rifle. The scope features a plain but useful reticle consisting of a single crosshair to prevent canting and a post that reminds me of the blade of a front sight. The P14 sniper rifle is long with its twenty six-inch barrel and heavy, being based on the P14 rifle, but it is a fair sniper setup. The optics are not good by today's standards, yet the rifle is as good as many sniper rifles seen in today's armies.

NO. 4 ENFIELD .303/.308

Caliber: .303 British/7.62x51mm   **Manufacturer:** Enfield & Stevens   **Typical Use:** Military

In the mid-1920s, the British wanted to replace the No. 1 Mk III rifle, which had served with distinction, but was expensive to make in terms of machine time, manpower, and materials. The British unveiled the No. 4 rifle, which used the standard Enfield action but had changes which facilitated mass production. The trigger system is the same, with a typical two-stage military take-up. The magazine system is the same but the magazines are not interchangeable. Capacity is 10 shots, and uses stripper clips, not spare magazines. Sights are much improved. The early No. 4 has an adjustable peep, but the final rush of war production saw this reduced to a simple L-shaped peep flip sight that lacks fine adjustments. The front sight is mounted on the barrel in a heavy barrel-band sight-protection unit, slightly back from the end of the barrel. The stock is a broad, two-piece affair. The forearms have no heat deflector, but the barrels on the No. 4 are so heavy it would be difficult to shoot long or fast enough to heat the stock. The No. 4 is the same length as No. 1 Mk III but slightly heavier. The safeties on both rifles are handy. After the war ended, Britain had vast stocks of No. 4 rifles that were basically obsolete. Once NATO adopted the 7.62x51mm, it was apparent that the No. 4 action was strong enough to be re-barreled to 7.62x51mm NATO. Both Sterling and Enfield developed modification kits for the No. 4. The development of the L1A1 (English copy of the FN-FAL), made modifying the No. 4 senseless.

Germany was first to have an active sniping program during World War I, but the British overtook them. The British wanted a new sniper rifle for World War II. The British military coupled the No. 4 rifles with the Bren scope aided by such excellent gunsmiths as Holland & Holland, and placed it on the battlefield as the No. 4T. It was the best available at the time. The rifles were modified with a detachable scope mount and a cheek piece. Excellent iron sights were retained, but the scope was mounted low. With the scope on, you can't use the iron sights, but the scope mount and scope can be removed by loosening the thumb screws. Removing and then reinstalling the scope will move the POI an average of two inches up and two inches to the side at one hundred yards. But if the scope is disabled, the iron sights keep the shooter in action. The cheek piece allows you to get your head high enough to use the scope, yet you are still low enough to use the iron sights if needed. The reticle consists of a very nice, dark, straight line and a heavy post. It is fast and easy to use. It is great at four hundred yards or less, so well suited to hunting, but too coarse for ranges of six hundred to eight hundred yards. Optics have greatly improved over the years. Compared to today's standard scopes, the No. 32 scope has a narrow field of view, and the images are dull. The detachable box-magazine avoids the single-loading feature of many sniping rifles that can be a problem in cold weather. The No. 4T is a heavy rifle, weighing close to twelve pounds loaded and it has a twenty five-inch barrel, which makes off-hand and kneeling positions difficult. Recoil is light, and blast and flash are both low.

The British needed a lighter version of the Enfield for jungle warfare during World War II. With their twenty five- or twenty six-inch barrels, the No. 1 Mk III and No. 4 rifles were too long. Modifications developed the No. 5, or the so-called "jungle carbine," mostly seen in Burma during late 1944 and 1945. This rifle appears to be a cut-down No. 4 but the action has also been lightened. The No. 5 action cannot be used safely with the 7.62x51mm cartridge. The No. 5 has a twenty-inch barrel and an elementary flash hider, which acts as a bayonet attachment point. The No. 5 bayonet can be used as a knife. As in previous Enfield rifles, the action is quick and the rifle holds ten rounds fed from a detachable magazine. The weapon was meant to be reloaded with stripper clips. The sights on the No. 5 are the best yet: they are peep sights with a big peep for rapid, close use and a finer peep for longer range, with a maximum of eight hundred yards. The sights are protected by wings and the front blade is a good size. The rifle is known for having an erratic zero problem; some will retain zero, some will not. The British withdrew them from service because of this issue. The butt stock has a pistol grip like other Enfields, but the swivel is fixed and mounted on the side of the stock. Attached to the butt is a rubber recoil pad. This not only takes up some of the recoil but also remains firm on your shoulder when firing quickly. The forearm on the No. 5 is shaped like a sporter rifle, except that an upper forearm is still present, which allows you to hold the weapon without burning your hand.

After World War II, the British needed a new sniper rifle and developed the L42A1. The British took the old No. 4T rifles that were in good shape and modified them to L42A1 specifications. They converted the weapon to fire the 7.62x51mm NATO rimless round, installed a fairly heavy straight-taper barrel, and cut the wood back to resemble a sporting rifle. The British designers kept the old sights, claiming that the velocity difference between .303 and 7.62x51mm NATO was such that one hundred yards equals one hundred meters on the scales (it is close). They retained the scopes. The example I tested was manufactured in 1971, although the action and the No. 32 scope had obviously been made before 1945. Optics have advanced exponentially since 1945. On a clear day, the L42A1 is fine, but when dark, can't compare to what we have now. The rifle seems very muzzle heavy and does not balance well. This impacts firing from the sitting or kneeling positions and firing off-hand. The barrel at twenty five inches was too long and heavy and not necessary for accuracy. An M700 Remington with a light eighteen-inch barrel would outshoot the L42A1 at every distance. The bolt-action system is typical Enfield and very fast. The safety is convenient for the right-handed shooter, but not suitable if you're left-handed. The L42A1 was the last Enfield rifle used by British forces. These actions served the British nobly for one hundred years or so, and should be commended for that.

Many people have criticized the L85A1, and it has a bad reputation, but I believe it to be a good rifle. It is short, with a twenty-inch barrel. Despite its weight, over ten pounds, it balances nicely between the hands and does not feel heavy, but alive and handy, allowing very fast repeat shots when fired in a semi-auto mode. Most bullpup rifles have a terrible linkage system resulting in poor triggers. The L85A1's trigger, while not perfect, is distinctly superior to the M16A2. The safety is conveniently located and can be flipped off quickly with finger pressure, even in the dark. You do not need to break your shooting grip to push it off. The trigger guard does not fold down or flip to the side but it is fairly big and would accommodate gloved fingers. The magazine release is a protected shelf and button. I found the magazine release quite quick. You remove your left hand from the foregrip, bring it under your chin, push the button, and drop your hand down, thus pulling out the magazine. The action has a dust cover and a handle on the bolt to assist in closing the action or pulling out a stuck case. The action has the same dual-spring system as the AR18/180 series. The springs seem soft; they do not spring closed with a rapid slam when the bolt is released. I anticipated malfunctions but none occurred. The flash hider is open on the bottom, and the blast will pierce sandbags, blowing up dust and sand, and alerting an enemy to your location. The selector is located at the rear of the rifle and cannot be flipped into position rapidly. I believe that semi-auto fire is more effective than full-auto, so the selector position does no harm. The real strength of the L85A1 is the SUSIT sight unit. This is a fairly massive, solid unit of 4X magnification. It has a translucent pointer system with a radioactive element whose red-orange glow allows you to fire at night. Adjustments for the SUSIT are in the mount rather than the unit itself. This makes for a stronger unit and substantially decreases the number of things that can go wrong with a scope. It takes practice to get used to the scope, but it allows fine accuracy.

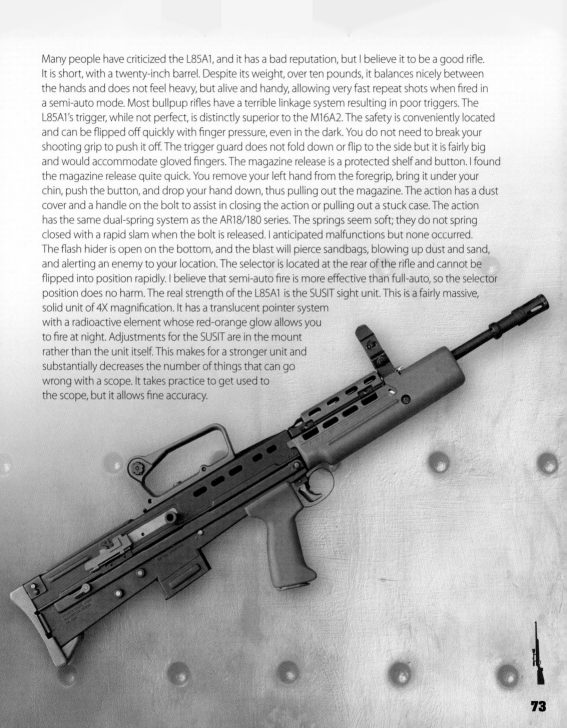

ACCURACY INTERNATIONAL

Caliber: .300 Winchester Magnum, .308 (7.62x51mm)   **Manufacturer:** Accuracy International
Typical Use: Military and police

The British labored from 1939 to the early 1980s with the Enfield No. 4T and its successor, the L42A1. Noted British marksman Malcolm Cooper developed a new rifle in the 1980s, which he named the Accuracy International. British and Swedish militaries adopted it as their standard sniper rifle. The rifle is very long with its twenty four-inch barrel and heavy at fifteen pounds. The trigger pull is quite good and broke cleanly and crisply. The scope was a 3x12 power Schmidt & Bender, which has a 92 percent light transmission rating. This is impressive, but costs twice as much as US scopes that come close to its power. The rifle is not fitted with iron sights. At the range, using 168-grain Federal soft point premium ammo, I got three-shot groups at one hundred yards of 9/16-inch and 2-7/16-inches at 505 meters. The rifle is muzzle heavy and thus poorly balanced. This weight and balance make it difficult to shoot off-hand or in kneeling positions. The Accuracy International has a slick action with a nicely-sized and shaped bolt knob. The safety is poorly positioned which slows response time. The rifle stock is made out of fiberglass and is merely a shell fitted around the action. The stock itself can be adjusted for length so the weapon can be used by different-sized marksmen and in different climactic conditions. The stock is too wide and the forearm is flat and uncomfortable. The bipod is heavy but is capable of multiple adjustments. The trigger guard is small and does not swing down or out of the way for winter use. The sling swivel rattled because it allowed metal-to-metal contact. The black stock and barrel were distinctive in appearance. The 3x12 power Schmidt & Bender scope is clearly the best part of this sniping rifle. It is very clear and bright. The only criticism of the scope I have (besides the cost) is the it adjusts in one-half MOA. This is really too coarse. This is crucial the closer you get to one thousand meters, and this rifle is a true one thousand meter man-killer. It is a very accurate rifle from the bench or prone position, but its weight and stock style make it difficult to carry in the field and slow to put into operation.

The Lewis was an air-cooled LMG in a day when water-cooled guns were common. It was a magazine weapon when belts were typical. It was half the weight of a water-cooled gun and did not need a tripod to fire effectively. It has a heavy, cylindrical metal shroud covering the barrel, making it muzzle heavy and rather awkward. The British used them in World War I, and kept them in limited use during World War II. The front sight is well protected and blade shaped. The Lewis gun is designed to be fired in the prone position, so is equipped with an integral bipod. This bipod is a well-machined heavy piece, which contributes to the weapon's muzzle heaviness. It swings back and forth loosely, shifting the balance of the weapon adversely each time. The weapon fired typically from a pan-shaped forty seven-round magazine. Such pans are slow to reload, but would be loaded before combat. They are heavy and awkward in size. They do allow a flat silhouette and permit a top-feeding gravity-assisted system. The pan avoids the problem associated with belts which shrink in the weather and drag in the mud. But the metal case hits the metal pan causing a rattle that is easy to detect on patrol. The rear sight is an involved peep unit that permits the weapon to be fired to very long range. But it lacks a tripod, which is needed to use a machine gun for ranges more than eight hundred yards. The Lewis gun fires from an open bolt and has those drawbacks; it clearly cannot be viewed as a rifle. It added to the firepower of the British infantry section to which it was issued. Lewis guns are common today in the United States because so many of them survived the war. They are finely machined and obviously durable as they approach their one hundred year mark.

BREN 7.62X51MM LMG

Caliber: 7.62x51mm (.308, .303 British)   **Manufacturer:** Royal Small Arms Factory, Enfield   **Typical Use:** Military

One of the best light machine guns to come out of World War II was the Czech ZB26 and its English alternative, the Bren gun. While heavier than the BAR found in US units, the Bren offered a detachable barrel so continuity of fire could be maintained. Made in Canada and England, many were supplied to the Nationalist Chinese forces in 8mm chambering. So the Chinese actually had a better LMG than the US military at the time! When the 7.62x51mm cartridge was adopted by NATO in the 1950s, in the English Army, the Bren, chambered for .303 British, was basically put away as obsolete since the MAAG58 belt-fed machine gun had been adopted. Soon, however, British patrols operating in a variety of post-war hot-spots found that toting a twenty six-pound, belt-fed LMG had severe drawbacks in comparison to the box-fed Bren guns. With some clever engineering, the Bren in .303 was rechambered for 7.62x51mm (or .308), the magazine for the new FAL rifle was used to feed it (modified to take thirty rounds), and an excellent patrol-friendly LMG was created. While no lightweight by any means, this box-fed, detachable-barrel LMG is much better for patrolling than available belt-feds and the chambering in .308 is better than any more modern design in .223.

LUGER M23

Caliber: 7.65mm   **Manufacturer:** DMW   **Typical Use:** Military and self-defense

Finland was part of Imperial Russia until the end of World War I, when it gained independence. Still, the new Soviet Union viewed Finnish territory as its own, and their German neighbors weren't too friendly, either. The Russian-manufactured 7.62mm Nagant was the first duty weapon of Finland before it adopted the 7.65mm Luger (known as their M23) in 1923. The M23 served the Finnish military well until it was replaced by the Lahti 9x19mm pistol. The M23 has the same standard Luger sight and safety system with the same problems—the 7.65mm cartridge has never been a successful military cartridge, but the Finns used it effectively. In testing, the 7.65mm shot very flat, which made hitting a distant target easier. But combat pistols are designed to hit close-range targets with good stopping power, which the 7.65 Luger lacks, although it does have good penetration. The trigger pull on the M23 is crisp, unlike many Lugers. The muzzle blast with Fiocchi ammo is very heavy. Recoil is considerably lighter than that found in similar 9x19mm Lugers. Like most Lugers, the trigger guard is quite small, which would hinder use when wearing gloves.

LAHTI L-35

Caliber: 9mm Parabellum   **Manufacturer:** Valtion Kivääruthedas Jyväskylä   **Typical Use:** Military and self-defense

The Finnish Lahti tested was similar to the Swedish M-40 Lahti and suffered the same shortcomings. It was quite heavy for its caliber, its magazines were difficult to load, and its sights were poor. The weapon's grip was too sharp, and the safety was difficult to rapidly disengage. Even so, the Finnish example shot good groups both with and without the shoulder stock. Trigger pull was quite crisp, partly because the weapon was well broken in. All Lahti pistols are rare, but can be seen in the northern parts of Europe. Swedish Lahtis have been sold for surplus, and they are not uncommon in the United States. Although rarer than Lugers, Lahtis generally are cheaper. In Finland, the Luger M23 7.65mm was used prior to the Lahti L-35, which became the classic Finnish Winter War weapon. All reports praised its ability to function in the extreme climate of northern Finland. Oddly enough, when the Finnish armed forces needed a new weapon, they bought Belgian P-35s rather than buying surplus Lahtis from the Swedes. They may have discovered problems with the L-35, as they were the only army to use it in combat. The Lahti, whether the Finnish L-35 or Swedish M-40, is an interesting collectible. Although clearly preferable to a Luger, it cannot be considered a top-of-the-line 9mm handgun.

SUOMI M1931 & SWEDEN'S M37/9

Caliber: 9mm   **Manufacturer:** Finnish National Factory and Husqvarna   **Typical Use:** Military and police

The Suomi M1931 SMG is one of the first-generation SMGs, which means the weapon is made out of machined steel parts instead of pressings, and has a wood stock. This SMG looks like a rifle but it shoots only a pistol cartridge. At fifteen pounds loaded with its seventy-round drum magazine, it is long and very heavy for an SMG. It was the star of the 1940 Winter War with Russia. When the Swedes needed an SMG during World War II, they bought Thompson SMGs from the United States, but that was not a dependable source. Sweden needed a locally-produced model, so they found the Suomi, modified the stock, and trimmed the barrel. The weapon was lighter and handier but lost little of its fine accuracy. With my Suomi gun, a M37/9 version made in Sweden, three hundred-yard chest-sized plates are reasonable targets. The Suomi has a bolt-cocking lever on the right side that does not reciprocate with the bolt. It crowds your shooting hand and can be uncomfortable when your right hand holds the pistol grip near the top. The safety is in a good central location and is combined with the selector. Pushing it halfway gets you to semi-auto; all the way forward out of the trigger guard gives you full-auto at about nin hundred rpm. The trigger guard is too small, particularly for cold weather climates where mittens are needed. The selector tends to get pushed to the full-auto position. It is difficult to stop it midway at the semi-auto position. The cyclic rate is nine hundred rpm, but the Suomi is so smooth in operation that it is very controllable. Keeping it set on semi-auto and cocking the bolt when ready to fire may be best. The magazine release is centrally located, but the lever is so small that leverage is slight. The magazine must be fitted carefully in the slots in the receiver. For these reasons changing the magazine is slow. The Suomi disassembles quickly, and the barrel can be quickly removed to allow easy cleaning with hot water. The M31 is heavier and longer than the M37/9, but both use the same seventy-round drum or fifty-round, four-column magazines. They are easy to shoot and very reliable. They are heavy but balance well. I believe the Suomi, both M31 and M37/9, the Owen, and the Star Z-63 are the best three military SMGs ever made.

Finland, Germany's ally in World War II, fought the Soviets for a second time in 1944. Seeking an alternative to the costly Suomi M31 SMG, they turned to the Soviet PPS43 SMG. They were probably familiar with it from their allies—the Germans had captured large quantities of them. The Finns decided to make their own version of the PPS43 firing the 9x19mm cartridge, but using either the M31 magazines or the drums they had used effectively in fighting the Soviets in 1940. This became known as the KP44 SMG, and it was used in the 1944 war and after. It differed from the Soviet PP543 in caliber and magazine. The grip was solid wood instead of plastic. The rate of fire was slower than on the PPS43 since the 9x19mm cartridge is less powerful. Sights were similar to the PPS43 but regulated for the 9x19mm cartridge. The safety is the same, it field strips the same—the weapons are close to identical. The bore is not chrome-plated, so corrosive ammo is an issue. It is easy to control due to the slow cyclic rate, with less blast and felt recoil. The KP44 is an excellent weapon and lighter than the M31. Until recently, few existed outside of Finland. The KP44 is one of the unsung weapons of World War II, and the lucky few who have used them praise them highly.

Most agree this was the best Mosin-Nagant rifle ever made. The M1928/30 is shorter than the standard M91, and has a thicker barrel to help stabilize the weapon and provide better performance. The blade-type front sight is well protected by sturdy wings. The rear sight, a shallow U-notch, is also well protected. Both are hard to use. The sights are graduated fromtwo hundred to one thousand meters and can be adjusted for interim ranges. You can adjust the sight for windage. Both factors are excellent for serious shooters. The action was quite slick for a Mosin-Nagant rifle, although not as good as an M91 Carcano, a Swiss M11/K31, or Krag rifle. Because of the nature of the action and construction of the bolt, I could not hit the bolt handle with the palm of my hand and raise the bolt. I had to grab it with my fingers, turn the rifle slightly to the left to improve my leverage, and pull up hard on the handle. Only with a great tug could I chamber a new round smoothly. After running the bolt home to get the bolt handle down. I had to pull hard on the handle or, better and faster, hit it with the palm of my hand. I almost had to take the rifle from my shoulder to pull the bolt up, which really slows down the process. The M1928/30's barrel is heavy compared to a standard M91 barrel. The rifle is muzzle heavy. Surprisingly, this weight helped steady the weapon, and was distributed it in such a fashion that it "hung" nicely between my hands with the sights centered on the target, aiding shooting.

M1873 ORDONNANCE REVOLVER

Caliber: 11mm   **Manufacturer:** French state factories   **Typical Use:** Military and self-defense

The M1873 I tested was made in 1880 but was in excellent shape. I was stunned at how modern many of its features are. The M1873 was a contemporary of the Colt Single-Action Army (SAA) and is far superior to it. The DA trigger system is like that of a modern Smith & Wesson revolver. The grip feels good and permits fine instinctive shooting, allowing the trigger finger to correctly fall into position for rapid DA work. The twenty-pound DA pull is heavier than necessary. All the parts on the weapon are serial numbered and the whole piece shows great care in manufacture. It is accurate; I fired a 1¹⁵/₁₆-inch group at 50 feet, equal to a modern Smith & Wesson. French ammo is slow—seven hundred fps as opposed to nine hundred fps for the Colt SAA. The ejection system slows reloading but the DA trigger is fast. The front sight has a McGivern-style bead that is useful for formal target work and quick acquisition on the cinema range. The light color of the front sight, due to absence of finish, allows for rapid pickup of the sight in poor light conditions. The French armies used the M1873 through World War I, and it saw service in French colonies. It was issued without any finish; amazingly, the example tested was almost 110 years old and still in excellent shape with no rust. I believe the M1873 was the finest combat revolver available in 1873.

The French developed the M1886 8mm Lebel small-bore rifle to shoot smokeless powder. The smokeless powder cartridge was a real breakthrough and envied by other European armies. Next, the French developed a handgun in the same bore to replace their M1873 11mm revolvers. The principles that applied to rifles did not apply to handguns, and the 8mm Lebel was simply a poor weapon due to this fact. The pistol was well designed and made of good materials. Most solid-frame revolvers were rod ejectors, but the Lebel had simultaneous ejection. It broke to the right (to the left is more common today), so the ejected cases are less likely to hit your body. The ejector rod has a large button on it, allowing you to eject the empty cases with a firm push of the hand. Recoil is quite light and thus rapid DA work is possible. The M1892 is a DA revolver and the DA action pull is smooth, if somewhat heavy, with a little stacking. SA pull is crisp and helpful on the formal target field. The front sight is high and has a bead formed into the front sight. That is difficult to hold on the formal target course, but shows up well on the cinema range and helped rapid indexing. The rear sight is good. They work well in poor light. The barrel is hexagonal in shape. The shape of the barrel helps indexing—the flat surface guides the eyes toward the front sight. The grip feels good and does not need any adapter. Recoil is light. The weak caliber doomed the Lebel from the start. This would have been a wonderful combat revolver if offered in a smokeless 11mm cartridge.

RUBY 7.65

Caliber: 7.65mm Browning (.32 ACP)   **Manufacturer:** Gabilondo & Alkartasuna   **Typical Use:** Military and self-defense

The Ruby 7.65 was a French wartime pistol. Many French servicemen took the Ruby home with them, as it was a common police and civilian weapon after World War I. Even today, the weapon is common and inexpensive. It is heavy, weighing thirty four ounces, and of standard design. It would be very hard to wear out if well cared for. It has a nine-round magazine capacity due to its long grip. The safety is certain, but you must shift the weapon in your hand to pull it back and off. It can be put on without shifting. This is backward; it is more important to remove a safety rapidly than it is to reengage it. There is no hold-open device when the last round is fired. Indexing is difficult due to the rear sight's pyramid shape and the small, shallow front blade. When fired rapidly, the rear sight has points that can cause confusion with the front sight. The trigger guard is small, given the large trigger, and could cause a problem with a gloved hand. There is not a lot to recommend this pistol: its sights are hard to use, its safety is hard to disengage, and it is heavy and underpowered.

M1935S

Caliber: 7.65mm French Long   **Manufacturer:** French state factories   **Typical Use:** Military and self-defense

The French used the M1935S in the colonial wars from 1945 to 1960 in Africa and Southeast Asia. In Algeria in the 1950s, the M1935A and S models were issued to civilians who were at risk from the guerillas because the newly-designed MAC 50 9x19mm pistol was in short supply. Only a few had been made prior to the German occupation, so they were not seen during World War II. About forty thousand were made during the war and procured by the Heereswaffenamt for Germany. As with all the French weapons tested, this one shot very good groups on the formal range. Although this weapon is not nearly as elegant as the M1935A, it seems rugged. The finish was painted flat black, easier to maintain than the blued M1935A finish. The safety is placed similarly to that of the M1935A, so it is slow and awkward. The M1935 has an underpowered cartridge; it should have been made in 9x19mm. As it is, the design is elegant except for the safety location. But the quality of design is lost with the odd 7.65 French long cartridge, which is slow in velocity, small in caliber, and light in weight—the opposite of what you want in a self-defense cartridge.

MAC 50

Caliber: 9mm Parabellum   **Manufacturer:** French state factories   **Typical Use:** Military and self-defense

The MAC 50 came into operation in the 1950s. It was the French Army service pistol for many years. The safety is located at the top of the slide. If using a one-hand hold, you have to break your grip to push the safety off or on. If you carry this pistol in condition three (hammer down, chamber empty) and rapidly retract the slide by pulling it with your left hand while your right hand pushes on the receiver, the safety may automatically disengage. Your finger can drag on it, causing it to slip off automatic as the slide closes on a loaded chamber. The magazine release is well located. The slide stop is well fitted. The slide moves forward with a simple touch. There is a loaded chamber indicator; the extractor pushes up when the weapon is loaded, though you can always see or feel if the weapon is loaded. Accuracy is adequate with this weapon :five-shot groups fired within 4¼ inches. As I've found in most French pistols, the trigger pull is wonderful. The weapon is well made and of high quality. The grip appears long, but it feels good in my hand. Sights are adequate for formal target work, but on the cinema range, they were gray and low, making indexing difficult. Even in the down position, the hammer looks as if it is half-cocked. This allows you to rapidly cock the weapon with the left, or weak, hand if you carry in condition two (hammer down, chamber loaded). The weapon's design also lets you carry it in condition one (hammer cocked, safety on, chamber loaded), handy when you continue moving after firing a shot. Overall, the MAC 50 was far superior to weapons previously used by the French military.

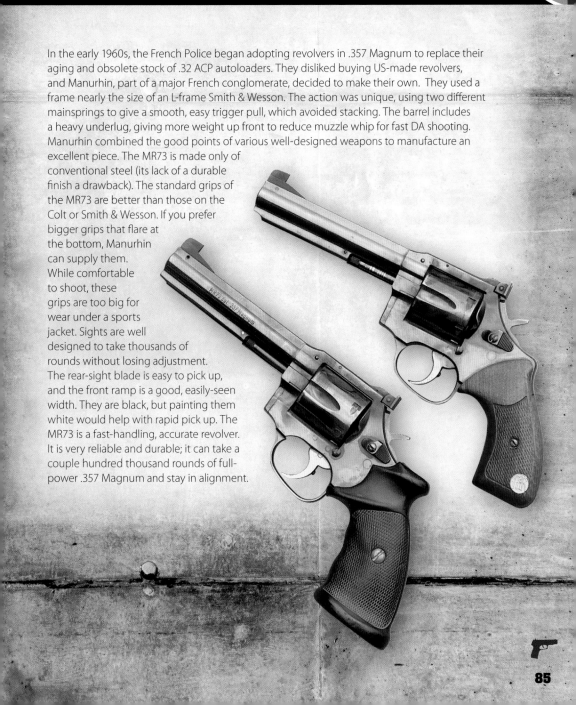

MANUHRIN MR73

Caliber: .357 Magnum   **Manufacturer:** Manhurin   **Typical Use:** Police and self-defense

In the early 1960s, the French Police began adopting revolvers in .357 Magnum to replace their aging and obsolete stock of .32 ACP autoloaders. They disliked buying US-made revolvers, and Manurhin, part of a major French conglomerate, decided to make their own. They used a frame nearly the size of an L-frame Smith & Wesson. The action was unique, using two different mainsprings to give a smooth, easy trigger pull, which avoided stacking. The barrel includes a heavy underlug, giving more weight up front to reduce muzzle whip for fast DA shooting. Manurhin combined the good points of various well-designed weapons to manufacture an excellent piece. The MR73 is made only of conventional steel (its lack of a durable finish a drawback). The standard grips of the MR73 are better than those on the Colt or Smith & Wesson. If you prefer bigger grips that flare at the bottom, Manurhin can supply them. While comfortable to shoot, these grips are too big for wear under a sports jacket. Sights are well designed to take thousands of rounds without losing adjustment. The rear-sight blade is easy to pick up, and the front ramp is a good, easily-seen width. They are black, but painting them white would help with rapid pick up. The MR73 is a fast-handling, accurate revolver. It is very reliable and durable; it can take a couple hundred thousand rounds of full-power .357 Magnum and stay in alignment.

The French Gendarme Nationale provides policing in the rural areas of France and enforces civilian law, yet the members are technically part of the military. They are more like the US Highway Patrol or State Police officers, though equipped more like the military than the police The Gendarme Nationale uses the French Service 9x19mm handgun. Until recently, this was the MAC50, a solid, steel-framed, single-column, SA pistol with good sights but with an unfortunate slide-mounted safety. Having to draw the slide to the rear slowed response time. In the late 1980s, France began replacing these weapons with the Beretta M92. This required the safety to spring back in place when released, solving the problem of accidentally leaving the safety on. It is otherwise the same as the US Standard M9 pistol. The French did not want to rely on Italy to supply their weapons, so obtained a license to build them from Beretta. GIAT, the large industrial group which makes tanks and other ordnance, manufactured the pistols. After extensive use, I have discovered that they are very accurate, pleasant to shoot, have good sights and triggers, and are incredibly reliable. They are wide, so not comfortable inside the waistband, but fine for a belt gun. I have one that I have put at least thirteen thousand rounds through and have yet to clean it. The locking block will occasionally break without warning, however, completely tying up the weapon, which is an alarming feature.

SIG 20/22

Caliber: 9x19mm   **Manufacturer:** SIG   **Typical Use:** Police and self-defense

The French Police have recently chosen the SIG 20/22 as their weapon in 9x19mm chambering. It is also available in .40 S&W and .357 SIG. It is viewed it as a low-price alternative to the SIG P226/9 series, and unpopular in the United States. But its popularity in France should tell you that it is a pretty good weapon. By design, it is a DA/SA weapon, but it can be modified to be a DAO. It has a polymer frame and holds fifteen rounds in 9x19mm. Sights are easily replaceable by pushing them in the slots in the slide, allowing the proper zeroing of the pistol. The trigger pull on DA is heavier and less smooth, and the SA seems heavy with a lot of overtravel to it. If you can fight the trigger into submission, accuracy is quite good as with all SIG pistols. It has a nice rust-resistant finish and overall presents a good business-like appearance. If it did not have to compete with its classier relatives of P226/9 heritage, it would be much more popular in the United States. It is a handgun for general defense purposes.

The MAS 38 SMG is light, handy, and short; it balances nicely between the hands. It has an excellent dust cover, good sights, and a straight-line stock to minimize muzzle rise. What it lacks is a proper cartridge: the 7.65mm French long caliber is insufficient for an SMG cartridge. If made in 9x19mm, it would have been a wonderful weapon. The stock is sloped slightly downward. That slight angle allows sights fitted to the top of the receiver to be mounted without projecting upward too much, unlike with such straight-line stocks as the M16 rifle. The front sight has a slot cut in it (like on the French 8mm carbine) that accommodates a thick front sight to allow quick pick up. It gives the shooter more time to center it in the peep for good accuracy. The rear sight consists of two peeps that fold down into the top of the receiver when not being used. It seems sturdy, although isn't protected by any wings. It takes time to remove the barrel on the MAS 38. Cleaning is difficult because you need hot water due to the corrosive primers typically used by French military and police. It is a no-nonsense barrel—short in length and unencumbered by cooling rings and other factors common to weapons of that period. The barrel is perfectly adequate for an SMG designed for 200 meters or less. Overall, the MAS 38 is a very handy, solid SMG with many good features. However, no positives can overcome the weak cartridge it uses.

The MAT 49 was the standard French SMG in the campaigns of Indochina and Algeria. It was a rugged and inexpensive piece of equipment. The MAT 49 offers a few "French" design features that distinguish its weapons. The magazine housing on the MAT 49 was designed to fold up, which makes storage easy while a soldier was riding a bicycle, still common in France. Similarly, the stock telescopes provide a short package for carrying on a bike or other vehicles, although this is not a good shooting platform. Extended, it is fairly stable, and the 9x19mm cartridge keeps recoil light so doesn't bruise the shooter's cheek. The pistol grip is nicely angled, and the grips have a palm well. A grip safety is incorporated, which helps guard against accidental firing if the weapon is dropped. The front sight is well protected by a sturdy hood and is a good blade shape. The rear sight, a notch, offers two positions, and is well protected against damage. Field-stripping is rapid and easy because the parts are big and sturdy. The weapon opens up easily so the barrel can be cleaned from the rear. The MAT 49 has no selector, but the cyclic rate on the MAT 49 is low enough that it is easy to fire single shots. The weapon is heavy between the hands and feels somewhat dead. As there is no safety other than a grip safety, the shooter must either carry the weapon with the bolt open ready to fire (always dangerous), or cock it when ready to fire, which slows reaction time. Fortunately, the bolt handle is on the left side, which allows the shooter to keep his right hand in the firing position.

M1886 R93 8MM LEBEL

Caliber: 8mm   **Manufacturer:** French state factories   **Typical Use:** Military

This was the first military rifle designed for smokeless powder, a major breakthrough in firearms technology. The M1886 R93 8mm Lebel was standard issue in World War I and was also seen in the field during the early stages of World War II. The rifle contains a tube under the barrel that holds eight cartridges. The Lebel avoids detonations by using a groove around the primer, and the head of the bullet fits into a groove rather than resting on a primer. The bolt-action is stiff and awkward, resulting in slow reloading. The bolt handle has an odd shape. You must grab the bolt handle with the fingers instead of manipulating it with your palm, as on most bolt-action rifles. You must loosen a screw to disassemble the two-part bolt for cleaning. The weapon's sights are calibrated from 400 to 2,400 meters, so the weapon shoots high at 100 yards. There is a small front sight and tiny U-shaped rear slot. Both are hard to see, and keeping proper elevation is difficult. The weapon lacks an upper forearm and gets hot with very few shots fired. The trigger is very straight, so my finger moved to the top of the trigger. This caused me to hit the bottom of the receiver, which impeded accuracy. Despite the long barrel, it balances nicely and has both a moderate report and recoil. You can short-stroke the rifle; that is, pull the bolt back far enough to eject an empty, yet not enough to chamber a new cartridge. You must pay careful attention to avoid being caught with no chambered cartridge. This was a rugged rifle during World War I, and the use of smokeless powder was a revolutionary step forward.

This was a standard battle rifle used by French forces during World War I. It saw limited use in early-World War II and some later by the French in Vietnam. The front sight is square, narrow, and hard to see. The rear notch is a shallow U and difficult to use. Neither sight has any protection. The rear ramp is calibrated from 400 to 2,400 meters, which is difficult to use at real combat ranges. The rifle lacks a safety. This may actually help in keeping the shooter alert and getting shots off quickly. The trigger on both the rifle and carbine versions is straight, which tends to cause your trigger finger to migrate to the top of the trigger and hit the bottom of the receiver, throwing off your shots. The trigger pull is heavy and the firing pin fall is long and heavy, but neither causes a problem. Recoil is mild and the report is low, especially compared to the carbine version. No butt trap exists to house cleaning supplies, nor is there a cleaning rod. The lack of an upper handguard must have been painful when using a bayonet, because the soldier would have to place his left hand over the front part of the barrel, which could burn it. The rifle is long but not heavy. Fortunately, it balances toward the rear, so both off-hand shooting and kneeling shooting are easy. For its purpose in World War I, the length would be an advantage when used with a bayonet, but awkward in a tight trench.

MAS 36—7.5 FRENCH

Caliber: 7.5x54mm French   **Manufacturer:** French military arsenals   **Typical Use:** Military

This was the last rifle adopted by the French Army before World War II. The MAS 36 uses a bolt with the locking lugs on the rear and an odd-shaped handle. In actual tests, this was not awkward, but you had to grip the handle rather than merely hit it with the palm of your hand. The action is smooth. Recoil and muzzle blast are heavy. A spike-style bayonet is stored in a container beneath the barrel; pushing the button allows you to withdraw it, invert it in the container (which becomes the mounting point), then affix the bayonet to the barrel. The bayonet is lightweight but rattles in the container. The MAS 36 lacks a safety, which may help the shooter be careful, and helps get shots off quickly. The sights on the MAS 36 are excellent. The front sight has a pyramid-style front, which is flat on top. The shooter can keep elevation consistent. It is protected by a sight hood. The rear sight is an excellent, sturdy peep unit with adjustments down to a practical two hundred meters. Both sights are quick to uses even in dim light. The rifle has stripper clips to load it and the system is very fast. The trigger was quick and reliable and that, coupled with the excellent sights and balance, allowed accurate shooting at two hundred and three hundred yards. The MAS 36 is a much-underrated rifle.

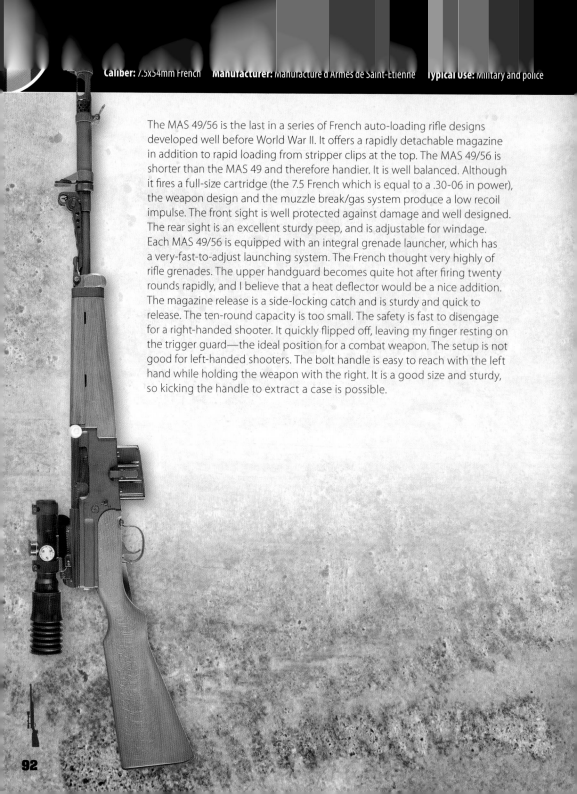

The MAS 49/56 is the last in a series of French auto-loading rifle designs developed well before World War II. It offers a rapidly detachable magazine in addition to rapid loading from stripper clips at the top. The MAS 49/56 is shorter than the MAS 49 and therefore handier. It is well balanced. Although it fires a full-size cartridge (the 7.5 French which is equal to a .30-06 in power), the weapon design and the muzzle break/gas system produce a low recoil impulse. The front sight is well protected against damage and well designed. The rear sight is an excellent sturdy peep, and is adjustable for windage. Each MAS 49/56 is equipped with an integral grenade launcher, which has a very-fast-to-adjust launching system. The French thought very highly of rifle grenades. The upper handguard becomes quite hot after firing twenty rounds rapidly, and I believe that a heat deflector would be a nice addition. The magazine release is a side-locking catch and is sturdy and quick to release. The ten-round capacity is too small. The safety is fast to disengage for a right-handed shooter. It quickly flipped off, leaving my finger resting on the trigger guard—the ideal position for a combat weapon. The setup is not good for left-handed shooters. The bolt handle is easy to reach with the left hand while holding the weapon with the right. It is a good size and sturdy, so kicking the handle to extract a case is possible.

FAMAS G2

Caliber: Submachine gun **Manufacturer:** Manurhin **Typical Use:** Military and police

The FAMAS G2 developed from the G1 model. One change is a special style of trigger guard, which lets the weapon's trigger be used without flipping the guard aside when wearing mittens. It uses NATO-style M16-style magazines rather than the unique FAMAS magazines originally needed. The weapon is equipped with a three-shot burst feature accessible from either side. It will fire in semi-only mode when the safety is pushed to the right side of the weapon by the trigger finger. Pushing it away from the finger puts the weapon off safe and on automatic fire. As shoulder-fired weapons are typically used in semi-auto, this seems odd. The three-shot burst system worked flawlessly and I found the full-auto cyclic rate quite controllable, allowing me to easily fire two-shot bursts. Despite using M16-style magazines, the weapon does not lock open with the last round fired. This is a drawback in combat situations. The sight picture and set-up are the same as on the G1. But the sights are rudimentary compared to optical sights available now to troops. The FAMAS G2 is superior to the G1. It has an unmistakably French flair to it, is handy in the field, and feels lively. It has proven itself reliable and durable. It's well balanced, and equal or superior to many iron-sighted rifles.

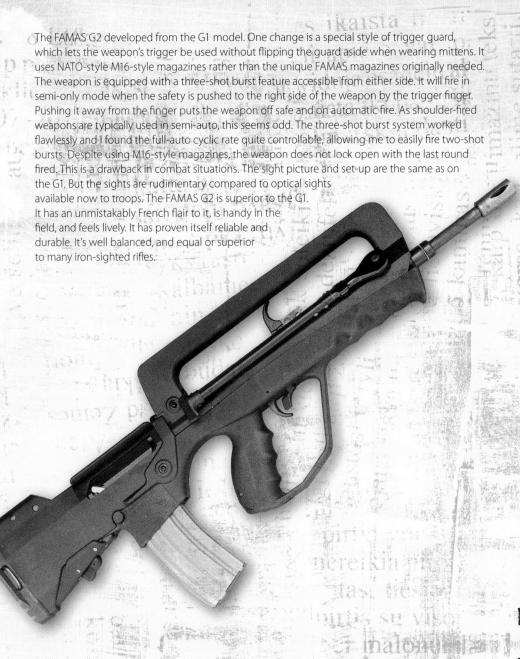

MODEL 1915 CSRG (CHAUCHAT) 8MM

Caliber: 8mm Lebel   **Manufacturer:** Gladiator SIDARME   **Typical Use:** Military

The CSRG, or Chauchat, is an undervalued weapon. Produced from 1915–1918, it was made from stamping and simple tubes. The CSRG was an infantry squad weapon not meant to be a gunsmith's masterpiece or fire thousands of rounds. The CSRG has some strong points. It does not need water as the German MG 08/15 LMG does. It is recoil-operated, not gas-operated, like the Browning Automatic Rifle (BAR). Its cyclic rate is low enough that you can easily fire single shots. It is lighter than a Lewis Gun, balances better, and was available in good numbers. The grip angle is straight so does not give a natural shooting grip. The combination selector/safety is stiff and difficult to operate. The shooting hand or the off-hand has to be removed from the firing position to operate it. Shooting carefully from full-auto is a solution. Recoil is high given the weapon's weight, and the shooter should place his cheek on the receiver tube, not the end cap. The receiver is black metal and was hot on my face. The front sight is an unprotected pyramid type and the back is a notch rear. Both blurred as soon as the first shot was fired and were hard to see. The magazine is flimsy sheet-steel construction. The rimmed 8mm French ammo and the magazine's curve make it difficult to load. You have to make certain that the cartridge lip is inserted properly. It holds only twenty rounds, not enough for combat effectiveness. Firing from an open bolt, the CSRG had limited fine accuracy.

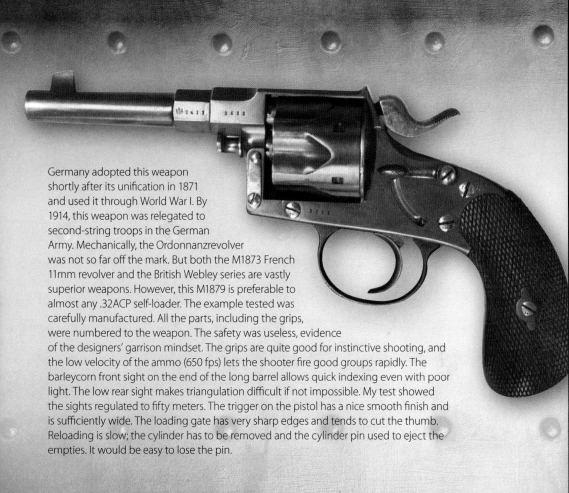

Germany adopted this weapon shortly after its unification in 1871 and used it through World War I. By 1914, this weapon was relegated to second-string troops in the German Army. Mechanically, the Ordonnanzrevolver was not so far off the mark. But both the M1873 French 11mm revolver and the British Webley series are vastly superior weapons. However, this M1879 is preferable to almost any .32ACP self-loader. The example tested was carefully manufactured. All the parts, including the grips, were numbered to the weapon. The safety was useless, evidence of the designers' garrison mindset. The grips are quite good for instinctive shooting, and the low velocity of the ammo (650 fps) lets the shooter fire good groups rapidly. The barleycorn front sight on the end of the long barrel allows quick indexing even with poor light. The low rear sight makes triangulation difficult if not impossible. My test showed the sights regulated to fifty meters. The trigger on the pistol has a nice smooth finish and is sufficiently wide. The loading gate has very sharp edges and tends to cut the thumb. Reloading is slow; the cylinder has to be removed and the cylinder pin used to eject the empties. It would be easy to lose the pin.

MAUSER M96

Caliber: 7.62x25mm (Mauser 7.63; .30)   **Manufacturer:** Mauser   **Typical Use:** Military and self-defense

The Mauser model 1896 7.63mm was one of the first serious semiautomatic combat pistols in the world. The Mauser M96 or copies are still commonly encountered and respected in many of the more remote areas of the world. On the formal target range, accuracy was unspectacular. Group sizes with the butt stock affixed were about half the size of those without it. The sights are very difficult to see. The rear sight is shallow (a narrow V shape), and the front sight is a large barleycorn, and this combination complicates the shooter's efforts to keep a proper target picture on the range. Although the sights are calibrated to some one thousand meters, this really is not a one thousand-meter pistol by any means. If in good condition and the butt stock is affixed, however, it might be a serious three hundred-meter pistol. It could be viewed more as a carbine than a pistol under those circumstances. Where this pistol really excelled was on the cinema range. I have shot Mauser military pistols before but, like many people, I fired them on casual or formal target ranges and never really fired them under combat conditions. Therefore, I always viewed them as obsolete. So when I took it to the cinema range, I expected the weapon to exhibit violent recoil and twisting in my hand and prove to be a very ineffective combat weapon. This is *wrong*! I was shocked, truthfully, at how well this performed on the cinema range. I found my performance with the Mauser to be as good as my performance with the Colt Government Model. The safety engaged and disengaged rapidly and my thumb could rest on the safety ready to be flipped off rapidly while covering suspects on the cinema range just like you do with a Colt Governement Model safety. First shot and repeat shots were also quick and on target. The high front sights on this weapon aided rapid indexing, which was apparent in the poor-light conditions of the cinema range. The grip did not shift in my hands as I had anticipated. The barrel gets hot after only thirty rounds, but that is not surprising in light of the small diameter. The pistol is bulky for the caliber, and it is too complicated to be made cheaply enough for modern militaries. But if you are going into a situation in which you have a Mauser military pistol loaded with factory-fresh 7.63 ammo, you are by no means at a disadvantage. This is a fine, well-designed combat weapon. It may look obsolete, but it is in fact a good fighting handgun. I recommend it highly.

The P.08 Luger is one of the most familiar silhouettes in the world. It was a much-favored souvenir of both World Wars and, to this day, has a large following, largely because it is a very accurate weapon. The design of the gun makes the action very strong. Triggers are often quite bad but an occasional good example does pop up. Sights are the typical European barleycorn front and V-shaped rear. On the darkened cinema range the front sight on the skinny barrel picks up fast, but the dark, shallow, low, and difficult-to-see rear sight slows your ability to triangulate on the range. The grip is quite good and is copied today in the H&K P7 and Glock 17 pistols. The pistol has a loaded-chamber indicator but it does not have a magazine safety. The standard P.08 does not have a grip safety, thus the shooter must depend on the side safety only, which is poorly situated for quick removal and reapplication. You have to break your firing grip to remove it or apply it. Many people have reported over the years that Lugers are unreliable, but I have never encountered any problems with functioning. Most problems that people report are traceable to poor magazines or low-power ammo. Assuming that you have a pistol with matching numbers, you should use good magazine and ammunition that is rated to what we in the United States call +P power levels. These are a lot of mismatched clunkers around which may have functioning problems. Lugers have been popular since they first came out. You can find commercial and military models all over the world; it has been manufactured in four countries in innumerable variations. Knowing how to work a Luger and what its strengths and weakness are can come in handy. Although I think a Luger pistol is one of the worst semiautomatic pistols for military purposes, many people like the mystique that goes with them, and they are generally very accurate.

"ARTILLERY" LUGER M1917-P.08 LANGE

Caliber: 9x19mm Parabellum   **Manufacturer:** Mauser, DWM   **Typical Use:** Military and self-defense

The Artillery Luger was designed during World War I to equip troops who could not carry a rifle but who needed an accurate weapon that provided more sustained-fire capability than a handgun. German machine gun troops used it, frequently with a thirty two-shot drum magazine. The six-inch barrel length of the navy model, no doubt, was familiar because it was adopted before the army used the P.08. I fired it both with and without the stock. Using the stock makes firing easier while running or crawling. During World War I, men typically shot one handed. The stock forced them into a Weaver-type stance, which helps accuracy. Even today, a lightweight butt stock would come in handy for a helicopter pilot, artilleryman, or combat engineer. The Artillery Luger has the same drawbacks as the common four-inch-barrel model. The sights are hard to see on both the conventional and cinema ranges. The safety is difficult to disengage rapidly, and the trigger is not very good. That said, the weapon shoots well and is surprisingly effective.

DREYSE

Caliber: 7.65 Browning   **Manufacturer:** German state factories   **Typical Use:** Military and self-defense

More than 250,000 Dreyse pistols were made by the end of World War I. The German military had eighty thousand of them. The Dreyse is an inferior pistol, especially compared to the same power-to-weight ratio pistols as the Model 03 Browning. The Dreyse has only one good feature: the quality of the machining is superb which makes stripping a breeze. A typical German gun, it has too many parts (all of them small) and too many springs. The sights are terrible. They are down in a dished-out groove in the top of the slide, and there is a tendency (particularly in fast combat-range situations) to pick up the side of the slide rather than the sight itself, causing you to be way off target. The serrations on the side of the slide are sharp and the spring is heavy, which sliced my thumb. The safety is awkwardly located. With practice, you can flip it off with one hand, but it is slow and uncertain. You cannot reengage it without using two hands, which is dangerous and inefficient. Carrying a cocked, loaded Dreyse pistol and shoving it back into my belt without putting on the safety is frightening. It has a poorly designed trigger pull; you pull through it to withdraw the firing pin and then it breaks very suddenly. It has a rounded grip that is sharp and simultaneously causes the weapon to shift in your hand. It kicks far more than it should for the little 7.65 cartridge it shoots.

This pistol is well made but its design is terrible. Removing the heel-butt-mounted magazine does not close the slide when withdrawn, but the slide does close when the magazine is inserted. The heel-mounted magazine release makes it slow to reload. The safety is extremely difficult to work; it is shrouded by a wood strip, and needs heavy, direct pressure on the small button to disengage. You can't withdraw the slide with the safety on. This is a dangerous feature if carried with the chamber empty and a loaded magazine, as it could seriously impact loading the weapon. You must choose a holster carefully because of this safety. The front sight is a European barleycorn design. Both front and rear sights are small and dark, which makes them difficult to use. The grip is comfortable except for a spur projecting from the magazine, which hit my little finger. You cannot grind off the spur as it's needed to retrieve the empty magazine due to its heel-mounted magazine release. The trigger has a considerable amount of slack before it fires.

MAUSER HSC

Caliber: .32 ACP (.380 ACP)　**Manufacturer:** Mauser　**Typical Use:** Military and self-defense

This is another German-designed 1930s commercial pocket pistol. It was similar to and competed with the Walther PP series. During World War II, Germany used thousands of these weapons as a substitute pistol and they are common today. They are no longer being manufactured. The slide on the Mauser does not cut your hand the way the Walther does, a major improvement. The Mauser HSc sights are hard to see, making rapid indexing difficult. Both front and back are low and small. It is difficult to hold elevation. The trigger has a funny little hook at the bottom that felt odd and cramped my finger. The magazine release is butt mounted which, though slow, prevents the holster from bumping out the magazine. The magazine has an extension on it to allow the larger hand to hold the pistol better. Unfortunately, the extension is designed backwards; it stretches the little finger awkwardly; it should be reversed. The DA trigger is heavy and hard to control when firing, but this makes it safer to carry with the safety disengaged. The pistol offers a hold-open device indicating when the last round has been fired, a desirable feature. The safety works like any slide-mounted safety but you must push it off firmly; it is not off when slightly ajar. Available in .32 ACP, they are also found in .380 ACP. At 20½ ounces, the Mauser is too heavy for its caliber. Still a Mauser HSc is a good pistol and is widely available, making it worthwhile to be familiar with it.

The German Army used the Sauer Model .38 pistol as a substitute weapon during World War II. The Sauer has a concealed hammer, so it stays clean. It uses a DA trigger system. It has a cocking lever. Subsequent shots can be fired in SA, but you can easily return to DA, by using the same lever to decock it. I encountered no slide or hammer-bite problems with the Sauer. The concealed hammer makes it easy to get out of a pocket and it has a loaded-chamber indicator. The M38 has a good safety, a nicely-located decocking lever, and it felt good in my hand. The sights are small but allow good indexing. The sealed action also remains clean. I would rate this the best of the .32 ACP pocket pistols tested from that pre-1945 period. Caliber is a serious issue with these pistols. Burst-fire methodology (emptying the magazine into the intended target) is the only way to offset this problem. By doing so, you are basically converting the pistols into single-shot shotguns. The Sauer Model .38 is preferable to a Walther PP/PPK.

WALTHER PP/PPK

Caliber: .380, .32 ACP, (.25 ACP, .22)   **Manufacturer:** Walther   **Typical Use:** Military and self-defense

James Bond made the Walther PP/PPK pistol famous. The Germans used Walther PP/PPK pistols as substitute pistols during World War II, mainly in .32 ACP. They also come in .380, .25 ACP, and in .22. These pistols were available commercially worldwide before World War II. A few years after the war, models made in France and Germany reappeared on the world market. The sights are hard to see for target work because of the small size and narrow notch. The SA trigger is good, but the DA pull was heavy and tended to stick before giving way without warning. The slide movement is notorious for slicing your hands. The non-selectable DA trigger-style is a liability after the first shot. You are faced with dropping the hammer and starting again with a heavy, DA pull, or manually recocking it. The alternative is to run with a loaded handgun with the safety off and finger off the trigger. The grip feels good even though it is short and I can get only two fingers on it. The size and weight of the pistol are good, but the .32 ACP caliber has poor stopping power, and the .380 is borderline in power. The Walther PPK is available in an alloy frame in .22 and .32 calibers, as well as steel framed.

WALTHER P38

Caliber: .9x19mm   **Manufacturer:** Walther and others during World War II   **Typical Use:** Military and self-defense

The German Army, growing in the 1930s, wanted a new service handgun in 9x19mm, and adopted the P38 Walther. It was the first handgun in 9x19mm with a DA trigger. Sights on the P38 are not great; the front is a European barleycorn type, and the rear has a shallow U-shape blade. This makes holding both elevation and windage difficult. On the cinema range, the front sight is quickly picked up, but triangulation is difficult because of the rear-sight setup. The pistol is wide and bulky for its cartridge size because the recoil springs are on the outside of the barrel rather than under it. Accuracy varies depending on how well the barrel and locking block are fitted to the frame. The SA pull on the tested example is short and light; the DA pull is heavy with a lot of slack. The safety can be applied to load the weapon, so the weapon does not have to be handled "hot." Most viewed the safety only as a decocker and kept it off so you could simply pull the trigger and fire the first shot. Although the P38 does not have a magazine safety, it does have a loaded-chamber indicator. The magazine release is located in the butt; you need two hands for release, making it slow. The weapon is easily stripped for field cleaning. The grip is comfortable and the weapon was designed for both left- and right-handed shooters.

In the 1970s, German police departments wanted a 9x19mm handgun suitable for uniformed and plainclothes officers in response to increasing terrorist problems. They specified that it have no manually-released safety, hold at least 8 rounds of ammo, fire 9x19mm cartridges, and meet certain weight and length requirements. Three weapons met the criteria: the Walther P5, the SIG P225 (P6), and the Heckler & Koch PSP (P7). The P5, while a traditional variant of the P38, is far less popular than the P6. Perhaps cost is one reason: the P5 is about twice as expensive as the P6. Despite this, these pistols are used by various paramilitary and police units worldwide. The slide on the P5 is solid on top unlike the P38 slide, which avoids the cracked slide problem. The decocker is on the receiver (instead of the slide) and easy to use. The sights are easy to pick up. The excellent trigger helps with accuracy.

The P5 has a built-in trigger stop with no overtravel and has a good surprise break. It is easy to load and drop the hammer. The DA pull is good and not as long in reach as many DA pistols. The heel-mounted magazine release slows reloading, and the magazine is single-column, limiting capacity. The slide is broad, not good for concealed carry, but fine for a military pistol. The P5 has an aluminum receiver, so it's lightweight. Recovery is fast. Overall, the P5 is large for its caliber, and neither as safe, due to the DA/SA trigger pull, nor as light as the Glock.

SIG P225

Caliber: 9x19mm **Manufacturer:** SIG **Typical Use:** Military and self-defense

The P220 was modified to shorten the weapon both in the slide/barrel and butt to make the P225. The German police tested it extensively and accepted it in the 1970s as one of three 9x19mm handguns to replace its aging fleet. While not representing any major technical breakthrough, it was the most common choice among German police agencies for years. Even with the shortened barrel and slide, muzzle whip was not an issue thanks to the 9x19 chambering. With a single-column magazine, the grip was quite handy. Available typically in a DA/SA model, it is also seen in DAO-style. Good sights, a fine single-action trigger system, excellent accuracy, and fine reliability are all typical SIG attributes found in this pistol.

The P7 was designed in response to the German police pistol trials of the 1970s. The P7 was unique because it had its cocking mechanism located in the weapon's grip. This pistol has no conventional safeties, per the police requirements. Grasping the weapon firmly cocks the weapon; letting go of the front strap allows the weapon to be decocked and thus completely safe. This design seems safe, but further use proves it is dangerous and should be avoided. The trigger is generally consistent, offering only a SA-firing. The size of the pistol is also fine for a 9mm handgun but the steel construction makes it too heavy. The fixed barrel allows for good accuracy. The sights were good both on the cinema and target ranges. The large, white front and rear sights facilitate good indexing and a quick response. The P7 can easily be used in either hand. But it still kicks as much or more than a .45 automatic. I have had four of these pistols break. Either the cocking mechanism or the firing pin broke after about three thousand rounds of full-bore European 9mm ammo. I've heard that now instead of fracturing, the mechanisms tend to be battered out of dimension, causing full-auto fire. The design of the P7 is not safe. As you pull the pistol out of the holster, you automatically cock it, so you are holding a cocked pistol with no safety and a very light trigger pull. Careful training would help, but there are much better options available, such as the Glock 17.

The Walther P99 has features that have been copied by its competitors. A hammerless polymer-framed pistol using a double-column magazine chambered in 9x19mm, it is also available in .40 S&W. It offers a number of different trigger systems in the same weapon. Set like a standard DA/SA weapon it has a heavy first DA pull followed up with light SA pulls. If the trigger is set all the way forward, it is pulled through the arc with very little pressure until you get to where you would normally feel the SA pull. You could carry it with the trigger set all the way to the rear using an SA-type trigger system. The safety is located on top of the side and actually is more of a decocker. This requires the shooter to break his grip. Sights are easy to change, which helps with getting the weapon properly zeroed for a given load and shooter. It has a good rust resistant finish. The most innovative, useful design on the pistol is the grip. By sliding panels in and out of the side of the grip, you can make it thicker or thinner. The rear portion of the grip also can be changed out to accommodate your hand size. Many others quickly copied this fine idea. Accuracy is quite good. So is the variety of trigger systems, but it is best to select one and practice with it. The short barrel does result in some muzzle whip when using high speed/pressure +P+ ammo. The felt recoil, thanks to the grip design, is quite manageable.

Starting in the mid-1970s, the SIG firm developed a line of DA (SA/DA) pistols made with alloy frames and pressed steel slides. Over the years, they have been modified with machined slides as technology has allowed them to be made quickly and accurately. First in this family is the P220. First available in 9mm and adopted in Switzerland in 1975 to replace the great but expensive P210 (known as the P49 in Switzerland), it is an accurate, dependable weapon. I have shot 2 ½-inch groups at fifty yards with my P220 and all have been are accurate. The sights are good, the SA pull quite crisp, although the DA seems heavy to me. Early ones had a heel-mounted magazine release, but soon the more desirable side-button release developed. They have been sold in .22 Rimfire, .38 Super, 7.65 Luger, and .45 ACP, as well as 9mm Luger. Recently, SIG has adapted the P220 to accept a higher capacity ten-shot magazine in .45 ACP while still keeping the grip area thin enough not to make it bulky and awkward. This is the new P227. If you don't have a P220 in .45 already and are in the market for such a weapon, it is hard to see why you would not get the P227 instead of a P220 since you gain a few rounds and lose nothing.

When the US military announced they wanted to adopt a new service handgun in the 1980s, SIG modified the P220 to accept a double-column magazine to hold sixteen rounds, making the P226 available. Slightly thicker but still quite nimble, it has been widely purchased by law enforcement and civilian self-defense proponents, and is a favored weapon of the US Navy SEALs. It is also available in .357 SIG and .40 S&W chamberings. These weapons are well known for being accurate and reliable. They are available with DA/SA triggers, DAO only (authorized as a duty weapon in New York City, most notably) and the DAK trigger system (which I think is the best option). It is an accurate, reliable, nimble weapon which can be carried concealed with a proper selection of holsters and a little effort, yielding a serious fighting handgun in time of need.

KORTH REVOLVER

Caliber: .357 Magnum   **Manufacturer:** Korth   **Typical Use:** Self-defense and target shooting

The Korth Company makes a variety of extremely well-made handguns. They are very expensive, but no one can fault the workmanship or materials used. They are popular in countries where shooters have money and are burdened by laws which limit their acquisition of firearms. In the United States, a Korth may cost 10 times as much as an Smith & Wesson, so the US consumer might prefer to buy 10 weapons. Where gun rights are restricted, the wealthy person might prefer to buy the best possible revolver for his firearms license spot, allowing one center-fire handgun. The Korth revolver illustrated is sized similarly to a Smith & Wesson K- or L-frame revolver and is chambered for .357 Magnum. It comes with a spare cylinder to shoot 9x19mm ammo. Accuracy is excellent. It has a very good SA pull and the DA pull was as good as a finely-done Smith & Wesson. The adjustable rear sight is precise and sturdy, bigger than a Smith & Wesson, more like the sight found on Colt or Ruger revolvers. The grip and stock fit perfectly but were poorly designed for rapid DA work. Upon firing full Magnum ammo rapidly, the weapon pounded the web of the hand and slipped downward, requiring me to pause and reposition my hand. For SA work, such stocks are acceptable but not for DA work. The cylinder release near the hammer is awkward. You can get used to it, but standard designs work so well, it is hard to justify this difference. The finish, a deep black, was excellent.

This P225 model was modified by the SIG Company to accept a double-column magazine, much as the P220 had been modified earlier, and became known as the P228. While SIG did not get the US Military award for a general-issue handgun, they did get the contract for a handgun to be issued to people needing a smaller, more concealable handgun. In this role, the P228 was given the military designation of M11. It has proven to be quite popular. Unlike the Beretta M9, no problems with breakage or functioning have ever been noted. With a thirteen-shot capacity and chambered for 9x19mm, it makes an excellent weapon for those who can carry a belt gun.

SIG P229

Caliber: 9mm (.40 S&W, 9x19mm)   **Manufacturer:** SIG   **Typical Use:** Military and self-defense

In the 1990s when the .40 S&W cartridge was introduced, many people thought they could simply rechamber 9mm pistols to accept the new cartridge. SIG soon realized that their existing platforms with pressed steel slides simply would not work, and developed a machined slide. It has replaced the stamped slides on the entire series except for the P225/228 models. SIG renamed the P228-sized pistol, after minor modifications in addition to the slide, the P229. All the good features of accuracy and reliability remained. The P229 is perhaps best known, in .357 SIG chambering, for its US Secret Service use. Any weapon good enough to protect the US President should be good enough for anyone. The Secret Service has been very smart in their choice of firearms. They have found the P229 to be a reliable, accurate weapon and are well satisfied with its performance in the field. It is also available in .40 S&W and even better in 9x19mm. This cartridge gives excellent stopping power while still offering cheaper practice ammo. It is available as a DA/SA weapon as well as DAO and with the DAK trigger system.

SIG P229 .22 RIMFIRE (DAK)

Caliber: .22 Rimfire   **Manufacturer:** SIG   **Typical Use:** Military, police trainer, and self-defense

While I have discussed the SIG P229 pistol, I want to mention this model separately. It is a standard P229 but instead of being available in a centerfire chambering, it is made in .22 Rimfire. This makes for a very useful and practical understudy or training weapon. It will fit in your standard holster, operates exactly the same as your centerfire model, and thus provides excellent, low-cost training to the shooter. Reliability, which can sometimes be difficult with a .22 Rimfire weapon, is excellent. Any difficulties with reliability are always traceable to the lead and lubricant residue building up on the face of the barrel near the chamber area. A few wipes with a rag using solvent will remove this residue and put you back in business. The weapon comes with adjustable sights which are very handy in allowing you to quickly and accurately zero your weapon. While not a target pistol, I have been able to put fifty shots into six inches off-hand at twenty five yards with it which is certainly good enough for a trainer. If you seriously use a P229 pistol, you should get a .22 Rimfire version. You will save the money it costs in ammo.

The M23 was designed to be an offensive pistol for the SOCOM. It is meant to be used in lieu of another weapon such as a rifle, carbine, or SMG. It did not need to be lightweight or easy to conceal. Like many Heckler & Koch designs, it is large in width, length, and depth. The slide of the weapon is heavy and thick. The polymer receiver, while large and thick, is light. The trigger guard is larger than normal to allow the use of gloves. The grip area is thick due to the double-stack, 12-shot magazine. It is difficult to load this magazine to full capacity. The decocker lever is convenient to the thumb. You can shoot this in the self-cocking mode (DA) or your can carry it cocked and locked. The safety is somewhat slow to remove but quick to re-engage. The DA trigger pull is typical for Heckler & Koch pistols—heavy and long. The SA pull is good, although not very crisp, and with overtravel. The sights were acceptable but not great. The heavy, thick slide coupled with the lightweight receiver caused recoil to feel odd, and I got a lot more muzzle whip than expected. Accuracy on the formal target range was acceptable.

After the German police trials in the 1970s, Heckler & Koch began selling a variety of personal defense handguns. Previously they had primarily made rifles and submachine guns. USP models were designed to be service-style pistols. Although they are blocky and thick, some have used them as concealed-carry weapons. The USP offers a wide variety of safety and trigger systems. It can go from the traditional DA/SA-style trigger to cocked and locked-style, to the constant pre-cocked LEM (law enforcement model) approach. All of the triggers seem heavy in pull whether DA or SA, and have a lot of overtravel, hampering accuracy on a weapon that is inherently accurate. The weapons are big in the grip area thanks to the double-column magazine. The USP Tactical is a standard USP equipped with an extended threaded barrel so a suppressor can be installed. High sights installed on the slide allow the shooter to align his weapon with the suppressor which would obscure standard height sights. The Heckler & Koch Elite version of the USP offers an extended slide and barrel which make for a different balance and less muzzle whip.

In an attempt to overcome the issues of fat slide and fat, awkward butt, Heckler & Koch developed the P2000 pistol. It is much thinner in the slide and narrower in the butt. It is an accurate pistol and if one works on mastering the LEM trigger, good results are achievable. I find the LEM trigger system slower for repeat shots than the Glock trigger action. Still, the P2000 is sufficiently convenient to carry that I can put one in a side pocket holster built by Rusty Sherrick and carry it with perfect concealment in business trousers. A shorter version of this pistol, called the P2000SK, is available and my friend, Leroy Thompson, likes his for pocket carry whereas I think it kicks and flips more.

The USP in .45 ACP is a large pistol. Heckler & Koch developed the HK45 and HK45C with a thinner slide and smaller butt to appeal to those who found the USP too large. This latter is a shorter version of the belt-holster-sized HK45 and holds eight rounds, compared with the standard ten of the HK45. The HK45 and HK45C are nice pistols, but have a lot more muzzle whip than a Colt Government Model, slowing repeat shots. A variety of trigger systems can be installed. The DA/SA system is not good, as the DA pull is very stiff and heavy with a lot of stacking. The LEM pre-cocked constant trigger seems best and is useful in these weapons. These Heckler & Koch pistols use a polygonal barrel rifling system, which is problematic. You cannot easily use lead bullets. While not a concern for the 9mm, with the .45s, cheap lead bullet reloads will let you afford to practice enough to master the weapon, yet they cannot be used in these weapons, making practice expensive.

HECKLER & KOCH P30

Caliber: .40 S&W, 9x19mm   **Manufacturer:** Heckler & Koch   **Typical Use:** Military and self-defense

The P30 pistol is slightly bigger than the P2000 and was designed to capture the police market that previously was using the USP models. It is thinner than the USP and can be made with an LEM trigger or standard DA/SA model. I find the safety system on the P30, with the decocker being at the end of the slide necessitating a shooter move his hand into a new position to activate it, a clear disadvantage. I am puzzled as to why anyone would accept it. But a number of European police agencies have adopted it and its slightly longer version, the P30L. I find the P30 with LEM trigger to be much better, although the LEM trigger is certainly not the easiest of the pre-cocked constant trigger systems to use. With lots of practice, you will get better but you need to keep it up as otherwise you will lose the skills so laboriously obtained to pull out good accuracy with an LEM trigger.

USP COMPAC

Caliber: .40 S&W, 9x19mm   **Manufacturer:** Heckler & Koch   **Typical Use:** Military, police, and self-defense

The USP Compac pistols are shorter in both slide/barrel and grip. They are reliable and designed to be concealed-carry pistols. The shorter slide increases muzzle whip. Thick in slide and fat in butt, they are less comfortable to carry even in an external belt holster, much less inside the waistband. The USP Compac in .40 S&W with an LEM trigger installed is the weapon authorized for federally approved pilots who are deputized as flight deck officers, which is an odd choice. The aggressive .40 S&W ammo coupled with the LEM trigger, which is long to pull and then suddenly goes off, makes getting good results difficult. Not surprisingly, none of the pilots I have instructed shot them very well, getting poor results in accuracy and speed.

The Bergmann M1918 set the pattern for SMG use that holds even today a short barrel, open-bolt firing, pistol caliber, high magazine capacity, and a marginal safety. SMGs today have gotten lighter, are made out of stampings, and are frequently more compact, but are very similar to the M1918. The Bergmann's cyclic rates are low, about 450 rpm. This allows for easy single shots and short bursts, even though the weapon lacks a selector. The safety on the M1918 consists of merely pulling the bolt to the rear and turning the handle in the cocking slot. This is slow to disengage and subject to slipping out of cold or wet hands. It also will jump out of the slot if dropped, causing inadvertent firing. The original M1918 SMG used the snail-drum Luger magazines. These drums are slow to load and expensive to make. They place the rounds farther out on the weapon, adversely altering the balance. In the post-WWI era, the M1918 SMG was modified to accept standard box magazines, which was a great improvement. The M1918 is a good, sturdy, durable weapon. With a few drawbacks, it has all the features necessary to make an effective SMG. This is quite a compliment to those original German designers in 1918.

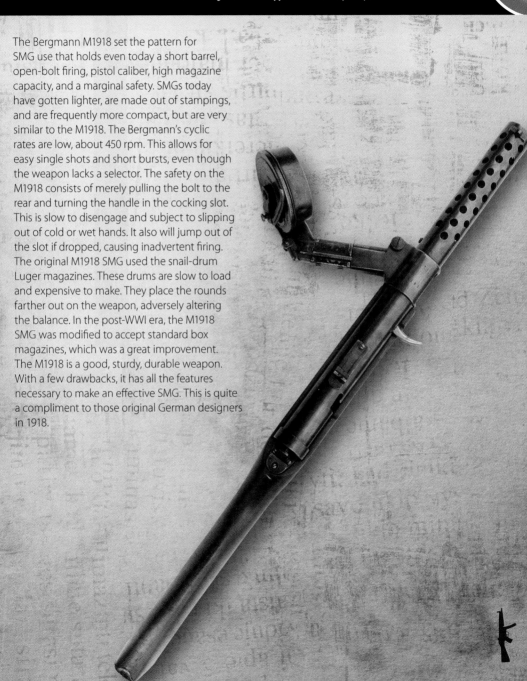

MP28

Caliber: 9mm **Manufacturer:** 9x19mm, 7.65 Luger, .30 Mauser **Typical Use:** Military and police

The MP28 is basically a slight refinement of the Bergmann M1918 used during World War I. Developed when SMGs were uncommon and the only real competition was the Thompson M1921, the MP28 was widely sold around the world. The MP28 was made with high-quality machining. The front sight is a typical European pyramid style and the rear sight is a small notch that blurs quickly upon firing the weapon. The MP28's safety is slow to disengage, slightly dangerous to engage if one's hands are slippery, and offers no safety to avoid accidental discharge if the weapon is dropped. The stock is a traditional wooden fixed stock with a solid butt plate. It is a very stable platform for shooting and is very durable. The MP28, like most SMGs, fires from the open-bolt position. The heavy bolt provides the only locking mechanism for the weapon, and the resulting heavy shifting weight makes sighted fire difficult, particularly at long ranges. The weapon can be quickly stripped for cleaning, and it is fairly resistant to mud and sand. The MP 28 uses a side-mounted magazine and the release button is not well protected. The side-mounted magazine allows for lower prone shooting, though it may be a problem going through doorways. The MP28 was not a great advance over the MP18, but it uses a much superior magazine system. Although it was heavy, it did fill its role for many armies in the 1920s and 1930s when the SMG was just coming into service.

The Bergmann MP35 is a typical first-generation SMG. It was made with great care out of machined parts and has a fixed, solid-wood stock. The Bergmann MP35 uses a reliable, two-position box magazine, which loads easily. It feeds from the right side, which allows for a lower prone position. The front sight is a European pyramid that can be adjusted to get the correct windage. The rear sight is a tangent with V-notch graduated in one thousand meters, too optimistic for a 9x19mm SMG. The weapon is accurate to three hundred yards. I easily and consistently shot ten x fourteen-inch metal plates at three hundred yards when firing on semi-auto. This is a heavy SMG—10.4 pounds loaded—so recoil is nil, and full-auto was easy to control and good. The bolt handle is located on the right side. Pulling it to the rear cocks the bolt, but it does not reciprocate with the bolt. It also is a closed unit, which helps keep dirt out of the system. The weapon has a safety lever on the left side. It is difficult to move positions rapidly; few likely used it, preferring instead to cock the weapon when ready to fire. The trigger system is selective by trigger squeeze. Pull it back halfway and it will fire semi-auto; pull it completely to the rear for full-auto. The weapon can be easily stripped to remove the barrel, making it easy to clean the barrel with hot water, necessary if corrosive ammo used. Although somewhat heavy, the Bergmann MP35 is a very well-made, highly-accurate, and controllable SMG.

MP40

Caliber: 9x19mm   **Manufacturer:** Erma   **Typical Use:** Military and police

The German MP40 is the most common version of the SMG series that began with the MP38. The weapon feels alive in your hands, unlike many SMGs. With good balance and lightness compared to other guns of the period, the MP40 is very nice to handle. The weapon fires from an open bolt. It has a bolt lock to avoid inertial firing, but has no safety except for a notch in the receiver. This is workable because it is faster to put the bolt home on an empty chamber than pull it to the rear to ready it, wrestle the bold handle from the safety notch, and then fire it. The front sight on the MP40 is protected by a hood that shields the front sight blade. The rear sight is a two-position leaf with a U-shaped notch, correct for one hundred and two hundred meters. It can be adjusted by the hammer-and-punch method. The rear sight is adequate for single shots, but when you fire burst, the rear sight is soon a blur lost in recoil. The cocking handle, located on the right side, projects far enough out that either hand can reach. The MP40 has a folding stock, which makes it easier to carry and store, but does not aid shooting. To open or collapse the stock on the MP40, you depress the button at the end of the receiver. The metal struts are uncomfortable on the cheekbone. Even worse, after much use, the locking points wear causing the stocks to wobble an inch or more. The pistol grip is nicely shaped and the panels are comfortable. The cyclic rate is low enough (about 550 rpm using standard military-grade ball ammo) that single shots are easily fired by trigger control. There is no selector. The MP40 makes a dandy carbine:three-shot bursts can be effectively delivered out to seventy five yards. You can easily hit chest-sized targets at two hundred yards with single shots. The MP40 has a plastic piece on the lower receiver designed to be the proper holding location. I find that location cramps my arms. The magazine release is a button, not a lever. Take care not to bump the magazine release or get a finger in the ejection port because it will tie up the weapon or hurt your hand.

WALTHER MPL/K

Caliber: 9x19mm   **Manufacturer:** Walther   **Typical Use:** Military

In the mid-1950s, Walther developed the MPL/K series of SMGs. The models differed only in barrel length; the K model was shorter than the L model. The Walther SMG used modern stamping techniques and designs to keep costs and production time down, and to produce a short overall length. The MPL/K has a few good points. The barrel, as well as other major parts, can be quickly removed to allow quick cleaning. The bolt cocker is easy to use and does not reciprocate with the bolt when firing. The pistol grip is nicely shaped and does have a flip-type safety, which can be used by right- or left-handed shooters. The safety selector is the typical German approach of safe, full-auto, and then a long stretch to semi-auto; most will have to adjust their grip to flip it. Cyclic rate is low enough to fire single shots easily. The trigger guard is big enough for gloved fingers but not mittens. The sights are well protected and offer both a peep and open sight at the same time. The rear is a peep unit, but the top has a wide-open slot for an open sight to be used in conjunction with the front sight. The standard front sight is a regular post, but the top of the circle of metal surrounding the post is a sight blade. It is very open and wide and, coupled with the open rear, is designed for rough work at night or

at very close range. This is an interesting concept and not seen on other weapons. There are drawbacks to the design. It is all metal so suffers from weather-related problems. It becomes too cold to hold comfortably in cold weather, too hot in summer. The magazine housing in front of the pistol grip lengthens the weapon. The magazine releases are stiff and difficult to operate on some tested, but not on others, as determined by the amount of wear. There is no protection against accidental dumping. The magazine housing is not beveled but is a straight-in type housing, so it takes time to insert magazines into the weapon. The stock folds and has two latches for stability. When collapsing it, it is easy to pinch your fingers in the latch area. Metal strut bar stocks are hard on the cheek, and the stock continually pounds the cheek when firing full auto. The Walther MPL/K offers very few, if any, improvements over such World War II designs as the MP40 or Sten.

HECKLER & KOCH MP5

Caliber: 9x19mm   **Manufacturer:** Heckler & Koch and other licensees   **Typical Use:** Military, police, and self defense

The MP5 is unusual for an SMG as it fires from a closed bolt. This aids accuracy as the bolt does not slam forward when you pull the trigger, jarring the weapon. The MP5, like all SMGs, should be used as a semi-auto short-barrel carbine, reserving full-auto fire for extremely close-range targets where the consequences of a stray round are not critical. The MP5 has two butt stocks: sliding and fixed. The sliding stock is uncomfortable because its metal struts hit the cheekbone. The fixed stock is better. The safety/selector on the MP5 is too short to be comfortably flipped with the thumb. You must shift the weapon in your hand. Because it fires from a closed bolt, you can use the safety and carry it loaded with a round in the chamber. The first stop is semi-auto fire, which is best for accuracy. The magazine release is centrally located. Different types of trigger housings are available. The standard provides for safe, semi-auto, and full-auto. Pistol grips now a come in two shapes: the older version and the tone that looks more modern. Forearms come in two types: the skinny version and the tropical version, which is fatter and allows you to fire more rounds without burning your hand. The trigger pull on the MP5 is as bad as that found on a G3, but is better than other SMGs. As with the G3, the weapon is designed so you could load it, put a round in the chamber, lock the safety off, throw it out of a helicopter at three hundred feet onto a steel deck, and it will not fire. This solves most SMG's common problem of accidentally firing if dropped, but it does make for a poor trigger pull. The MP5 is light, well balanced, handy, and reasonably accurate. Cleaning it is often difficult because of the small nooks and crannies in the receiver. It serves its intended purpose well: to provide low-penetration, short-range, reasonably-precise fire over a limited period. The MP5 is a fine if somewhat over-engineered SMG.

HECKLER & KOCH UMP

Caliber: 40 S&W (.45 ACP) **Manufacturer:** Heckler & Koch **Typical Use:** Police

The Heckler & Koch UMP (Universal Machine Pistol), available in both .40 S&W and .45 ACP, is designed for the "U.S." law-enforcement market. It is a good police SMG as it is lightweight and fires from a closed bolt. The tested UMP .40 SMG was an early gun. It functioned perfectly firing one thousand rounds of Wolf-Brand, 180 grain, .40 S&W ammo. The model was equipped with a two-shot burst system, but I got better groups firing on fast semi, which allows for better control. The UMP in .40 is accurate, easy to handle, and feels very lively in the hands. The selector switch is ambidextrous. It is long enough and positioned to permit it to be rapidly flipped off. The magazine on the UMP is clear plastic so you can determine ammo status. The magazine housing is nicely funneled and the release lever is well positioned for use by either hand. Removal and insertion are quick. The UMP has a hold-open device when the last shot is fired. The UMP is equipped with excellent sights, front and rear. The rear sight offers a peep and an open-notch rear. The weapon is readily stripped. The folding rear stock with its rubber-cushioned top is pleasant to use. The UMP stock is firm. The weapon has a plastic frame which seems to absorb recoil. The weapon offers a variety of hard mounting points for add-ons like laser-aiming devices, flashlight, or optics via its Picatinny rail system. Trigger pull was typical Heckler & Koch: heavy with lots of creep and overtravel.

The Gewehr 88 (GEW 88), also called Commission Rifle M1888, was the first Mauser rifle used to equip German troops. The M1888 resulted from a military commission attempting to selectdesirable features in a military rifle. It was a different design from subsequent rifles and used a different bullet diameter, .318 inches rather than .323, and produced a clip-loading repeater that shot a high-velocity, smokeless cartridge, superior to the single-shot, large-bore, black-powder rifles used previously. The M1888 uses a muzzle jacket and has no upper handguard. These designs rust and get hot in the sun. The Germans quickly realized this was a bad idea and discarded the muzzle jacket. The front sight is a typical unprotected, pyramid type, and the rear sight is also unprotected. In the lower position, the rear sight has a battle setting of four hundred meters. The V-shaped narrow rear sight is hard to see through. The safety is the wing type and locks the action when applied. It is very stiff and slow. It is best to leave the bolt handle up slightly and close it when ready to fire. It has a single-column magazine extending beyond and below the stock and has a bolt handle positioned between the receiver front and back. The bolt handle and knob are big enough to allow fairly fast use of the bolt. On the test example, the trigger pull had some slack in it but was very light. Even though this rifle was long and unwieldy, it was not muzzle heavy. Both of these traits are helpful for off-hand and kneeling shooting.

Caliber: 7.92x57mm Mauser   **Typical Use:** Military
Manufacturer: Mauser, Imperial Arsenals of Amberg, Danzig, Erfurt, Leipzig & Spandau

This was the standard infantry weapon of the mainline German forces in World War I and was used to a limited extent in World War II. This rifle is sighted from four hundred to two thousand meters. The rear sight has large ears on each side of the blade, which slows sighting. The front sight is the unprotected pyramid shape, which is difficult to use. The rifle is muzzle heavy, which makes shooting off-hand and while kneeling difficult. The long barrel minimizes muzzle blast and flash, but recoil is surprisingly high, given the weapon's weight. The M98 action has no bolt-hold-open device. In my rapid-fire drill with this rifle, I managed to close the bolt on an empty chamber and snap it empty. Combat weapons need a bolt hold to alert the shooter that it is time to reload. The rifle has other drawbacks: the safety is slow to operate, the butt plate is smooth and tends to slip off the shoulder (which slows reloading speed), and there is no trap to contain cleaning supplies (although a cleaning rod is slung under the barrel). Even though the rifle tested was made in 1912 and appears to be well broken in, the action was very stiff which slows shooting speed.

M98 MAUSER

Caliber: 7.92x57mm and others of similar length   **Manufacturer:** Mauser & others worldwide   **Typical Use:** Military

The Mauser M98 was the final development of the Mauser bolt-action rifle design. Even today, almost 100 years later, no more reliable bolt-action rifle has been designed. A discussion of the M98 is really a discussion of the action only. Any length or shape barrel in many different calibers can be added to it. A wide variety of sights and stocks can be put on that barreled action. They may look and feel slightly different, but all are M98 rifles and have the same basic reliability and quality. Considering the hundreds of M98 designs available, I reviewed my Mauser reference books and decided that I could fairly analyze the M98 using the Gewehr 98, Kar 948 K, M98 rifle in 7x57mm, Gewehr 33/40, and the Iranian M30 or Model 49 Carbine. Here are the points they have in common.

1. All chamber a real rifle cartridge.

2. All have pyramid front sights coupled with tangent rear sights.

3. All the various M98s evaluated take bayonets.

4. The M98 cannot be readily removed from the stock for cleaning. So maintenance is a problem.

5. The bolt handles on M98 come in a variety of patterns from turned down to straight out. The straight-bolt handle is slightly faster to use and operate.

6. Trigger pulls pull up through the slack to about 6 pounds. These two-stage pulls are safer and more reliable.

7. All have clip guides and hold five rounds, fed from the magazine. Five rounds and a stripper clip-loading system are slow compared to a detachable box magazine.

8. The safety is slow but certain. Turning the wing up halfway allows you to work the bolt but still prevents the weapon from firing. Flipping the safety all the way over locks the bolt and keeps the weapon from firing, but you need to use your shooting (strong) hand to take it off. Placed in the middle position, you immediately see it. When properly broken-in, you can flip the safety off with your thumb so won't need to break you grip on the weapon.

9. Recoil and blast are factors based on weight and muzzle length as well as caliber rather than design feature. The early M98s, like the Gewehr 98 with its 29.3-inch barrel, are much more pleasant to shoot than the 17.91-inch barrel of the Persian Model 30/49 carbine. You burn more powder in the barrel rather than the air with the longer barrel, and you move the blast further from your ears. The heavier 8mm rifles are much nicer than the lighter ones from the standpoint of felt recoil.

10. All the M98 stocks have metal butt plates, which make them rugged and durable. The rifles usually have cleaning rods slung under the barrels or they carry a jointed rod in the butt. Metal butt plates do not soak up recoil as rubber pads do, but they will last longer.

11. Except for rare examples, the stocks on M98s are wood. The stocks have a substantial wrist and are unlikely to break. An M98 rifle is a rugged and dependable piece of equipment. It may not be as fast as a Lee Enfield or Schimdt Rubin, and may not have as good a set of sights and safety as a Pattern 14/17 Enfield, but it still is a fine weapon.

The G33/40 was nothing other than a standard prewar Czech design that the Germans reinforced by adding some metal around the butt stock to allow the mountain troopers to use it as a climbing aid. The rifle uses a smaller diameter receiver than the standard Mauser action which makes it slightly lighter. The barrel is shorter and lighter in general. This results in a much lighter, handier weapon than the standard K98 Mauser rifle. The sights are standard Mauser: the front is the typical pyramid style, though well protected from accidental damage. The rear ramp has a V-shaped notch. The G33/40 is sensibly sighted with graduations from one hundred to one thousand meters. The sights are difficult to see and slow to use on fast situations and in dim light. Because of the rifle's lighter weight and shorter barrel length, recoil is heavier than usual for a K98, by about a 15 percent margin, not enough to cause a problem. The G33/40 is well balanced and not muzzle heavy, which offsets the increased recoil.

This is the German counterpart/competitor of the M1 Garand rifle. The K43 is as heavy as a Garand and is gas operated, and the recoil is accordingly lighter than the M98K. The trigger pull was gritty and not very precise. The front sight is a blade which was easy to see. It has a hood to protect it. The rear sight was U-shaped and shallow making it difficult to keep proper elevation. The magazine catch is usable but too small to allow speedy reloading. The bolt handle is conveniently placed to allow the shooter to pull the bolt to the rear with the left hand, while holding the rifle by the pistol grip with the right hand. It can be used with either hand, yet is canted enough to clear the scope when one is mounted. It has a dust cover that gets pushed back automatically when the first shot is fired. The safety, located on the rear of the receiver, is slow to engage and disengage. The stocks seem to be made out of laminated wood, which has proven to be stable and durable. The weapon is not particularly well balanced for off-hand shooting because the balance point is toward the back. The K43 represents an odd dead-end for German service rifle development. It uses the standard rifle cartridge, which makes it powerful, yet the designers limited the effective range of the weapon with poor sights.

GEW 98/40—8x57mm

Caliber: 8x57mm   **Typical Use:** Military
Manufacturer: Hungarian State Arsenal, modified by German Military Arsenals

The GEW 98/40 is a German wartime modification of the 8x56R Hungarian M35 rifle. By changing the magazine to a double-column type and re-chambering it for the rimless 8x57mm cartridge, a standard caliber, they avoided ammo complications. This rifle uses the split-receiver Mannlicher-style of action coupled with the Lee Enfield-type of two-piece stocks. The bolt handle is half-round with the bottom half checkered. It is not particularly fast and you tend to lift it with the heel of your hand then place your fingers around the knob to draw it to the rear. Since the knob is in the middle of the receiver rather than at the end, as typical on Mausers, you must reach forward an extra inch and a half to grab it, slowing the reloading process. The sights are a pyramid front sight coupled with a small notch rear open sight. The sight elevations are reasonable: they are graduated from one hundred to two thousand meters. The front sight has a large front sight hood to keep it shaded and avoid damage. While helpful on a sunny day, it is difficult to pick up when dark. Accuracy is typical for this type of rifle, but the sights make it difficult to get consistently good results. The trigger pull is as good as found on many factory rifles today. The safety is the standard wing Mauser type. It is safe, but removing it to permit a rapid shot is difficult. The stock feels surprisingly square in my non-shooting hand, and is less comfortable than a rounded stock. The stock gets squarer as it gets closer to the muzzle.

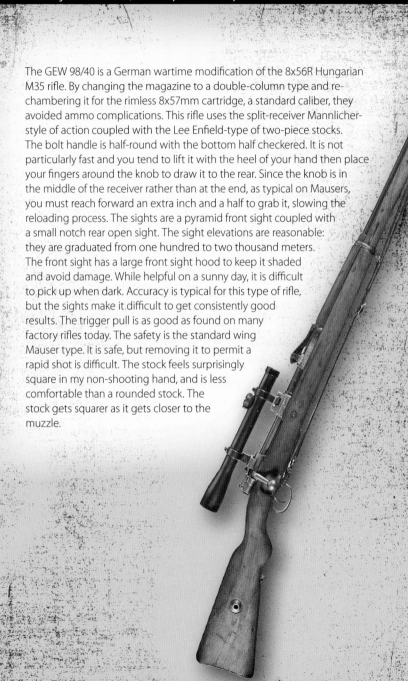

The German High Command during World War II apparently decided to ignore the battlefield request for a 4X scope to be used by snipers and developed instead the 1.5X unit. These were to be mounted on standard K98 Mauser rifles. The Mauser 98 rifle selected was not modified in any way. The trigger pull was standard and no special fitting was evident. The regular iron sights on both front and rear retained a pyramid front that was well protected and a V-shaped notch rear sight. On the test example, the scope is a 1.5X unit that has a long-eye relief, allowing it to be mounted on the right about where the ramp rear sight is located on an M98. The reticle consists of a post reticle coupled with a crosswire to help the shooter avoid canting. The sight is dark and has a narrow field of view. The scope is detachable, but once removed and replaced the POI shifts. The forward mounting of the scope allows the normal safety to be used, and this also preserves the option of clip loading. The scope is graduated from one hundred to eight hundred meters. The rifle tested was ill balanced and muzzle heavy. Off-hand and kneeling work were very difficult and my results were poor. The M700 Remington with a 1.5X5 power scope turned down to 1.5X will get better results. The M98 set up this way can't be considered a good sniper rifle. Perhaps this combination was meant to give normal frontline troops a rifle that was easier to shoot than the standard M98 rifle.

MP 43/4—7.92x33mm

Caliber: 7.92x33mm   **Manufacturer:** Walther   **Typical Use:** Military and police

The 7.92x33 cartridge was a real breakthrough in military weapons. During World War I, German ordnance came up with the idea of a reduced-range cartridge that would be lighter than normal rifle rounds yet still have adequate power for infantry. They came back to this idea in World War II, and developed the 7.92x33mm cartridge, which fired a spitzer 8mm bullet of 125 grains at 2,247 fps. The MP 43/4 is better designed than the AK47. The German rifle's safety is convenient for right-handed shooters and can be removed without noise. The weapon can be left with the selector in semi-auto and the safety fixed. Simply flipping the safety off will allow the shooter to fire, faster than the AK47. The rate of fire is about four hundred rpm, a third lower than the AK47, and the ammo has a lower recoil impulse. The slower rate of fire and lower recoil level make the weapon much more controllable in semi-auto, and especially so in full-auto fire. Although the MP 43/4 has a selector to allow burst fire, the design and German manuals clearly state it should be used as a semi-auto carbine. The front sight, a typical European pyramid, is unprotected. Pyramid-style front sights are hard to use accurately, especially when coupled with the V-notch rear sight blades. The rear sight is graduated from an intelligent one hundred meters to an unrealistic eight hundred meters. When firing in semi-auto, your finger must allow the trigger to go all the way forward after pulling the trigger, thus firing a shot. You cannot simply let the trigger go forward enough to catch the last sear engagement; the weapon will not fire. You must let it go all the way forward and pull again through the double-pull system. There are metal handguards on the weapon. After shooting forty five rounds, the weapon was too hot to hold. The MP 43/4 is heavy at ten pounds or more, but has many excellent features not seen on other German small arms of the period.

Developed in the last days of World War II, the German VG 1 represents an excellent piece of engineering. A need to arm the "people's army" caused local political leaders to develop their own weapons to arm these last-ditch troops. It is impossible to know how many VG 1 rifles were made but a good estimate is nine thousand. They are quite rare in the United States. The stock and forearm are wood and only roughly shaped. The safety is a lever that falls nicely under your thumb; you can disengage it and fire quickly. The sights are well-protected, typical blasé in the front. The rear sight is a single-position blade. Both sights are adequate. Trigger pull is full of creep, slack, and overtravel, but no worse than many Heckler & Koch military rifles. The trigger guard is small. The weapon is relatively short and lightweight. Using 7.92x33mm, it would easily fulfill its intended purpose. The German VG 1 is a retarded-gas-operated weapon. Surrounding the barrel is a sheet-metal jacket. At the end of the jacket, the bolt for the rifle is placed and it is pinned to the jacket. Upon firing, the gas pushes the jacket back entirely and the bolt in the rear of the jacket moves along with the entire sheet-metal jacket. The effect of the heavy bolt in the rear of the sheet-metal shroud going to the rear with each shot is rather a "chunk-chunk" feel to the rifle as the weight is shifted back and forth rapidly. While an odd sensation, it is something that a shooter will get used to quickly and causes no real handling problem. A large handle is welded on the left side of the receiver to permit the action to be worked chambering a round. Overall the VG-1 is quite an interesting rifle.

The HK G3 is a very reliable weapon. However, I find many drawbacks. The recoil is much stiffer than in gas-operated weapons because of the G3's roller-lock mechanism. It is jerky, especially when firing in full-auto mode. The safety is hard to disengage unless you shift the weapon in your hand. The trigger system is heavy and full of creep and slack. The G3 is too heavy and not well balanced; it does not feel alive in the hands. The magazine release is acceptable, but the G3 has no hold-open device so you do not know when it is empty. There are two styles of handguard. The slim-line one is comfortable but overheats so badly that after firing four or five magazines, you cannot hold it. The tropical unit is triangular in shape and stays much cooler, but is so big that it is difficult to hold securely. The flash hider works decently, but no better than similar units. There is a ring around the front sights on the G3, which can be distracting, and shades the front sight, so shooting in the dark is more difficult, but in daylight, it avoids glare. The front blade is thick: it completely covers man-sized targets at three hundred yards. The rear sight is tapered the wrong way permitting sunlight into the eyes. It appears to be rugged. The mechanism for cocking or loading the weapon is awkward. It takes a strong hand to pull it to the rear to chamber a round. With no hold-open device, the time needed to withdraw the magazine, insert a new one, and then pull the cocking lever back is unacceptable. The sling mounting, which does not swivel, is permanently mounted on the left side of the weapon, and is very difficult to use. The G3 butt stock is short and rigid, which adds to the already high felt recoil of the weapon. It is not shaped to allow quick mounting for fast shots. The G3 also has a sliding butt-stock assembly. As with all such metal stocks, it is uncomfortable to use. The metal struts hit your cheekbone and the rear butt plate draws all the recoil into a very small area. This stock is stable when extended and does not rattle when closed. The grip on the G3 feels okay, but would not be easy for the left-handed shooter. Although reliable, the G3 is simply too difficult to use.

The post-World War II German government armed its military with US-supplied M1 rifles. Soon, however, it selected another design, the G3, which was reliable but very hard to shoot well. The Germans immediately saw a need for a sniper rifle. The designers at Heckler & Koch were forced to convert the G3 into a sniper rifle. The G3 had good intrinsic accuracy, but the designers knew the trigger was a problem. A proper sniper rifle should employ a good telescopic sight. It should gather light to extend the shooting day, and be rugged. If it is removable, it needs a mount that will allow it to maintain its zero position; re-sighting is impractical. The resulting scope was a very high-quality unit of rugged design, although it is heavy and expensive to make. The Schmidt & Bender telescopic sight installed on the STG 1 has a variable power from 1.5X to 5X. The scope includes a reticle that can be used for range estimation. The mount on the STG is a typical German-style claw mount. It allows the shooter to take off the scope for storage or transit and yet returns to POA when reattached. To use the scope, the stock has a cheek piece installed to elevate the shooter's eye. The forearm installed on the STG is the tropical model. The STG comes with a bipod. Although it helps steady the rifle when firing prone, it shifts the POI. The Heckler & Koch engineers managed to get a trigger on the STG that is almost as good as the M14 rifle. Unfortunately, it lacks take-up so you must only rest your finger on it when you are ready to fire.

KKMPI 69

Caliber: .22 Long Rifle   **Manufacturer:** German state arsenal
Typical Use: Military, police, self-defense, and trainer/understudy

This rifle is a dedicated .22 RF version of the East German version of the AK47 rifle—they call their model the MPI 69. The large number of students under eighteen who were part of the militia program and the low number of shooting ranges in East Germany also encouraged the development of the KKMPI 69. This is not a conversion unit. This rifle functions the same as the MPI 69 and is designed to be a trainer for the new soldier and youth groups. While it looks a lot like the standard .30 caliber rifle, it is not identical by any means. The rear sight looks and acts the same, but it is only adjustable to a much shorter distance. With miniaturized targets and ranges, this works perfectly in teaching shooting skills. The weapon loads the same, although it holds less ammo than the MPI 69. But unlike a lot of similar .22 rimfire rifles, the KKMPI 69 fires in both semi and bursts, just like its bigger-caliber brother. Of course since it is a blowback only weapon, no gas system exists and the rifle is lighter than the standard MPI 69. The safety/selector, the sights, the trigger pull work the same, and the stock and grip are identical, allowing a shooter using a KKMPI 69 to get lots of inexpensive practice to either learn the skill needed or to keep those skills sharp. This is a valuable training weapon.

HK 53

Caliber: 5.56x45mm   **Manufacturer:** Heckler & Koch   **Typical Use:** Military and police

The HK 53 is a shortened version of their 5.56x45mm rifle, the HK 33. As with all Heckler & Koch weapons in this series, it is a roller-locked weapon. Accordingly it has more felt recoil than one would expect for a cartridge-fired rifle. As with the other H&K weapons, the sights are hard to use, adjust with difficulty, and the safety is impossible for a person with normal length thumbs to use, unless you shift your hand. The stock is a collapsing unit with metal struts and, thanks to the felt recoil generated when the bolt hits the rear of the receiver, it will hurt your cheek bone when firing multiple shots rapidly. The small, thin forearm gets very hot when only two or so magazines are rapidly fired; it becomes almost impossible to hold the weapon. Blast is sharp and depending on the ammo used, muzzle flash is an issue. Even with ammo that individually did not have a lot of flash, it seemed to build up in the flash hider and about every six-eight rounds, the residue would light up in a big ball of fire. More critically, the HK 53 feels very "dead" in my hands. It is not at all a lively weapon and, while almost the same size as an MP5, it is not nearly as nice to handle. Slow to operate with substantial felt recoil and blast, it is not nearly as handy or good weapon as a Colt Commando with a similar length. More powerful than the 9x19mm MP5, it is not as good a fighting weapon as the 10mm version of the MP5 which retained the handiness of MP5 while still providing a bigger, heavier bullet.

HK 36

Caliber: 5.56x45mm   **Manufacturer:** Heckler & Koch   **Typical Use:** Military, police, and self-defense

Heckler & Koch developed the HK 36 rifle to replace the G3 in German service. It was released about the time the Berlin Wall collapsed and reunification occurred. This distraction may have kept agencies from purchasing it. Spain has adopted the HK 36. German troops in Afghanistan use it. The rifle has been well received. One problem is dust which is so abrasive that plastic trigger parts have been worn out. The HK 36 trigger pull, even before abrasion, is poor. One serious drawback is that the safety/selector lever is too short and you must shift your grip to operate it. The magazine release is convenient. The magazines are reliable and can be clipped together, which is handy. You can see how many rounds are in the magazine—a good, if not essential, feature. The weapon is piston operated, and when you take the handguard off, it looks frail and unprotected, but it does hold up well. The rifle comes with different types of sights including an integral red-dot-type unit and an optical sight. If you do not like those, removing the factory unit and replacing it with a rail and newer optical or red-dot-sights will yield better results. The folding stock is solid and easy to use, but it limits the shooter to one length. The weapon has a very "plastic" feel in my hands, which is uncomfortable. As the weapon has a trigger pull that is hard and heavy and sights that are slow and difficult to use, the M4 or SCAR are better choices for a combat rifle.

MG 08/15

Caliber: 7.92x57mm   **Typical Use:** Military   **Manufacturer:** Deutsche Waffen und Munitionsfabriken (DWM); Spandau & Erfurt arsenals

During World War I, the tripod-mounted machine gun dominated the battlefield. The German Maxim 08 MG proved to be an extremely reliable, hard-hitting weapon, but it was not light or easy to carry. It could fire long bursts but was too heavy to carry forward and provide close-range support work in an attack. Much thought went into developing the MG 08/15, but the Germans had little time to design it, and it is disappointing in many ways. The MG 08/15 basically is the MG 08 with a slightly modified receiver, a separate, smaller water jacket, and a butt stock plus pistol grip. It is still water cooled and has a belt to hold the ammo. Belts are awkward to use and web belts can lose shape due to moisture. The weapon weighs forty three pounds (with water) and is long at fifty three inches overall. The MG 08/15 is not something I can hold off-hand and fire. It is very heavy at the muzzle end. Firing from the kneeling position is a little better, but it is only in the prone position that the MG 08/15 can be used with ease. The rear sight is a nicely-calibrated peep unit. The front sight is dark and difficult to pick up rapidly. The shoulder stock is awkward looking and quite massive but feels surprisingly good. The pistol grip is small and too ropelike in feel. The grip's cylindrical shape allows the weapon to twist in your hand. The safety falls readily to the thumb. The slow cyclic rate of about 450 rpm (depending on ammo) allows firing single shots without needing a selector.

The MG 34 was one of the standard machine guns used by German forces in World War II. This MG was designed to circumvent the provision in the Treaty of Versailles that prohibited Germany from manufacturing heavy machine guns. By providing a quickly-removable barrel, the weapon avoided the heavy water jacket. The gun weighs 26.5 pounds with the bipod attached, and many claim this is a "light machine gun." In comparison, a Maxim weighs 40.5 pounds. I found MG 34 difficult to fire off-hand because of its weight and poor balance, which is a result of its length, its weight out front, and its open-bolt firing cycle. Firing it from a kneeling or bipod prone position is quite easy, however. The cyclic rate on the tested gun ran a little over nine hundred rpm, probably higher than ideal, but the gun does fire in a semi-auto and full-auto mode. Belts on the MG34 do not have the disintegrating links. Belts can be linked together (theoretically) endlessly; in static positions, one thousand rounds are not uncommon. As a squad automatic weapon, the MG 34 is not successful because of its weight and cyclic rate. At the platoon or company level, when used with the heavy tripod, it is quite effective. If manned by a proper three-man crew, replacing the barrels at 250-round intervals, you can keep up a steady stream of fire. The German tripods allow for automatic traversing fire, good when attacked. The telescopic sight on the tripod helps the shooter firing over the heads of his own troops. During World War II, German sources claimed they could effectively fire out to 3,800 meters with this combination. The ability to quickly replace barrels on the MG 34 is a strong point. The lever is flipped and the whole action is turned on its side. The barrel comes loose and gravity should cause it to fall out. If that fails, you need to fish into the barrel jacket and pull it out, and it is hot. Shove the new one in, close the action and resume firing. This represented a breakthrough in 1934.

MG 42

Caliber: 7.92x57mm Mauser (7.52x.51mm in MG 3)
Manufacturer: Various German and other countries' factories   **Typical Use:** Military

Germany developed the MG42 to meet the needs of the battlefield, and it proved to be a very successful design. The MG 42 and MG 3 (the 7.62x51mm version) are very reliable and durable. The late Kent Lomont, America's foremost Class 3 dealer and machine gun expert, set an MG 3 on a Lafayette tripod. He fired a continuous ten thousand-round burst in seven minutes! The barrel got white and the receiver got red. He removed and replaced the barrel, and fired another one thousand round burst. There were no problems. Some older MG 42s will fire out of battery, especially dangerous when used with wartime ammo of questionable quality. Removing the barrel is fast and easier than on the MG 34 because you do not have to turn the weapon receiver, but you are still dealing with hot metal on the receiver and the barrel. The other chronic problem with the MG 42 is its cyclic rates. They can fire up to 1,500 rpm. There is no provision for semi-fire and its cyclic rate is too high for single shots. Cyclic rates at the high end are too high for a ground machine gun unless it is used with the tripod. Many guns you encounter will have the fast-rate

springs installed, although even a well-trained skilled shooter will most likely get eight–ten shot bursts when so set up. I have read that the German theory was to throw a shotgun-like burst of bullets out, killing by saturating the area with bullets. Perhaps, but the MG 42 is so hard to control that I lose concentration. Today, more than a half century later, the MG 3 is manufactured in Germany, Italy, Turkey, and other countries, and soldiers are using the same weapon that their grandfathers used. Such longevity is almost unheard of today.

FG 42

Caliber: 7.92x57mm Rifle   **Manufacturer:** Krieghoff   **Typical Use:** Military

The German FG 42 may well be the best, and is certainly the most interesting, German weapon I've encountered. There are two models which have the same name but are very different. They were made during World War II at the request of the German Air Force Airborne Forces. The FG 42 fires the full-power 7.92x57mm rifle round. When the selector is set on semi, it fires from a closed bolt, and when the selector is set on auto, it fires from an open bolt. I tested both models, and the rate of fire was under five hundred rpm. This low cyclic rate allows good control, thanks to a very effective muzzle break. The weapon did not climb upon firing bursts, but actually the muzzle went down! It was easy to control when firing bursts, even off hand. This is not possible with rifles like the FAL, HK G3, M14, or even AK47. Yet the FG 42 shoots a more powerful cartridge. The sights are conveniently sitting on top of the receiver, and I did not have to raise my head to use them. A scope mount is provided, which works easily. Two more features make the FG 42 highly desirable. First, the magazines, ten and twenty shots, are inserted on the left side. This does not disturb balance, and I could easily maintain low position due to the lack of a projecting magazine. Second, the weapon weighs less than nine pounds, very light for its power level. It is short in overall length and it felt lively and nimble in my hands.

COLT ARMY SPECIAL

Caliber: 9x29mm (.38 Special)   **Manufacturer:** Colt   **Typical Use:** Military and self-defense

This Colt handgun was used by the Greek Army and Navy in World War I, and France bought over ten thousand of them. The Army Special has a steel frame; its parts are well made of good material, and are subject to low stress due to the relatively low power and recoil of the .38 Special cartridge. The grip is large (slightly smaller the New Service), and does not fit the hand well without an adapter. When rapid DA strings are fired, it tends to shift in the hand. Although the trigger pull on SA is quite good, on DA it is heavy and tends to stack. I find the cylinder release mechanism on all Colts awkward. You pull the release to the rear and push the cylinder out. This is much slower than the method found on Smith & Wessons where you push the release in and push the cylinder out. The extractor rod does not lock and is subject to damage if struck hard. The front sight is dark, but lines up well in dim light because it is high on the barrel, aiding indexing. The rear sight is low and does not help much. The ex-Greek Army Special revolvers I have seen are battered and worn, proof they were much used. The Army Special was better than many military revolvers used during World War I.

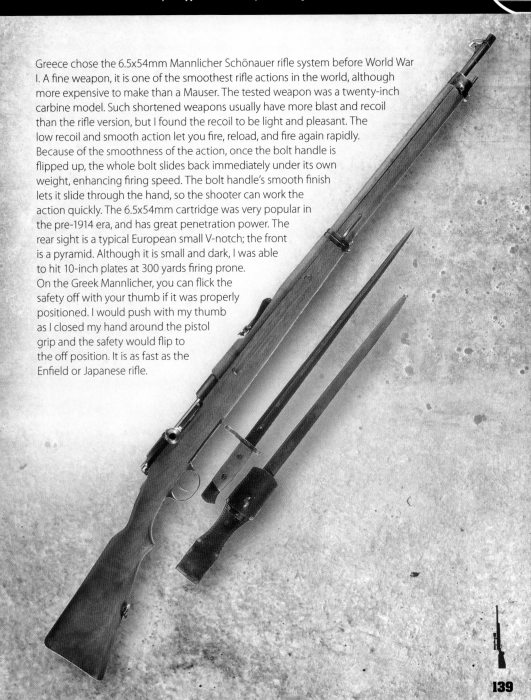

Greece chose the 6.5x54mm Mannlicher Schönauer rifle system before World War I. A fine weapon, it is one of the smoothest rifle actions in the world, although more expensive to make than a Mauser. The tested weapon was a twenty-inch carbine model. Such shortened weapons usually have more blast and recoil than the rifle version, but I found the recoil to be light and pleasant. The low recoil and smooth action let you fire, reload, and fire again rapidly. Because of the smoothness of the action, once the bolt handle is flipped up, the whole bolt slides back immediately under its own weight, enhancing firing speed. The bolt handle's smooth finish lets it slide through the hand, so the shooter can work the action quickly. The 6.5x54mm cartridge was very popular in the pre-1914 era, and has great penetration power. The rear sight is a typical European small V-notch; the front is a pyramid. Although it is small and dark, I was able to hit 10-inch plates at 300 yards firing prone. On the Greek Mannlicher, you can flick the safety off with your thumb if it was properly positioned. I would push with my thumb as I closed my hand around the pistol grip and the safety would flip to the off position. It is as fast as the Enfield or Japanese rifle.

M37

Caliber: 7.65mm (.32 ACP) **Manufacturer:** Metalwares Small Arms and Machine Works, LTD.
Typical Use: Military and self-defense

There is nothing spectacular about the Hungarian M37. I tested a standard model without the Germany Army side-safety modification, so it had only a grip safety. The hammer is small and shrouded by the slide and length of the receiver, making it difficult to cock rapidly if carried with a loaded chamber, hammer down. You either trust the grip safety or carry the weapon chamber empty and load immediately prior to firing. Moving with such a weapon if loaded and cocked is dangerous. You must hold the weapon *loosely* because a firm grip disengages the grip safety, raising the possibility of accidental discharges. In fairness, you need a firm grip to deactivate the safety. The heel-butt-mounted magazine prevents rapid reloading. The front sight is dark and small and the rear is small, so proper indexing is difficult. The grip is very straight and the weapon tends to point low, causing low bullet strikes. The M37 functioned perfectly during the firing test and recoil was light, typical for a .32 caliber steel frame weapon.

RK 59

Caliber: 9mm Makarov **Manufacturer:** Hungarian state factory **Typical Use:** Military, police, and self-defense

The RK 59 is the lightest, most powerful PPK-type pistol ever made. This excellent military handgun was issued to members of the Hungarian military and police forces. Although the RK 59 is the size of the Walther PPK, the recoil shoulder is slightly higher over the web of the hand; all the hammer bite-and-slide slashing so common with Walthers is absent. This pistol has an alloy frame, making it lightweight. It is chambered for 9mm Makarov, which is better than .380. The bare-metal finish on the alloy frame is fine for civilian use, and the blued slide is acceptable. On the formal range, the DA pull was typical of a Walther PPK: very heavy with a lot of stacking. The SA was crisp but suffered from the typical autoloader problem of substantial overtravel. The sights are small, dark, and hard to pick up; I was able to achieve only a 3¾ inch group at fifty feet. Painting them white would help. The weapon performs better on the cinema range. It was quick to put into operation and fast to shoot. Still, indexing was slowed by the poor front sight. The size, weight and caliber combination of the RK 59 makes this an excellent weapon.

This AK47-style rifle is Hungarian made. The stocks were typically light-colored wood, the forearm did not cover the gas assembly, and it had a forward pistol grip. The weapon otherwise was the same so far as accuracy, trigger, and safety features. Hungary developed the AMD 65 for troops needing a shorter weapon. This weapon had the same style exposed forearm with pistol grips, a shorter barrel with a flash hider/compensator use, and a single strut folding stock. It is much shorter than the standard fixed-stock rifle when folded. The single strut folder was easier and quicker to use than the double strut under-folder commonly encountered with AK rifles. The twenty-shot magazine was commonly issued with these rifles, again aiding compactness. It will accept all other AK magazines. The weapon is louder than the standard example. It feels nimble in the hands, and is well balanced. The weight falls nicely between the two grips. When firing multiple rounds rapidly, the single strut wire folding stock was painful on my cheek. I tested the AMD 65 in semi-only and the stock slammed hard, so full auto would be worse.

UZI SMG

Caliber: Submachine Gun   **Manufacturer:** Israel Military Industries & others   **Typical Use:** Military, police, and self-defense

The Uzi is one of the most popular submachine guns in the world. Famously used by the Secret Service after Hinkley shot President Reagan, it has been the official military issue in numerous armies besides Israel's. For many years, the German Army used Fabrique Nationale-made examples and many other organizations have used them. With a nice, low 550 rpm cyclic rate, they are very controllable. Firing single shots even when the selector is set on full-auto is easy. Magazine changes are fast and convenient in the dark, thanks to the "hands-find-hands" location of the magazine in the grip. The barrel can be readily removed for cleaning. Popping off the top cover allows you to quickly remove the bolt for cleaning and gives immediate access to the interior of the weapon for cleaning. The sights are well protected and adjustable, and the sling swivels are conveniently located. The original models were equipped with detachable wood stocks, but most models now seen use the metal folding stock. It is a little complicated and can pinch your fingers but is certainly sturdy and acceptable. While not the best SMG in the world by any means, the full-size Uzi is a fine weapon, good enough to guard the US President, and to guard you as well.

The Mini Uzi was produced in response to a demand for a small SMG to compete with various MAC10-types. Based on the original Uzi, it is smaller, a little lighter, but truly not as controllable due to its higher cyclic rate when fired on full-auto. The stock deploys more quickly than the standard model, which is convenient. The Mini Uzi keeps the original Uzi magazine release system and sights. It can be quickly fieldstripped to permit cleaning, and it is just as rugged and dependable as its bigger brother. Due to the shorter bolt operating area and lighter bolt, the Mini Uzi will typically run three hundred or so rpm faster than a standard model. This makes it still feasible, although difficult, to fire single shots while set on full-auto. It is also much less controllable when firing bursts on target at standard engagement distances. In an attempt to reduce the length of their standard model Uzi SMG to 8¾ inches, the US Secret Service trimmed the barrel so it would fit into a brief case. When you do that, the standard Uzi is no longer than a Mini Uzi, and yet you still retain the more-controllable, lower rpm of the original mode. This may be a better solution.

MICRO UZI SMG

Caliber: 9x19mm Submachine Gun   **Manufacturer:** Israel Military Industries   **Typical Use:** Military and police

Many people like the idea of a really small SMG. The MAC11 was popular as soon as it was available. The Micro Uzi was made to compete with it. It is modeled on the standard Uzi but is much shorter. It uses the stock of the Mini Uzi, which is convenient. Unlike the normal Uzi, it uses adjustable open sights so it can be zeroed. Produced in 9x19mm, it is superior to the other "little SMGs" like the MAC11 and Czech M62, which are available in .380 and 7.65. The Micro Uzi's main problem is its cyclic rate. When fired in full-auto mode, the cyclic rate runs about 1,800 rpm with the closed-bolt version and slightly slower with the open-bolt version. The normal Uzi's cyclic rate is 550 rpm. With this high cyclic rate, firing single shots when set on full-auto is impossible and even 3-shot bursts are a challenge in training. In real world use, such bursts get five–ten shots. Some people like this saturation, but not me. The Micro Uzi can be fired on semi-auto only and in that mode, makes a nice, short carbine, albeit of pistol power. But it is short enough to be carried where other pistol-powered carbines cannot be used, which makes it handy and useful.

The Israelis needed a battle rifle that would work in sand and desert conditions. They developed the Galil, one of the finest AK47s ever made. It uses a solid machined receiver, which helps with durability for a squad automatic weapon; sixty thousand rounds or more is the common figure mentioned for the lifetime of the rifle. The machined receiver and the smaller bore make the Galil .223 rifle approximately nine pounds, heavy for that caliber. The sights on the Galil are superior other AK47-type rifles. The rear sight is an adjustable peep with night-sight capability, and the front is a protected post with night-sight capability. The design does not permit the easy addition of optical sights. The bolt handle is shaped to allow either hand quick access. The stock is not particularly comfortable to shoot with, but it folds easily, opens even faster, and is rock steady. The safety system on the Galil surpasses that of the AK47. You can remove the safety from the right side, but there is also a pistol-grip-mounted safety that can be flipped off with thumb pressure. It is loud, but fast to operate. The magazines on the Galil rock in and are released just like the AK47 magazines. Galil magazines are sturdy, but heavy, as they are steel; M16 aluminum magazines are far lighter. The pistol grip on the Galil is comfortable and allows good control of the weapon. The forearm comes in two distinct styles: the standard rifle group and the heavier squad auto with bipod unit. Both have heat deflectors and are open at the top to allow the heat to escape. You can fire a large number of rounds rapidly before the weapon gets too hot to hold. The flash hider on the Galil, which seems to work well, is also used as a grenade launcher. The trigger design and weight are drawbacks. The trigger is so straight that it tends to hit my finger when firing and hurt it. Firing off a magazine in winter leaves my cold fingers stinging and throbbing. At almost ten pounds, the Galil 5.56 rifle simply weighs too much.

MODEL 1889 ORDNANCE REVOLVER

Caliber: 10.4x20.2mm   **Manufacturer:** Glisenti   **Typical Use:** Military and self-defense

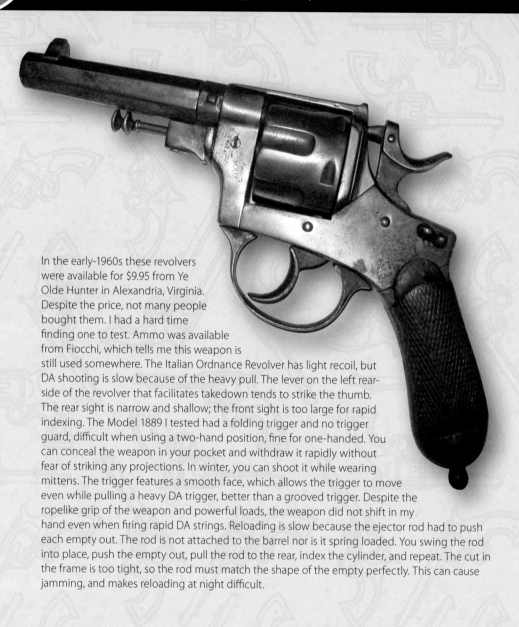

In the early-1960s these revolvers were available for $9.95 from Ye Olde Hunter in Alexandria, Virginia. Despite the price, not many people bought them. I had a hard time finding one to test. Ammo was available from Fiocchi, which tells me this weapon is still used somewhere. The Italian Ordnance Revolver has light recoil, but DA shooting is slow because of the heavy pull. The lever on the left rear-side of the revolver that facilitates takedown tends to strike the thumb. The rear sight is narrow and shallow; the front sight is too large for rapid indexing. The Model 1889 I tested had a folding trigger and no trigger guard, difficult when using a two-hand position, fine for one-handed. You can conceal the weapon in your pocket and withdraw it rapidly without fear of striking any projections. In winter, you can shoot it while wearing mittens. The trigger features a smooth face, which allows the trigger to move even while pulling a heavy DA trigger, better than a grooved trigger. Despite the ropelike grip of the weapon and powerful loads, the weapon did not shift in my hand even when firing rapid DA strings. Reloading is slow because the ejector rod had to push each empty out. The rod is not attached to the barrel nor is it spring loaded. You swing the rod into place, push the empty out, pull the rod to the rear, index the cylinder, and repeat. The cut in the frame is too tight, so the rod must match the shape of the empty perfectly. This can cause jamming, and makes reloading at night difficult.

M1910 GLISENT "BRIXIA"

Caliber: 9mm (9x19mm)   **Manufacturer:** Glisenti   **Typical Use:** Military and self-defense

The Italian military has often made poor choices in handguns, and that includes the Brixia. The Brixia lacks the grip safety found on the Glisenti and has a reinforced sideplate. Although the Brixia was a commercial pistol, some were bought for government trials and designated the "M1912." The cartridge is the 9x19mm Italian loading. The case had slightly different dimensional specifications but lower power level, like a sub-normal 9x19 cartridge in pressure. A standard 9x19 cartridge will fire in the M1910, but depending on the pressure may damage the weapon. The Brixia pistol looks good and the interior is finely engine-turned. The grip has an angle to it similar to the Luger Lahti, HK P7, and Glock. Sights are the European barleycorn type. Keeping elevation on the formal range is demanding; on the cinema range, the sights pick up faster since they get up in the air at the end of a slender barrel and allow good indexing. The rear sight is too shallow and narrow, making firing tedious. Both sights are dark and would benefit from being painted white. The poor sights and trigger pull resulted in groups on the formal range of 4⅝ inches, over twice the average size. The trigger pull was gritty and hard. The Brixia recoils violently, for no reason I can fathom. There are better choices available than the Brixia.

BERETTA M1919

Caliber: .25 ACP   **Manufacturer:** Beretta   **Typical Use:** Military and self-defense

At one time, this was the issue handgun of the Italian Air Force. I assume that the weapon was merely a "badge of office" and not really designed to be a fighting handgun for downed airmen. However, perhaps the Italians felt that its light weight and small size made up for its caliber limitations. This is the weapon fictional spy James Bond was armed with in Ian Fleming's early novels, oddly enough. I have noted that many real-life intelligence people are not very sharp on guns, either! As with all similar hammerless designs, the safety on the M1919 is difficult to disengage rapidly, worse to put back on, and dangerous to carry loaded with a round in the chamber without the safety on. Enough said. Sights on the weapon are similar to those found on pocket pistols of similar caliber the world over. They are made small to fit in your pocket. Unlike the Soviet PSM 5.45mm pistol, no special ammo is available to save this weapon from the apparent deficiencies caused by its caliber.

The Beretta Model 1934 is an all-steel weapon, single-column, butt-magazine-release pistol with a multitude of problems. This weapon recoils heavily for its caliber. The sights are hard to see, the front is too shallow, the rear too narrow, and the front sight is a pyramid, which makes target work grueling. My groups ran approximately five inches, roughly twice that of a Model 19. This was basically because the sights are also hard to use on the target range, not because of any intrinsic inaccuracy in the weapon. I do not think the method of holding the barrel to the side is conducive to accuracy but certainly it is adequate for this type of weapon; it is difficult to shoot accurately. The slide on the M1934 closes when the magazine is removed. Although the heel-butt-magazine release slows reloading, once you disengage the magazine release and pull the magazine out, the slide will close, making it a little more difficult to load properly. If you attempt to load this weapon with the safety on, it will jam. Therefore you are forced to load it, dangerously, with the safety off. The poor sights also are a drawback on the cinema range. They are too shallow with no contrast, so indexing becomes arduous, and recoil was negligible. On the formal target range, the recoil seemed to be heavy compared to the power factor. The safety was nearly impossible to disengage quickly with a strong-hand thumb. You have to push it up as far as possible with your right thumb, then shift your thumb and push off the remainder with the thumb. This is very slow. If it is not all the way off, the hammer will sometimes, but not always, fire the weapon. For instance, if you pull your weapon out (cocked and locked) and push on the safety with your thumb but not flip it the whole 180-degrees, the hammer will sometimes fire the weapon. The location of the safety is ineffective: it is too far forward, making it awkward for your thumb to hit and disengage it rapidly. Although the M1934 is well made, it is not well designed for military purposes. It is too slow to reload, difficult to use in low light, and not particularly powerful. Other .380 weapons, such as the CZ38/39 DA series, are much better suited to the tasks of a military weapon.

BERETTA M1951

Caliber: 9mm Parabellum **Manufacturer:** Beretta **Typical Use:** Military and self-defense

The M1951 is Italy's current service weapon and a standard military handgun in Israel (M951) and Egypt (Helwan). Frankly, it has not seen much combat use, and the United States imports commercial Helwans made in Egypt. The reliable design is similar to the Beretta M92. The M1951 Beretta uses a single-column magazine, which features a SA-trigger. It has a straight-line feed increasing its reliability. The single-column magazine avoids grip bulk and the SA trigger makes it easy to shoot. The magazine release is on the butt, which makes it slow. It requires two hands to use and tends to get pushed off by car seats. The front sight is narrow and low, and the rear sight is small and shallow, making indexing slow. Painting the sights white helps. The trigger is gritty. The safety on the M1951 is a crossbolt variety. Rarely used, this safety is one of the pistol's best features. You can flip the safety off and on rapidly without shifting your hand at all. It was faster to operate than a Colt Government Model. With your thumb resting on the knuckle of the button, extending the thumb slightly will bump the safety off. To reengage, straighten the trigger guard finger, flex the finger straight out, hit the button with the inside of your knuckle, and it will flip on. In actual practice, this works well for right- and left-handed shooters. No other safety is needed. Since the pistol grips are flush with the safety, you avoid flipping the safety off while in the holster.

BERETTA M92 D MODEL

Caliber: Caliber: 9x19mm **Manufacturer:** Beretta **Typical Use:** Military and self-defense

The D Model Beretta is a variant of the standard M92 Beretta. The standard D model has no manual safety on the slide as a standard M92 does, causing it to be called the "slickslide model." It fires only with a long trigger pull. The hammer follows the slide down with each shot. The hammer lacks a hammer spur since none is needed as the weapon cannot be manually cocked to get an SA lighter-type pull. The safety can be depressed to deactivate the trigger hammer system, then left in that position rendering the weapon incapable of being fired until the safety is once again manually raised. Many people like this approach, as a weapon like the Beretta carried on safe in this manner will be very resistant to "snatch" problems, since assailants who gain custody of an officer's pistol will find it will not fire. I prefer this style of safety. Some are seen where the safety simply flips back and forth and accomplishes nothing. Some early St. Louis Police Department M92D models were found to be of this type—a worthless approach. The trigger pull on a Beretta M92 D is long like the DA pull on a standard M92 but seems quite smooth. Thus while heavy, it is an easy weapon to shoot well. Thanks to the trigger system, it has little overtravel and anticipated shots are avoided. While it would seem that such a heavy, long trigger pull would be a drawback, it is not. In fact, the consistent smooth pull yields quite good results. While not quite like an old, long-action pre-war Smith & Wesson, it is close.

BERETTA BRIGADIER

Caliber: 9x19mm   **Manufacturer:** Beretta   **Typical Use:** Military and self-defense

The Beretta Brigadier is a variation of the standard M92 series, differing only in the slide. The Brigadier slide is thicker and reinforced at the side near the barrel to address two issues. First, certain high-pressure loadings in the 9x19mm pistol started breaking the slide, and the rear portion hit the shooter's face. This problem was traced to a bad lot of steel, but Beretta reinforced the slide to resolve this. Second, when the M92 was altered to take the new .40 S&W cartridge, there was more involved than just using a different chambered reamer, as the .40 S&W is a high-pressure round and it affects the weapon differently. The Brigadier-style slide helped Beretta cope with this cartridge in the M92-style pistols. The thicker slide weighs more, which helps reduce both felt recoil and muzzle flip allowing a fast repeat shot. The rear sight is the same as on a standard M92 slide but the front sight is also contains in a dovetail, so it can be easily changed. Additionally, the weapon is equipped with night sights which can easily be changed out when they dim.

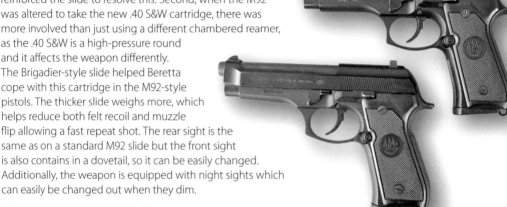

BERETTA PX4 "C" MODEL

Caliber: 9x19mm Parabellum; .40 S&W; .45 ACP   **Manufacturer:** Beretta   **Typical Use:** Military and self-defense

The Beretta PX4 pistol series uses a rotary barrel system, which has a lot of movement to it. Dust and dirt penetrating the system could impact its functioning and tie up the weapon. I found the PX4 accurate, and it had a good trigger pull with the "C" or constant trigger system. It's terribly heavy, and with little overtravel at the end. It holds seventeen rounds, but thanks to the polymer grip firm, it did not feel bulky or wide, but rather comfortable and nimble. The slide was nicely beveled so it was not "fat" when holstered on your belt. My only concern was dirt impacting function. I sent it to my friend, the late Kent Lomont, a tireless tester. If Kent can't break something, I want two of them. He took my Beretta PX4 "C" Model worn in a belt holster on a 1,500 mile ATV trip into the Idaho Mountains. Firing some eight thousand rounds in it without cleaning, it worked fine, although toward the end he said it was getting a bit sticky and he had to hit the back of the slide with his off hand. He was using lead bullet reloads, so lead residue and bullet lubricant added to the powder residue and dust and dirt. From this I concluded the rotating barrel system would work, and my concerns were groundless.

BERETTA M38/42

Caliber: 9x19mm **Manufacturer:** Beretta **Typical Use:** Military and police

The M38/42 was the last in a line of wartime SMGs. The M38/42 had all the best features of the earlier models, but was easier to produce. The Beretta M38 series has one of the best magazines ever made to fire 9x19mm ammo, critical for any self-loading machine gun. It is very reliable. All models are sturdy and use a full-sized wood stock, so they present firm shooting platforms. The safety is located on the left side of the receiver and is essentially worthless. The M38/42 is selective fire, but it uses two separate triggers rather than a selector switch. By using the dual-trigger system, the shooter can quickly decide which system to use and rapidly shift between them as tactical needs arise. Sights are an open U-notch rear with an unprotected blade front. The sling swivels are well positioned to permit a proper carry strap to be installed. Weight and size of the weapon make a nice package. Its cyclic rate is slow enough that single shots are easy even if you pull the full-auto trigger. The weapon is solid, well-made, and effective at two hundred yards or more, depending on the ammo and the shooter. It is an excellent weapon and a credit to its designers, even a half century after it was created.

BERETTA M93

Caliber: 9x19mm　　**Manufacturer:** Beretta　　**Typical Use:** Military, police, and self-defense

The M93 is a SA pistol. The trigger guard is larger than most SA pistols because you need to put the thumb through it when using the front-mounted foregrip. The safety is similar to the M1911 Colt. The weapon does not fire full-auto, but rather semi-auto or three-shot bursts. You must push a button before the selector can be depressed to the three-shot-burst mode, which helps prevent flipping the safety off and firing bursts when you want only single shots. The sights are similar to the M92 and are quick to pick up. The stock is a collapsing, single, metal strut unit. When affixed, it is rigid and nicely shaped to hit the shoulder. The Beretta M93 can be used in burst fire without a stock, The barrel on the M93 is longer than the M92 and is ported. The slots are designed to hold the weapon down, but they only increase noise and muzzle flash. The foregrip is attached to the weapon's trigger guard. By putting his hand on it and pressing down, the shooter pulls down on the foregrip, resulting in greater control. Although the foregrip is clever, it makes the weapon bulkier. Most double-column, 9mm pistols are fat because of the double-column magazine. The M93 Beretta is fatter than even the M92 due to a set of wood grips that are thicker than plastic, and the ratchet system found on the selector that gives the weapon its three-shot-burst capacity. This makes the M93 grip bulky, uncomfortable, and reduces instinctive shooting ability. Once mastered, the machine pistol becomes the single most deadly close-range weapon available. It is not a machine gun or even an SMG, but in its unique role as a close-range, defensive/offensive weapon, nothing comes close.

This modification of an original Swiss design was adopted by the Italian Army shortly after Italy was united. Originally a single-shot design, the rifle was modified in 1887 to use a three-shot magazine, and this is what I tested in 10.4mm Italian caliber. People tend to think that these old-time rifles are obsolete and underpowered. This rifle is not underpowered: it shoots a 313-grain, 10.4mm bullet at 1,430 fps, akin to a heavy .44 Magnum load. I killed a 2,200-pound bison with a 330-grain bullet at 1,200 fps in an M29 S&W four-inch barrel, and the bullet went completely through the animal. This is a long rifle: fifty four inches overall with a thirty four-inch barrel. Long barrels burn black powder more efficiently. Its length makes the rifle unwieldy, but its barrel diameter kept the rifle from being muzzle heavy, so you can shoot it easily both off-hand and when kneeling. The action is smooth and it has a very light trigger pull. There is no two-stage take-up, so you must take care to not fire prematurely. There is no practical safety on the rifle; instead, a decocking system is used. The rifle has no upper handguard, but with black powder you would likely only fire a few rounds at a time, so this is not a problem. When in the down position, the rear sight is set for 275 meters; when raised, it is graduated from 400 to 1,800 meters. It is not protected by wings. The front sight is a dark pyramid type located off center, also not protected. They are hard to see. The Model 1871/87 has an additional three-shot magazine, making a four-shot weapon if including the chambered round. A magazine cutoff was included to keep the contents of the magazine ready for an emergency. You insert the rounds manually—no clips or chargers. By 1891, the Italians started to issue Carcano rifles in 6.5mm so these large, black powder Model 1871/87s became obsolete.

M91 CARCANO 6.5mm RIFLE

Caliber: 6.5mm   **Manufacturer:** Bressica, Beretta   **Typical Use:** Military

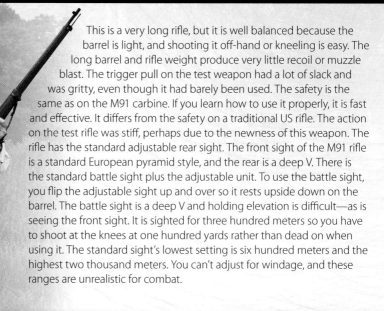

This is a very long rifle, but it is well balanced because the barrel is light, and shooting it off-hand or kneeling is easy. The long barrel and rifle weight produce very little recoil or muzzle blast. The trigger pull on the test weapon had a lot of slack and was gritty, even though it had barely been used. The safety is the same as on the M91 carbine. If you learn how to use it properly, it is fast and effective. It differs from the safety on a traditional US rifle. The action on the test rifle was stiff, perhaps due to the newness of this weapon. The rifle has the standard adjustable rear sight. The front sight of the M91 rifle is a standard European pyramid style, and the rear is a deep V. There is the standard battle sight plus the adjustable unit. To use the battle sight, you flip the adjustable sight up and over so it rests upside down on the barrel. The battle sight is a deep V and holding elevation is difficult—as is seeing the front sight. It is sighted for three hundred meters so you have to shoot at the knees at one hundred yards rather than dead on when using it. The standard sight's lowest setting is six hundred meters and the highest two thousand meters. You can't adjust for windage, and these ranges are unrealistic for combat.

M91 CARCANO 6.5mm CARBINE WITH FIXED SIGHTS

Caliber: 6.5mm   **Manufacturer:** Bressica & others   **Typical Use:** Military, police, and hunting

Many people have a poor opinion of the Italian 6.5 carbine, especially the fixed rear sight model. Once you use the weapon, you may change your mind. My test group at one hundred yards went into 3¼ inches, which is acceptable, but it was hitting about twelve inches high, indicating it was sighted for an unrealistic combat range of three hundred meters. The recoil of the 6.5mm Italian cartridge was light, yet the bullet's weight, size, shape, and ballistic coefficient offer good penetration. The 6.5 Italian rifles all use stripper clips inserted into the rifle action. When the last round is chambered, the empty clip falls through the magazine slot to the ground. This is a very rapid reloading

method as well as a very handy way to carry spare ammo. The trigger on the test example had the typical double pull of a military rifle and the trigger's final pull was quite gritty, but shooting is still accurate and easy. The carbine stock contained a butt trap for cleaning equipment. The bayonet was a "sticker" rather than a "slasher." The action on the rifle is fast and the bolt handle is properly designed to allow rapid reloading. The safety seems hard to engage and disengage. To use it easily, place your hand on the side of the weapon, not around the grip. With practice, your thumb will be able to flip it on and off rapidly. The M91 Carcano carbine is very light and handy to carry and use. It is easy to shoot in the off-hand, kneeling, and sitting positions. It offers light recoil with plenty of power to stop assailants.

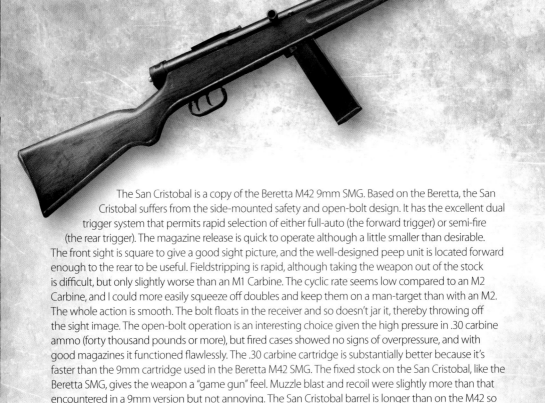

The San Cristobal is a copy of the Beretta M42 9mm SMG. Based on the Beretta, the San Cristobal suffers from the side-mounted safety and open-bolt design. It has the excellent dual trigger system that permits rapid selection of either full-auto (the forward trigger) or semi-fire (the rear trigger). The magazine release is quick to operate although a little smaller than desirable. The front sight is square to give a good sight picture, and the well-designed peep unit is located forward enough to the rear to be useful. Fieldstripping is rapid, although taking the weapon out of the stock is difficult, but only slightly worse than an M1 Carbine. The cyclic rate seems low compared to an M2 Carbine, and I could more easily squeeze off doubles and keep them on a man-target than with an M2. The whole action is smooth. The bolt floats in the receiver and so doesn't jar it, thereby throwing off the sight image. The open-bolt operation is an interesting choice given the high pressure in .30 carbine ammo (forty thousand pounds or more), but fired cases showed no signs of overpressure, and with good magazines it functioned flawlessly. The .30 carbine cartridge is substantially better because it's faster than the 9mm cartridge used in the Beretta M42 SMG. The fixed stock on the San Cristobal, like the Beretta SMG, gives the weapon a "game gun" feel. Muzzle blast and recoil were slightly more than that encountered in a 9mm version but not annoying. The San Cristobal barrel is longer than on the M42 so its overall length is greater. It's a dandy weapon with much to offer.

After World War II, The United States, believing Italy needed to help stop the spread of Communism, gave the military the M1 Garand. The Italians modified it to fire bursts, and to take the new 7.62x51mm round, and to weigh less. The result was the M59 Beretta. The M59 offers an integral grenade launcher that serves as a muzzle break for recoil reduction, important for burst-firing on shoulder-fired weapons. The sights on the Beretta M59 are similar to the M1 Garand and are very good. The front is a well-protected blade and the rear is a good-sized, well-protected peep. The safety is centrally located and easily removed by either hand. The trigger guard does not fold down, but there is a fitted winter trigger. The selector is on the side of the rifle and not designed for rapid use. You must break your shooting grip to change the mode of fire. Experience shows that firing full, auto with 7.62x51mm ammo is not effective; semi-auto is more productive. The cocking handle is on the right side, so you must break your firing grip to cock it. You can kick it open to clear rounds. The magazine release is centrally located and quick to use, although the magazine must be rocked into position, not simply jammed into the magazine well. The stock is wood, which can warp. Accuracy on the M59 when fired on semi-auto is like the M14: two inches at one hundred yards. The M59 is a good, user-friendly rifle, although it may not be as rugged as Heckler & Koch's G3.

Beretta developed the AR-70 in the 1970s to meet the demand for a rifle to fire the NATO 5.56x45mm cartridge. These rifles were sold to various small armies and police agencies and, in modified form, have now been adopted as the duty weapon in Italy. The AR-70 has one serious drawback. The safety works backward. Instead of flipping it down with the thumb to put it off and pressing upward to apply the safety, it works just the opposite. You flip it up to go off, and it works only on one side, difficult for the left-handed. The small trigger guard is also flawed, as it does not fold down or to the side. The AR-70 has a good, centrally mounted magazine release, and a bolt-hold-open feature. The trigger pull is adequate for the type of rifle. Sights are useful for 300 to 350 meters, which is all you need for the fifty five-grain one-in-twelve-inch twist 5.56x45mm ammo. The rear sight has a two-position flipper set of 150 and 300 meters, and the markings are painted white. The front sight is a cylindrical post. Both sights are protected by excellent wings. The front handguard got warm after firing only one hundred rounds and does not have a heat deflector. The handguard can easily be removed and replaced. The rifle has a bolt-release lever like the AR-15. Insert a loaded magazine, hit it with your fist, and your rifle is loaded and ready to go. The flash hider is short and open at the bottom, so kicks up dust when the rifle is fired from the prone position. The AR-70 has a dust cover like the AR-15: it opens automatically upon firing, does not rattle, and will help seal the action from rain as well as dust. The rifle takes down quickly for cleaning.

The Beretta ARX100 is the semi-auto version of the latest Beretta military rifle in 5.56.x45mm. This weapon disappoints for several reasons. The gas system is a piston-style rather than direct impingement-type but, unlike many such systems, the Beretta does not feel heavy. The barrel comes out readily and can be changed to other chambered units such as .300. A shorter barrel can be inserted if desired. I tested a short-barrel version and found it quite nimble. Adding a suppressor makes the overall length equal to the sixteen-inch barrel full-sized weapon, but you can shoot it without ear-muffs for comfort and safety. The stock both folds to the side and extends. The stock's latch seems flimsy; you push down on the stock and hit it to close, then pull to open. The stock extends to only three positions. More alternatives would help different sized shooters. The weapon has the typical set of rails on all sides, tempting the shooter to weigh down his weapon. The top rail holds the peep rear sight and front adjustable sight, which gives a sight picture similar to the M4. One rail will mount an optical sight. The trigger pull is typical for a semi-auto military-style rifle. The safety and its lever are small, so difficult to remove or apply with either speed or certainty. The bolt release is also difficult to apply or release.

Italy used the M1930 Breda 6.5 as their standard light machine gun during pre–World War II campaigns in Africa and through the war. This is surprising, as far better designs were available. The Breda M1930 LMG fires from a closed-bolt position, but only a little metal plug keeps the firing pin from following the bolt home, which would keep the weapon from detonating the cartridge primer. The weapon is fed by a side-mounted integral magazine, but has a top cover that houses an oiler. As each round is fired, a drop of oil drops onto the next cartridge so the case will not stick in the chamber. The feed mechanism is intricately machined and practically designed to create malfunctions. The weapon operates from the short recoil principal. The barrel itself and the locking lug area are quite complicated. One good point is that the barrel can be rapidly changed when it gets hot. The Breda M1930 uses an integral magazine hinged at the side to fire. The metal box is filled by stripper clips, then put into position. It is then swung aside and loaded by means of stripper clips and swung back into the firing position. This limits the ability to keep up any continuity of fire, and loading it in challenging conditions is difficult. This system creates the possibility of damage to the integral magazine, effectively sidelining the weapon. The weapon is too long, poorly balanced, and there is no good way to carry the weapon on patrol that will let it be used rapidly. The safety is located at the rear of the receiver and on top—impossible to release quickly. The cyclic rate was low enough that short bursts are possible. But there are so many bad design elements on the Breda that one cannot understand why it was used.

BERETTA M1918/30 CARBINE

Caliber: 9mm   **Manufacturer:** Beretta   **Typical Use:** Police and self-defense

The Beretta M1918 was an earlier submachine gun (SMG) and quite a good one. Many police agencies do not want their officers armed with a full-auto weapon, yet wanted something better than a handgun. The Beretta M1918/30 was a great choice. The copy tested resembles the M1918 SMG in all aspects save two. First, it is a closed-bolt weapon. Beretta figured a policeman firing in semi-auto only with a twenty-shot magazine would have no problems with "cooked-off" rounds firing. The closed-bolt system makes the rifle easy to shoot and safe to handle. Second, the M1918/30 fires only one shot with each pull of the trigger. The sights have a nice post in front and open adjustable rear. The butt stock permits the insertion of a cleaning rod. The safety is difficult to operate: To cock the weapon and chamber a round, you must pull the large ring on the back of the bolt all the way to the rear, and release. Recoil with the M1918/30 is light. The weapon is lightweight yet feels sturdy in the hand. It is quite nimble, which is unusual for a military weapon. The twenty-shot magazine is a good size. Unfortunately this magazine is unique to the weapon, so spares are difficult to find.

NAMBU (PAPA)

Caliber: 8mm   **Manufacturer:** Tokyo Gas and Electric   **Typical Use:** Military and self-defense

Kitiro Nambu, a Japanese Army officer, designed this weapon as a commercial pistol. There were four variations. It was purchased by individual officers; the only "army" order was some five hundred purchased by Siam before World War I. When evaluating the Papa Nambu, keep in mind that Japan had no tradition of handgun use prior to 1850. This pistol is made of good materials. The sights allow quick indexing on the cinema range; they are high and obvious in semidarkness, but are harder to use on the formal range. The caliber is light but as good as the 8mm Roth used in the Roth-Steyr 07, one of the top three World War I–era combat handguns. The weapon cannot be safely carried loaded with a round in the chamber. Instinctive/reactive shooting is more difficult than with a Roth-Steyr 07, but no worse than a Luger. Accuracy on the formal range is surprisingly good. The low recoil and low flash generated by the 8mm Nambu cartridge in a medium-weight weapon, coupled with a trigger system that is light if not crisp, permit accurate shooting and rapid repeat shots. On the cinema range, the angle of the grip, similar to the Glock, allowed good instinctive shooting. The design is weak for reaction/instinctive draw and shooting courses. The Papa Nambu was expensive to produce, and most of the production machinery was destroyed in a 1923 earthquake.

TYPE B "BABY" NAMBU

Caliber: 7mm   **Manufacturer:** Tokyo Gas and Electric   **Typical Use:** Military and self-defense

The "Baby" Type B Nambu was designed as a pre–World War II commercial venture to be sold to Japanese officers who were required to purchase their own sidearms. It used a cartridge that was low in stopping power and unique to this weapon. The 7mm Nambu pistol is made of good materials. A miniature of its predecessor, the Papa Nambu, it shares those design limitations and successes, including a good trigger and a front sight that is quick to index on the cinema range. The safety features of the Nambu 7mm are poor. The pistol works well enough on rapid repeat shots and quick indexing. The caliber lacks power, partly because the 7mm Nambu ammo does not have the benefit of a steel penetrator. The 7mm Nambu seems better than a .25 ACP and slightly less powerful than a .32 ACP. Despite firing from a locked-barrel position, the 7mm Nambu does not have the power of a .30 Luger or a .30 Mauser cartridge. Factory-loaded 7mm Nambu ammo is difficult to find, expensive since it is a collector's item, and of questionable quality since it is so old. I had ammo custom-loaded to test the weapon. Results were typical for a small-caliber pocket pistol. Because it is a lightweight weapon, recoil was surprisingly sharp but not unpleasant. Although it will never be a quick-reaction weapon or a "stopper," it is more powerful and of much better manufacture and materials than the .25 Beretta used by the Italian Air Force at that time. It is far superior to many European autoloaders of the period.

TYPE 26 REVOLVER

Caliber: 9mm   **Manufacturer:** Tokyo Gas and Electric   **Typical Use:** Military and self-defense

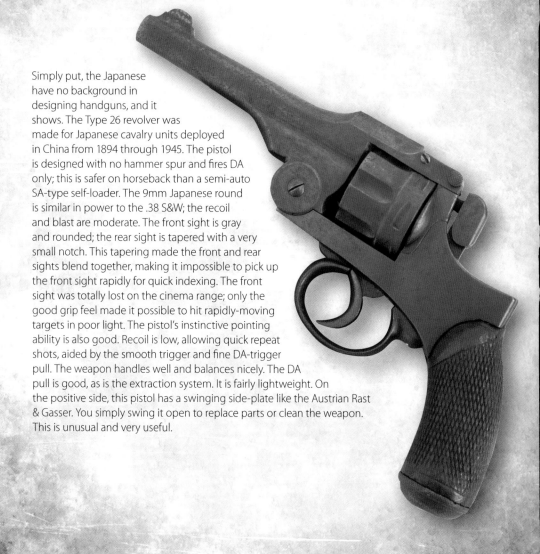

Simply put, the Japanese have no background in designing handguns, and it shows. The Type 26 revolver was made for Japanese cavalry units deployed in China from 1894 through 1945. The pistol is designed with no hammer spur and fires DA only; this is safer on horseback than a semi-auto SA-type self-loader. The 9mm Japanese round is similar in power to the .38 S&W; the recoil and blast are moderate. The front sight is gray and rounded; the rear sight is tapered with a very small notch. This tapering made the front and rear sights blend together, making it impossible to pick up the front sight rapidly for quick indexing. The front sight was totally lost on the cinema range; only the good grip feel made it possible to hit rapidly-moving targets in poor light. The pistol's instinctive pointing ability is also good. Recoil is low, allowing quick repeat shots, aided by the smooth trigger and fine DA-trigger pull. The weapon handles well and balances nicely. The DA pull is good, as is the extraction system. It is fairly lightweight. On the positive side, this pistol has a swinging side-plate like the Austrian Rast & Gasser. You simply swing it open to replace parts or clean the weapon. This is unusual and very useful.

TAISHO TYPE 14

Caliber: 8mm Nambu   **Manufacturer:** Tokyo Gas and Electric   **Typical Use:** Military, police, and self-defense

The first official-issue Japanese pistol, the Type 14 was designed by an ordnance board working from the Papa Nambu model. It is an unusual, well-made pistol of good materials. My test groups at fifty feet ran approximately 5½ inches, roughly twice that of the Model 19. I fired ten-shot groups and all ten went into six inches; clearly acceptable combat accuracy. The trigger pull on this Type 14 is very light. The sights are small. They are fine for formal target work, but on the cinema range, they get lost in the dark. I could not see the back sight at all, and indexing ability was seriously impeded. The angle of the grip is quite good, allowing some natural pointing ability. The safety may be its worst feature. You must flip it through an arc of 180 degrees, and this can only be done with two hands. However, when using a normal two-handed hold, you can flip the safety off with your weak hand quite rapidly and fire the pistol with your other. The safety seems very certain and would not be accidentally turned off. The Type 14 has a magazine disconnector, desirable in a military pistol, but the spring that holds the magazine in place is so strong that you have to yank the magazine out with your spare hand. The magazine's short overall length keeps the trigger-reach short, critical for use by people with small hands or short fingers. The cartridge fired is nearly as good as any 7.65 Luger. It is a moderate-velocity, small-caliber, lightweight projectile of round-nose design, so does not have much stopping power with conventional ammo. The Nambu is an underrated pistol. It is nearly as good as a Luger P08, and the one I tested has a better trigger pull than any Luger I have tried.

Although by no means a wonderful pistol, the Type 94 is as good as many European 7.65 pocket pistols that I tested. The sights are low, small, and hard to see in poor lighting, but are acceptable in good light. The front sight is small, short, and dark which made indexing difficult. The rear sight is too shallow. It produced a lot of flash on the cinema range. The recoil is high for the power of the cartridge—104-grain .30 caliber bullets at nine hundred fps velocity. The pistol is light, but I think the grip design causes the recoil. The rope-like grip tended to shift in my hand; control is difficult, and repeat shots are slow. The conveniently located safety in this particular pistol falls readily to hand, much like the Colt Government Model, and you can carry this pistol cocked and locked. There is a detent that goes into effect after you push it off making it difficult to flip it back on with your thumb alone. But it is more important to be able to flip it off readily than to engage it quickly. It allows you to quickly engage your targets. Toward the end of the war, quality control deteriorated dramatically in Japanese arms. Type 94 pistols that show rough workmanship should be checked before firing. They will fire out of battery, and without the breech locked. They are not safe.

The Japanese developed the M1944 Type 100. It is as well made as any Sten and is as well finished as many European SMGs produced in later years. The Japanese were slow to develop SMGs for a variety of reasons. First, they purchased some German or Swiss-pattern M1928 Bergmanns, likely encountering a variety used by Chinese forces in the 1930s. The poor performance of the Chinese weapons may have made them conclude SMGs were not effective. Second, SMGs were not popular until after 1941. Last, the Japanese had some excellent LMGs, such as the Type 96 and Type 99, both of which had much greater penetration in the jungle than any SMG. The SMG may not be the ideal jungle weapon. Most fire from an open bolt, which affects accuracy, has limited range, is heavy, and suffers from limited penetration. The Type 100 has a nice fixed peep sight but is not protected from damage. The Type 100 has a vector-type compensator on the muzzle, although I did not get to test it. The 8mm Nambu cartridge, which is not powerful, may not have enough muzzle velocity to really make a difference. The Type 100 can be taken down quickly and the barrel removed for cleaning. The safety, which is located in the trigger guard, is convenient and quick to remove. The Type 100 is a fairly lightweight weapon that is nicely balanced.

TYPE 30 6.5mm

Caliber: 6.5mm   **Manufacturer:** Koishikawa Arsenal   **Typical Use:** Military

This rifle, the so-called hook safety model, was the standard infantry rifle during the 1904-1905 Russo-Japanese War and was issued to Japanese soldiers stationed in China. The rifle has the typical European-style pyramid front sight, with no protection. The rear sight is a shallow U-shaped rear on an open-ramp-style. The rear notch is so small that it is difficult to get a proper sight picture even in the bright light. Light can hit the sight from either side, which can shift bullet impact because you see the sights differently from different angles. The trigger pull is good and both report and recoil are light, which makes the weapon a pleasure to shoot. The rifle is muzzle heavy, which makes off-hand shooting difficult. No butt trap is fitted to the stock. The action was smooth, and I could quickly reload after a shot by rapid bolt work. The smoothness of the butt plate coupled with the ill balance of the weapon caused it to occasionally come off my shoulder as I rapidly worked the action. You must use an atypical approach to work the hooked safety. You pull the hooked safety with the little finger of your right hand; then you do not hit the stock, and working it is fast. It would be difficult to use if wearing gloves or mittens.

TYPE 44 6.5mm CARBINE

Caliber: 6.5mm   **Manufacturer:** Arisaka   **Typical Use:** Military

The Type 44 6.5mm Japanese carbine was introduced in 1911 and was issued mainly to cavalry units. All Japanese rifles of this pattern have a very fast safety. It is convenient, free from projections, sturdy, and most importantly, it can be disengaged rapidly. You push in with your thumb only and twist your hand to get it off. The rifle has a well-protected pyramid front sight. The rear sight is a shallow V-notch and is calibrated from four hundred to two thousand meters, too far for realistic combat ranges. The sights are hard to see, slow to use, and almost worthless in dark conditions. The action offered a bolt hold-open device. The action was very smooth, so you can fire quickly. The bolt handle is well positioned and can be operated properly with the handle in the palm of the hand, rather than having to pull the handle with your fingers. The trigger pull is heavy, which affects accuracy, especially when shooting off-hand. The weapon is light, short, and well balanced. The rifle has a butt trap that holds the cleaning rod and does not rattle. The rifle has a sling mounted on the side so the cavalryman can carry the weapon diagonally across his back. It has a dust cover to protect the bolt, which also makes little noise. Recoil is light and accuracy is good. The ballistics of the cartridge ensure a low blast. The integral bayonet makes the weapon slightly muzzle-heavy.

TYPE 11 LIGHT MACHINE GUN 6.5MM

Caliber: 6.5mm   **Manufacturer:** Japanese state arsenals   **Typical Use:** Military

"U.S." veterans nicknamed the Type 11 LMG "the Woodpecker" for its distinctive sound when firing with its light report and five-shot bursts. The weapon is short, making it handier than many similar weapons, but it is not easy to handle. There is no forehand to hold on to when firing off-hand or from the hip, and the bipod legs are not easy to use. Your hand can slip and hit the hot barrel shroud. It is most suitable for prone-position shooting. The cartridge hopper system avoids the problem of magazines and permits a low profile for the weapon. It is convenient to operate and allows the shooter to use the rifleman's stripper clips without any delay. But the ammo is exposed to rain and contaminants, which would eventually affect reliability. Recoil is low and the weapon fires accurate bursts. The front sight is a pyramid type. It is well protected by wings which had holes in the side to allow light to fall on the sight. The rear sight is V-shaped and difficult to use. The safety is difficult to use. The bolt-retrieving lever has to be comfortably pulled all the way to the rear or the bolt will not catch sufficiently to pick up a cartridge. The stock is an odd shape and offset to the right. The grip is wrapped in metal as is the front part of the stock. You can easily place your cheek on the metal, not the wood, and be burned. The grip is cramped and the shooter must hold his hand at an odd angle to fire it. Although I began this test with a poor opinion of the Type 11, I ended up liking it. The ability to fire long bursts with accuracy is the selling point.

MODEL 99 7.7mm

Caliber: 7.7mm   **Manufacturer:** Japanese state arsenals   **Typical Use:** Military

The Japanese forces in China encountered problems with their 6.5mm machine guns and rifles, so they introduced the Model 99 in 7.7mm, which is the ballistic equivalent of the .30-06 cartridge. The Model 99 shares many design features with the Model 38. The front sight is a blade shape and the rear includes a peep sight. The sights were calibrated from 300 to 1,500 meters. The butt plate is solid metal and a metal strap through the grip ensures that the stock will not break at the wrist. It has a bolt cover. Trigger pull is good for a military rifle. The rifle has a flush magazine, but you can unload it by pushing the latch in front of the trigger guard. A cleaning rod is slung under the barrel. The bore is chrome-lined, making maintenance much easier with corrosive primers and in humid jungle conditions. There is a monopod on the rifle. Although the legs are thin, they do allow the shooter to rest his rifle on it for a steadier shot, but too much pressure will bend or warp them. The bolt handle sticks straight out, which is faster to operate than curved handles and that, coupled with the 5-shot stripper clip loading mechanism, yields a fairly continuous stream of fire. The bolt handle is smooth. The safety system is the same as the Model 38; very practical once you practice and discover its secrets. With its shorter barrel at 25-¾ inches and 7-¾ pounds, the Model 99 is convenient to handle and it balances well. The recoil is greater because of the more powerful cartridge, and the noise level is higher because of the shorter barrel than earlier Japanese service rifles.

DAEWOO DP 21 9MM

Caliber: 9x19mm   **Manufacturer:** Daewoo   **Typical Use:** Military, police, and self defense

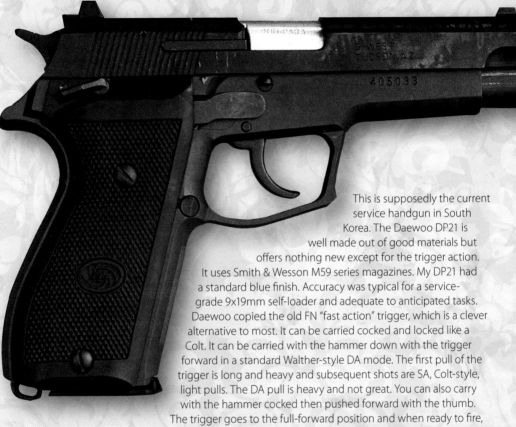

This is supposedly the current service handgun in South Korea. The Daewoo DP21 is well made out of good materials but offers nothing new except for the trigger action. It uses Smith & Wesson M59 series magazines. My DP21 had a standard blue finish. Accuracy was typical for a service-grade 9x19mm self-loader and adequate to anticipated tasks. Daewoo copied the old FN "fast action" trigger, which is a clever alternative to most. It can be carried cocked and locked like a Colt. It can be carried with the hammer down with the trigger forward in a standard Walther-style DA mode. The first pull of the trigger is long and heavy and subsequent shots are SA, Colt-style, light pulls. The DA pull is heavy and not great. You can also carry with the hammer cocked then pushed forward with the thumb. The trigger goes to the full-forward position and when ready to fire, lightly pull the trigger through the arc and the hammer jumps back, allowing the standard, SA-pull mode, then complete the cycle to fire the weapon. This has potential to improve accuracy, but is so different from other systems that you must work to master it. While this might be easy for Korean troops trained in it from the start, it would be difficult for those used to conventional DA weapons. The DP 21's safety lever, located only on one side, is frame-mounted like a Government Model. The shooter can engage the safety with the pistol cocked, allowing him or her to move safely without dropping the hammer down all the way, as you need to do with a slide-mounted system or frame-mounted decocker pistol like the SIG.

DAEWOO K-1

Caliber: 5.56x45mm   **Manufacturer:** Daewoo   **Typical Use:** Military

The Daewoo K-1 is a South Korean–made rifle designed to be the equivalent of M16 rifles. It is lightweight, fairly nimble, and reliable. The K-1 rifle tested was a semi-auto variant of the Korean selective-fire weapon, but otherwise identical. It uses the M16 gas system and magazines. The safety is not as easy to use as the M16's, but it is acceptable if you cant your hand a bit. The safety is not ambidextrous. The magazine release is fast and handy, like the M16's. The front sight is a cylindrical pyramid, gray in color, and difficult to use, but the rear is a peep sight and works well. The K-1's stock is modeled on the collapsing wire stock of the M3 SMG. This creates a compact package, but it is not incredibly sturdy. If you pull it past the catch at the rear, it comes loose. Thanks to the mild recoil of the 5.56x45mm cartridge, the rounded rods of the stock do not bruise the cheeks. The weapon recoils oddly because the stock flexes each time it is fired. Recoil is light, but you must reposition your eye on the sight, which slows subsequent shots. The forearm is made out of a sturdy plastic material but lacks a double heat-liner. Firing a couple of fast magazines makes it too hot to hold. The pistol-grip stock feels good, but the winter trigger guard cannot be laid flat.

DAEWOO K-2

Caliber: 5.56x45mm   **Manufacturer:** Daewoo   **Typical Use:** Military, police, and self-defense

The Daewoo K-2 differs from its predecessor by using the Kalinskov gas system and a folding, full-plastic stock as opposed to the collapsing wire unit. The stock design offers a much more stable shooting platform, while still giving the shooter a rifle that can be stored readily in confined places. The sights on the K-2 are similar to those on the K-1, offering a pyramid-shaped cylinder front sight and an excellent rear peep. The front sight is gray and difficult to rapidly pick up on field targets. But a rudimentary front sight exists on the top of the rounded hood covering the front sight, which lets you align at close range with poor visibility. The magazine is identical to the M16's and the magazine catch is speedy. The safety/selector is convenient to the shooting hand but the levers are small and short—you must shift your hand in the grip to manipulate them. The gray metal finish and black plastic stock are very similar to the M16. The bolt offers a good cocking handle to be kicked open when malfunctions require clearing. The winter trigger guard system does not fold flat against the pistol grip. Today the Daewoo K-2 is rarely seen outside of Korea. It is simply out-marketed by the AK47 and M16. More's the pity as the K-2 is an excellent rifle.

Caliber: 5.56x45mm   **Manufacturer:** Daewoo   **Typical Use:** Military

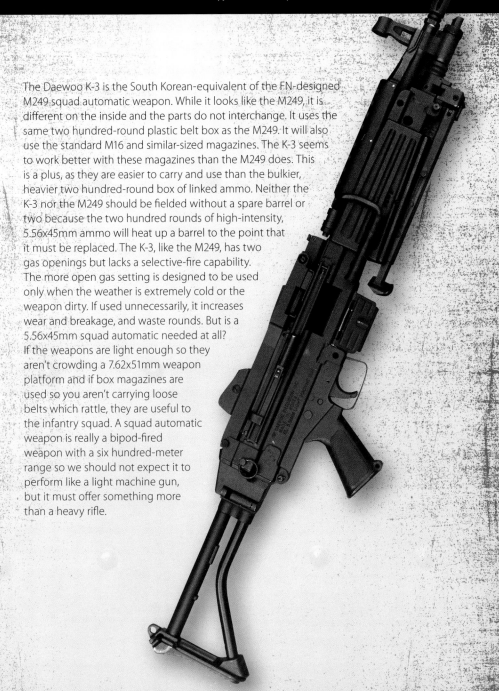

The Daewoo K-3 is the South Korean-equivalent of the FN-designed M249 squad automatic weapon. While it looks like the M249, it is different on the inside and the parts do not interchange. It uses the same two hundred-round plastic belt box as the M249. It will also use the standard M16 and similar-sized magazines. The K-3 seems to work better with these magazines than the M249 does. This is a plus, as they are easier to carry and use than the bulkier, heavier two hundred-round box of linked ammo. Neither the K-3 nor the M249 should be fielded without a spare barrel or two because the two hundred rounds of high-intensity, 5.56x45mm ammo will heat up a barrel to the point that it must be replaced. The K-3, like the M249, has two gas openings but lacks a selective-fire capability. The more open gas setting is designed to be used only when the weather is extremely cold or the weapon dirty. If used unnecessarily, it increases wear and breakage, and waste rounds. But is a 5.56x45mm squad automatic needed at all? If the weapons are light enough so they aren't crowding a 7.62x51mm weapon platform and if box magazines are used so you aren't carrying loose belts which rattle, they are useful to the infantry squad. A squad automatic weapon is really a bipod-fired weapon with a six hundred-meter range so we should not expect it to perform like a light machine gun, but it must offer something more than a heavy rifle.

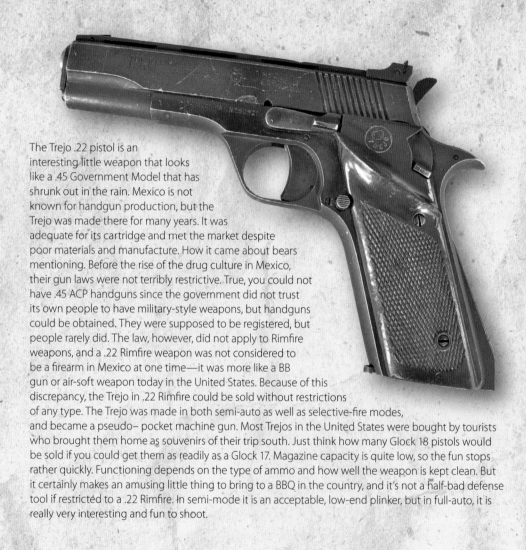

The Trejo .22 pistol is an interesting little weapon that looks like a .45 Government Model that has shrunk out in the rain. Mexico is not known for handgun production, but the Trejo was made there for many years. It was adequate for its cartridge and met the market despite poor materials and manufacture. How it came about bears mentioning. Before the rise of the drug culture in Mexico, their gun laws were not terribly restrictive. True, you could not have .45 ACP handguns since the government did not trust its own people to have military-style weapons, but handguns could be obtained. They were supposed to be registered, but people rarely did. The law, however, did not apply to Rimfire weapons, and a .22 Rimfire weapon was not considered to be a firearm in Mexico at one time—it was more like a BB gun or air-soft weapon today in the United States. Because of this discrepancy, the Trejo in .22 Rimfire could be sold without restrictions of any type. The Trejo was made in both semi-auto as well as selective-fire modes, and became a pseudo– pocket machine gun. Most Trejos in the United States were bought by tourists who brought them home as souvenirs of their trip south. Just think how many Glock 18 pistols would be sold if you could get them as readily as a Glock 17. Magazine capacity is quite low, so the fun stops rather quickly. Functioning depends on the type of ammo and how well the weapon is kept clean. But it certainly makes an amusing little thing to bring to a BBQ in the country, and it's not a half-bad defense tool if restricted to a .22 Rimfire. In semi-mode it is an acceptable, low-end plinker, but in full-auto, it is really very interesting and fun to shoot.

REMINGTON ROLLING BLOCK CARBINE

Caliber: 7x57mm   **Manufacturer:** Remington Arms Company and others   **Typical Use:** Military, police, and hunting

After the US Civil War, the Rolling Block was popular in the United States, Latin America, Egypt, and Turkey before Mauser developed its repeating rifle. The Rolling Block comes in many calibers and lengths. Large black-powder cartridges are common, but I tested an example in 7x57mm, a popular caliber in the late nineteenth and early twentieth centuries. Most Rolling Blocks are rifles, but I tested a military saddle ring carbine. The carbine version is lightweight and yet shoots a fairly effective round. Because the Rolling Block has a shorter receiver (it lacks a bolt), it is shorter than other rifles with the same barrel length. Sights on the Rolling Block are typical of the period. The front sight is a pyramid that is difficult to pick up, and the rear sight has a very small, shallow notch that makes holding consistently a challenge. The rear sight offers elevation to long distances that were appropriate at that time before indirect-fire weapons. The Rolling Block only has half-cock notch as a safety, which could easily break if the rifle were dropped. The trigger pull was heavy but it was crisp. The hammer must be pulled manually to the rear. It had a strong spring, so it takes a lot of muscle to pull it. When the hammer hits the block, it is jarring and impedes accuracy. To load and fire the Rolling Block you must cock the weapon, pull down on the back of the block, insert the cartridge, close the block, and pull the trigger. If you do not want to fire immediately, you pull the trigger and lower the hammer to the safety notch. You extract the empty cartridge by cocking the hammer and pulling back on the block. This pulls the case clear of the chamber, flinging it out, and then you load a fresh round. Once down, slam the block closed with your palm and you're ready to fire. The trigger guard is small, but the rifle can be used with either hand. This is a very simple weapon with big parts. It is easy to operate and maintain. This rifle was handy to carry in the field, and it balanced well for off-hand, sitting, or kneeling use. The short barrel and short sight radius coupled with the poor sights made long-range work more difficult. By the time the test weapon was made, the Rolling Block action was obsolete and cannot compare to the Mauser bolt action, which was then available as a battle rifle. However, in its prime (1867-1888), it was one of the best rifles in the world.

RAST & GASSER "MONTENEGRIN"

Caliber: 11mm   **Manufacturer:** Rast & Gasser and various Belgian manufacturers   **Typical Use:** Military and self-defense

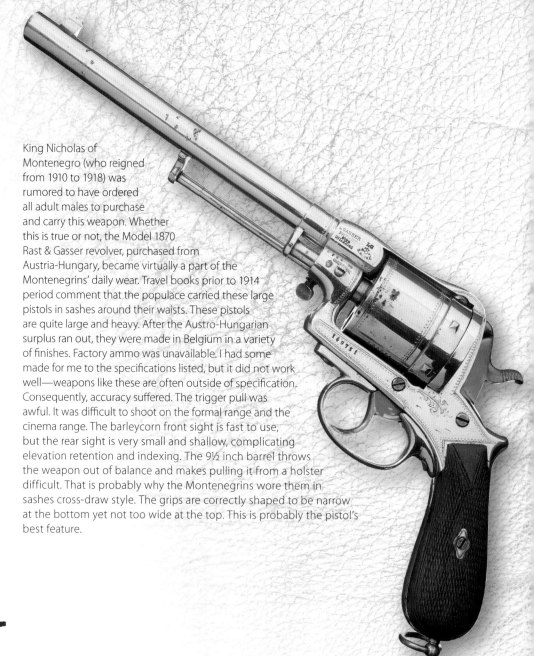

King Nicholas of Montenegro (who reigned from 1910 to 1918) was rumored to have ordered all adult males to purchase and carry this weapon. Whether this is true or not, the Model 1870 Rast & Gasser revolver, purchased from Austria-Hungary, became virtually a part of the Montenegrins' daily wear. Travel books prior to 1914 period comment that the populace carried these large pistols in sashes around their waists. These pistols are quite large and heavy. After the Austro-Hungarian surplus ran out, they were made in Belgium in a variety of finishes. Factory ammo was unavailable. I had some made for me to the specifications listed, but it did not work well—weapons like these are often outside of specification. Consequently, accuracy suffered. The trigger pull was awful. It was difficult to shoot on the formal range and the cinema range. The barleycorn front sight is fast to use, but the rear sight is very small and shallow, complicating elevation retention and indexing. The 9½ inch barrel throws the weapon out of balance and makes pulling it from a holster difficult. That is probably why the Montenegrins wore them in sashes cross-draw style. The grips are correctly shaped to be narrow at the bottom yet not too wide at the top. This is probably the pistol's best feature.

M1894 ORDNANCE REVOLVER

Caliber: 9.4mm   **Manufacturer:** Artillerie Inrichtungen   **Typical Use:** Military, police, and self-defense

The M1894 was adopted in the 1880s–1890s when armies wanted smaller-caliber rifles and pistols, and smokeless powder was developed. The Netherlands used a 9.4mm bullet larger than those other countries used, but only equal to a .38 S&W or .38 Long cartridge, so not very powerful. The heavy DA-trigger pull forced me to place my arm at an angle to get enough leverage after six shots to fire the pistol. This heavy pull may have been a safety feature, but caused firing to be very slow on DA strings. The trigger surface is smooth, which normally helps rapid DA work, but the pull limited its usefulness. The ejector rod is attached to the ejector housing and spring-loaded. Each chamber has to be indexed to accomplish ejection. The small cutout on the frame at the cylinder's rear has to be carefully aligned in order to eject the cases, which slowed the procedure. The rear sight is too low and shallow for rapid pick up. The front sight is tall and has a bead built into it which would normally help pick up, but due to the angle on it toward the muzzle, light causes it to fade out. For its period, the Ordnance Revolver is a decent military revolver, and fares well when compared to the Colt M1878.

Most of these rifles appear to be heavily used and abused from having served in the Netherlands and East Indies for many years, but the rifle tested had apparently been spared this fate and was in good condition. One feature I especially like about this rifle is the wood fitted to the left side of the magazine; it took some care and attention to do that, and I am certain it was done to avoid the metal hitting the soldier when he carried this weapon slung across his back. I know of no other rifle where such care was taken. The Model 95 uses the standard Mannlicher-style action, which is somewhat slow in comparison with a Mauser action because the bolt handle is located farther from the hand. The safety is also slow to use. The Dutch carbine has a good-sized ball on the bolt handle, which allows the shooter to get a solid grip on the bolt and thereby improve the speed at which the bolt is operated. Still, it was slower than a Mauser bolt system and much slower than a straight-pull rifle. The rifle has no butt trap but it does have a cleaning rod which I value on any combat rifle. The sling swivels are mounted on the side of the stock. Unfortunately, the leather of the sling hits the shooter's face when he takes a proper shooting position. This impedes aiming somewhat and is especially uncomfortable when snap shooting is used on close-range targets. The sights are the typical European pyramid front sight with no protective wings and a V-notch open rear sight. The lowest setting is four hundred meters and is calibrated to two thousand meters. The shallow V-notch and pyramid front sight combination is very hard to use effectively and slow to acquire. The Model 95 No. 4 N.M. carbine is a nice rifle to use from the standpoint of balance and feel. Recoil is light, yet due to the construction of the bullets and the coefficient of the loads, it has adequate penetration and power for military purposes. The action is not particularly quick to use and the safety is awkward and slow, but it feels "alive" in the hands. It has a good balance for both off-hand and kneeling shooting.

M1914

Caliber: .45 ACP   **Manufacturer:** Arsenal, Kongsberg   **Typical Use:** Military, police, and self-defense

This pistol is basically a Norwegian-manufactured copy of the Colt M1911. The slide stop is lower than on the Colt, allowing quicker release of the slide, and the wooden grip panel is cut out to accommodate the lower slide stop. Otherwise it is a standard M1911. The Norwegian M1914 shoots exactly the same as the M1911. The short tang causes some hammer bite if not held correctly, just as with the M1911. The Norwegians made these pistols in small quantities up to World War II and a small number were manufactured for the German occupation forces. The Norwegian Army picked a good handgun to replace the 7.5 Nagant revolver. The Colt automatic was a giant step forward in power, reloading ease, and maintenance. At that time, there were few suitable self-loading pistols. Interestingly, they were issued with three spare magazines, one more than offered in the US military.

M1894 KRAG

Caliber: 6.5mm   **Manufacturer:** Swedish state factories   **Typical Use:** Military and sporting

I like Krags because they have a very slick action. I could eject the chamber and load a new cartridge before the ejected one hit the ground. As battle rifles, they have some flaws. The trigger on the M1894 is the typical two-stage military unit with a lot of slack and a heavy pull. The sights are adjustable to hit on target from one hundred meters out to the long ranges typical of the days before machine guns and mortars. It has a small, narrow V-shaped notch that tends to blend in with the wood on the forearm, making it very difficult to see the front sight properly. The barrel and forearm get very hot after firing very few shots. The rifle has a butt trap to contain cleaning equipment. The Krag cannot be reloaded with stripper clips. It can be loaded with a round still chambered by flipping open the gate and dropping in a round. At its time, this was an advantage, but it became a liability once stripper clips came into existence. Krags manufactured in Norway were made well into the twentieth century when metal standards had improved. A 6.5x55mm Krag made in the 1930s is likely to be much stronger than an 1896 US rifle. The Germans re-chambered them for 7.92x57mm and used them during World War II. I think a Krag action makes it the ideal sporting rifle. As a military rifle of the period, however, it cannot compare to the M93 Mauser, M91 Carcano, or Schmidt Rubin.

175

RADOM MODEL 35

Caliber: 9mm Parabellum   **Manufacturer:** Fabryka Broni, Radom   **Typical Use:** Military and self-defense

The Polish government adopted the Radom pistol in 1935 and manufactured it for the Polish Army through the beginning of World War II. After Germany conquered Poland, the Germans produced this pistol in Poland for their army; Steyr also produced some in the last days of the war. Prewar Poland had many cavalry units, and the Radom was designed to be fired one-handed from a horse. It is a reliable, though heavy, pistol, and has only a grip safety. The lever on the side that looks like a safety is merely a hammer drop. Pushing this lever down drops the hammer; releasing it permits it to spring back into the original position. The weapon that I tested had a poor trigger pull, which caused large groups. The sights are too small with the U-shaped rear notch and a very small front, making them difficult to see and decreasing accuracy. There is no cock-and-lock safety. You can carry it with the hammer down and then try to cock it, but it's difficult because of the burr hammer and because the side of the slide covers a lot of the hammer. You can carry it with the chamber empty and hammer down, but you will need both hands to get the weapon to operate. Or you can carry it cocked and trust the grip safety, which could allow accidental discharge. The grips flare at the bottom, which breaks your hold.

Caliber: 9x18mm   **Manufacturer:** Polish state factories   **Typical Use:** Military, police, and self-defense

The Soviet Union demanded standardization from her Eastern European "allies," but allowed them to design their own weapons as long as they used the standard cartridges. The Poles developed the P83 for the 9x18mm to use like the Makarov. It appears similar in size and construction, but the Makarov is made from machined parts while the P83 is constructed with more stampings. It also strips differently. The P83 has a nice set of sights. The front is black and square-faced, which helps with pick up. The grip feels good in the hand, and should not get too hot or cold as it's made out of a synthetic material. The pistol has a rear butt-mounted magazine release. This slows speed reloads, but allows both right and left-handed people to use the weapons with equal facility. The safety was quite stiff to start but smoothed out with use. The safety system worked like that of the Makarov, which is the reverse of the system on the Beretta and Smith & Wesson. The lever on the side looks like a hammer drop but is actually the slide release. The P83 has a chrome-lined barrel but a plain blued finish. Testing the weapon at fifty yards from the back-rested position, I was able to get groups small enough to stay in a man's chest. By comparison, I did shoot groups one third that size with a M92 Beretta that day. I found the P83 to be a good pistol within the limits of the cartridge for self-defense purposes.

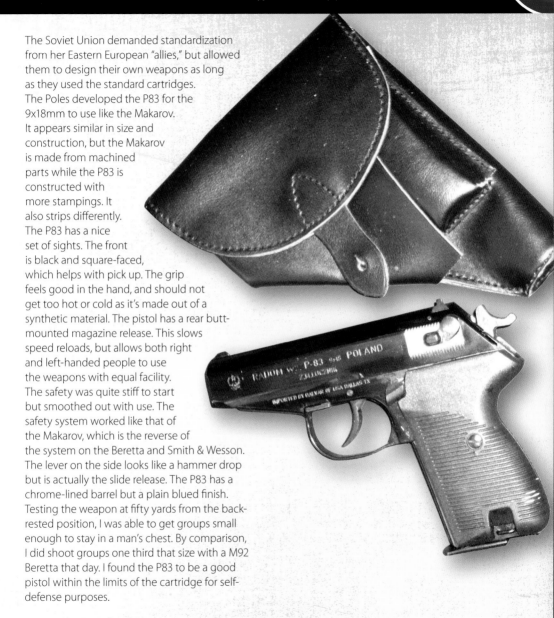

The Polish PM63 is a 9x18mm machine pistol, meant to be better than the typical handgun soldiers carried. It should not be judged as a true SMG or short carbine. The PM63 fires semi only by pulling the trigger part way back, or full-auto with a full pull of the trigger. A sliding stock allows it to be deployed from the shoulder, or you can fire it off-hand without the stock. Unlike most true machine pistols, the PM63 fires from an open bolt. Using it off-hand without the stock extended is very difficult. With the stock extended and firing from the shoulder, it is a very effective weapon, easily hitting man-size targets at two hundred yards off-hand. To load and fire the weapon, insert a double-column magazine into the grip. Short magazines and longer, higher-capacity models are available. When pulled back, the slide will stay back as this weapon fires from the open-bolt position; it won't move forward like most handguns until you pull the trigger. If only one hand is available, pushing the muzzle of the weapon at the compensator position will allow you to cock it. The safety can be flipped on and off readily with the thumb. Sights are good on the front and are sturdy. The rear is protected by wings and while open, it does flip to compensate for different distances. The trigger pull is very light for an open-bolt weapon, and thanks to the lightweight slide, there is little jarring. The low cyclic rate allows good control for two-three-round bursts.

The HK 21 is an extremely lightweight machine gun that is designed for the platoon or company level and is also a major-caliber squad automatic weapon. The HK 21 uses a belt for sustained fire but can take a box magazine, and has a rapidly-changeable barrel. The barrel is heavy enough so that overheating is minimized even though it fires from a closed bolt. Additionally, it fires the 7.62x51mm NATO round giving a better, longer-range gun.. The HK 21 offers a fine tripod that helps it in its sustained fire mode.. The HK 21 has many similarities to the G3 rifle and also suffers from many of its failings. The sights on the HK 21 are the same as the G3's, except that the rear sight is graduated to one thousand two hundred meters rather than four hundred meters. The sights are on the gun rather than the barrel. The butt stock on the HK 21 is the same design as the G3: both lack a butt trap and have the same pistol grip and safety/selector setup. The safety is not positioned in such a way as to allow it to be flipped off rapidly. You can set the selector on semi-auto and fire rapid semi-auto shots the same as you would with the G3. Because the weapon is heavier, the recovery time is faster, and because the belt can contain more ammo than the twenty-round box, you do not have to break the rhythm of your shooting. Barrels on the HK 21 can be exchanged rapidly, and as long as you are somewhat careful, you should not burn your hand. The HK 21 barrel uses the standard G3 flash hider. It is acceptable but does nothing to control muzzle rise. Given the light weight of the weapon and the considerable recoil generated because of its cyclic rate, a muzzle brake would prove useful. Probably the worst two features of the HK 21 are the cocking mechanism and the loading mechanism for the belts. The cocking lever is similar to the G3's except that the spring fitted to the bolt is much heavier and the whole thing is much harder to operate. I cannot cock the HK 21 while lying on my stomach by merely reaching up and pulling the cocking lever to the rear—it is too strong. The second bad feature involves the belt loading. Most machine guns use a top latch and tray system; with the HK 21, you push the belts upside down from the normal position because the bolt is opposite the normal position in an LMG into the feed tray. Furthermore, as the weapon gets hotter, pushing belts into the receiver with your fingers gets to be less and less fun. I am not sold on 5.56x45mm squad automatic weapons but given a choice between an M249 in that caliber and the HK 21 in 7.62x51mm, I think I would prefer the M249 because it is easier to cock, offers a box magazine carry without an adapter, and makes loading belts much easier and less painful. But I do like the ability to fire sustained semi-auto fire at long range that the HK 21 offers, as well as the power the 7.62x51mm provides once the range gets long and the wind gets stiff. With a suitable tripod, the HK 21 can be used as a general-purpose LMG rather than a mere squad automatic.

AIM

Caliber: 7.62x39mm   **Manufacturer:** State arsenals   **Typical Use:** Military and police

The standard AKM 7.62x39mm rifle modified only in the forearm is the standard infantry rifle in Romania. The Romanian variants have a vertical forearm pistol-grip stock which lends them a very distinctive look. When the Romanian military wanted a weapon more easily concealed, they developed the AIM. It uses a side-folding stock similar to those on standard East German-manufactured AKM rifles. The stock seems sturdier than the typical AKM under-folder, and it hits the cheek less than the narrower struts of the under-folder. The release is a good-size button that can be rapidly depressed and swings forward and back with little effort. The action is typical AKM, as is the rear sight. The barrel on the AIM is thirteen inches long and effectively ends at the end of the gas system. A short, fairly effective flash-hider is added to the barrel. Because of this barrel length, the weapon doesn't need a special gas system, nor does the bolt system have to be modified. While it is not as compact as the Soviet AKSU, it's much less expensive to make. I found the operation of it and results the same as other AKM. You must actively grip the forearm, yet the best rifle work is not done with the support hand holding the forearm but merely resting on the palm area. Carrying it for long periods may cramp the wrist, but it lets the shooter hold the weapon through the firing of many magazines, when heat build-up would normally make the forearm too hot to hold.

Z88

Caliber: 9x19mm Parabellum   **Manufacturer:** Denel   **Typical Use:** Military and self-defense

The South African Z88 is a Beretta-licensed copy of their M92 pistol. It differs in lacking the slide capture feature designed to catch the rear slide if it breaks off. The hammer is shaped differently and the grips are slightly different. I found both SA and DA trigger pulls to be gritty and heavy. The safety also felt quite gritty. Perhaps with shooting, the parts will wear in and become smoother. The sights were standard Beretta-style and easy to pick up in dim light. In good light on the formal range, you need to align the top of the rear and front sights and not take the top of the white dot, as that will cause your bullets to strike high. The grips on the Z88 look like the Beretta's but have a slight ridge, unlike the rounded-off Beretta. Shooting is fine with a two-hand Weaver hold, but when firing with one hand, the pistol slipped with each shot, so I had to reposition my hand for the next shot, slowing me down. This does not happen with the Beretta. The finish on the Z88 looked like a traditional blued finish but may be more rust resistant, like the Brunerton finish found on the Beretta.

MAUSER M1896

Caliber: 7x57mm   **Manufacturer:** Mauser   **Typical Use:** Military, police, and hunting

The Boers surprised the British with their powerful resistance during the Boer War. This was due in part to the fact they were well armed. They used the Mauser M1896 carbine, a very modern weapon at that time. It used a stripper clip to load, which was faster than the British Enfields. It had a sling swivel on the side. The example tested was a captured Boer War piece in excellent condition. The sights are the typical pyramid front but without any guard, coupled with a low V-shaped open rear sight. Adjustment ran to one thousand four hundred meters, but the lowest setting was four hundred meters, so the rifle hit twenty four inches high at one hundred yards. This is typical of the European battle zero of the period. There is no bolt hold-open feature, so the shooter has no alert and can easily pull the trigger on an empty chamber. The carbine uses a straight-grip stock with a thick wrist that is very sturdy. The carbine balances well in the off-hand, kneeling, and sitting positions. The action is slick and quick to use. The safety is slow to operate and many would carry it with either an empty chamber, or the bolt handle slightly out of position, safety off and round in the chamber. The Mauser is lightweight, handy, flat shooting, and dependable. If the sights were adjustable to allow more practical results, both in terms of range and quick acquisition, the M1896 would be a fine battle rifle.

ASTRA 900

Caliber: 7.63 Mauser (.30 Mauser) **Manufacturer:** Unceta & Co. **Typical Use:** Military, police, and self-defense

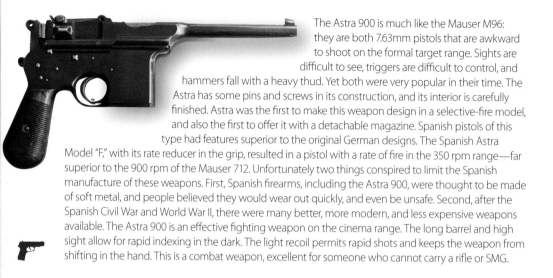

The Astra 900 is much like the Mauser M96: they are both 7.63mm pistols that are awkward to shoot on the formal target range. Sights are difficult to see, triggers are difficult to control, and hammers fall with a heavy thud. Yet both were very popular in their time. The Astra has some pins and screws in its construction, and its interior is carefully finished. Astra was the first to make this weapon design in a selective-fire model, and also the first to offer it with a detachable magazine. Spanish pistols of this type had features superior to the original German designs. The Spanish Astra Model "F," with its rate reducer in the grip, resulted in a pistol with a rate of fire in the 350 rpm range—far superior to the 900 rpm of the Mauser 712. Unfortunately two things conspired to limit the Spanish manufacture of these weapons. First, Spanish firearms, including the Astra 900, were thought to be made of soft metal, and people believed they would wear out quickly, and even be unsafe. Second, after the Spanish Civil War and World War II, there were many better, more modern, and less expensive weapons available. The Astra 900 is an effective fighting weapon on the cinema range. The long barrel and high sight allow for rapid indexing in the dark. The light recoil permits rapid shots and keeps the weapon from shifting in the hand. This is a combat weapon, excellent for someone who cannot carry a rifle or SMG.

STAR MODEL B

Caliber: 9mm Parabellum **Manufacturer:** Star Bonifacio Echeverria SA **Typical Use:** Military, police, and self-defense

The Star Model B is a Colt Government Model-style pistol manufactured in 9x19mm. Star pistols all follow traditional designs and are well made. Although they always look good, occasional batches of Stars are made of soft steel. This causes parts to misalign and the weapon to wear rapidly. Any ex-military or police Star will be of excellent quality. The Star Model B has all the good and bad points of Colt Government Model. There is no grip safety, which is fine—it accomplishes little, and many people pin them off on a Government Model. It has a magazine safety, and the safety locks the hammer rather than the sear. The steel construction allows rapid repeat shots. The Star MMS (a 7.63X25mm version) is available with a butt stock and extended magazine. For someone not equipped with a rifle, this weapon can be used as a short rifle due to its 7.63mm ammo. German forces used the Star Model B during World War II as a substitute standard pistol. After the war, the Germans used the Star for their new paramilitary border police. South Africa bought the Star Model B to replace an aging stock of Webley and Enfield revolvers until an embargo began in 1964.

The Star DK is a mini-sized Government Model-style pistol in .380 chambering. As with a Government Model, it is a SA trigger-style firing from a locked breach. The sights are nice and visible, especially given the fact that the DK is really designed to be a pocket weapon, not a belt gun. Trigger pull is around six-eight pounds with some overtravel and the safety is a good size to permit it to be rapidly removed. The hammer has a nice spur on it which may encourage some to carry the weapon in condition two, but you should not do so as it has no firing pin safety and, like all Stars, can fire if the chamber is loaded and the weapon falls on the hammer spur when the hammer is lowered. No grip safety is present, which is a good feature. Accuracy is acceptable with achievable results of 6-inch, 5-shot groups at twenty five yards off-hand. It is not a match weapon, nor are the sights or trigger pull meant for fine accuracy work. Carrying the DK is always an issue, for your pocket holster must be made such that the safety is not inadvertently released. With the advent of 9x19mm pistols in a size similar to the DK in .380, the DK .380 is now more a collectible firearm rather than a serious self-defense piece. But if you already have one and do not want to spend the extra money replacing it with a more powerful weapon, the DK will perform just as well today as it did fifty or more years ago.

The Star MD is a modification of the standard Star military model but is modified to fire bursts. The weapons are often fitted with a hollowed-out butt stock similar to those used on Broomhandle Mauser pistols. These stocks are quite effective as they make shooting easier. The Star MD is a 9x23mm pistol and the PD version shoots the .45 ACP cartridge. The Star MD is a pistol chambered for the 9x23 mm cartridge and also shoots the 38 ACP cartridge. It is also chambered for the 9x19mm and 7.63 Mauser cartride and is known as the PD model when chambered for the .45 ACP cartridge. It comes with either standard fixed sights or a graduated leaf rear unit. You get full-auto fire by pushing the selector on the right side of the slide down where it hits the disconnector, which allows the weapon to fire in bursts. The weapon should be carried in the full-auto position and changed to semi-auto for a more distant target. These weapons are often equipped with extended magazines but as they are single column, they can get very long. It may be better to carry the shorter eleven- or sixteen-round magazine on the belt and carry the weapon with the standard magazine flush in the weapon. With practice, you can get two or three bursts before reloading. Controllability of the Star MD/PD depends largely on the cartridge used and the shooter's stance, so is harder to control than the smaller-caliber examples. The sights are small, shallow, and dark. The magazine release is handy and the side safety quick to operate from the holster. The design is great for well-trained and alert shooters but dangerous for inexperienced, less well-trained ones.

The Z-70 is rare in the United States. It has a folding cocking handle that can be used easily with either hand. It does not move back and forth with the bolt, which is distracting. The front sight is a simple post but protected by sturdy ears. The rear sight is a simple L-shaped peep adjustable for a realistic one hundred and two hundred meters. Sturdy ears protect the rear sight as well. The weapon has a short overall length and a very sturdy folding stock which extends and collapses easily. Once extended, it is quite sturdy and rigid. It feels more comfortable than many metal stocks with thinner or rounder struts but is not as comfortable as wood. The grip is angled nicely and does not cramp your hand. There is no grip safety to tie up your weapon. The safety is incredibly fast; simple inward pressure with the knuckle of the thumb will remove it, and extending the trigger out slightly more and pushing inward with the knuckle reapplies it. You needn't shift your hand, and it's secure from accidental bumping or snagging. The Z-70 is a well-designed selective fire weapon. It uses a trigger mechanism to change the mode of fire. Pull on the top of the trigger for semi-auto; pull the bottom for full-auto. It's very fast, and you needn't shift your hand. Right-handed shooters can easily use the magazine release with the left hand. The magazine housing is not flared, so it slows magazine insertion. The magazines are sturdy, hold thirty rounds, and are easy to load without a loading tool. The barrel comes out of the weapon so you can clean it properly. The parts on the Z-70 are big and sturdy. The Z-70 is light, short, handy, and feels alive in your hands. The cyclic rate at 550 rpm is low enough to allow single shots to be fired even if a selective-trigger system did not exist. On full-auto, the Z-70 is quite controllable, even in long bursts. I have dumped an entire magazine with one full-auto burst at fifty feet into a chest-sized target. The Star Z-70 is eminently superior to the Uzi and rivals the Owen.

M93 SPANISH MAUSER

Caliber: 7x57mm   **Manufacturer:** Mauser   **Typical Use:** Military

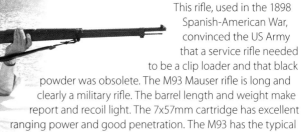

This rifle, used in the 1898 Spanish-American War, convinced the US Army that a service rifle needed to be a clip loader and that black powder was obsolete. The M93 Mauser rifle is long and clearly a military rifle. The barrel length and weight make report and recoil light. The 7x57mm cartridge has excellent ranging power and good penetration. The M93 has the typical Mauser winged safety; slow to engage or disengage unless you carry it in the halfway position, which prevents firing but does not lock the bolt. The best way to carry these rifles is with the safety off and the bolt handle up; simply close the bolt to fire. The rifle is sighted for four hundred meters as a first setting. It has the typical pyramid front coupled with a shallow V-shaped rear ramp graduated out to great distances. The sights are hard to see even in bright light, and it is difficult to keep the elevation. The front sight has no protection, so the sun affects your use of it, shifting your POI. The stock is well made out of wood. The action is smooth. It has a cleaning rod under the barrel, but no butt trap for cleaning equipment. The long barrel makes it muzzle-heavy, making it difficult to shoot off-hand, but is adequate for kneeling and other positions.

M93 SPANISH CARBINE

Caliber: 7x57mm   **Manufacturer:** Spanish arsenals   **Typical Use:** Military

It was during the Spanish-American War of 1898 that US forces first encountered smokeless powder and clip-loading Mauser rifles. Spanish forces may not have been well led or supplied, but they were brave and had the better weapon. The clip-loaded Mauser M93 rifle and carbine in 7x57mm wreaked havoc on US forces, and to this day, it remains a fine rifle in a good caliber. Bannerman had Spanish rifles captured in Cuba and Puerto Rico in his catalogs as early as 1900, which were aimed at buyers who wanted the latest in military hardware. Many people tend to look at the M93 Mauser and wrinkle their noses because the action is not as strong as the later M98. They are correct that the M93 is not as strong, but it is perfectly adequate for 7x57mm because it fires at a lower pressure than 7.92x57mm or .30-06. Accompanying this lower pressure is lower recoil, which is always nice for a rifle used by low-skilled soldiers. The caliber has an excellent ballistic coefficient, allowing superb penetration and low trajectory. The ammo is slightly lighter round for round than 7.92x57mm or .30-06. It might well be likened to the 7.62x51mm NATO round, in fact, and it is not short on power.

AR10

Caliber: 7.62x51mm   **Manufacturer:** Fairchild ArmaLite   **Typical Use:** Military, police, and hunting

The AR10 preceded the AR15 (later called the M16). The AR15 was a scaled-down model of the AR10. The AR10 arrived after the FAL had been perfected and the M14 had been adopted by the US military, which impacted its popularity. The aluminum receiver and plastic stock of the AR10 were radical advances. Weighing seven pounds at a time when most rifles weighed closer to eleven pounds was a breakthrough. Few AR10s were produced; some sold in Sudan, Burma, and a few other areas. The weapon I tested was in good internal condition but the exterior was battered. Because it is so lightweight, I feared the AR10 would suffer from heavy recoil, but it does not. I could not feel the spring in the stock in operation, unlike with an AR15 or M16. The front sight is a nicely shaped blade. The rear sight is adjustable for both elevation and windage. The controls on the AR10 all fall nicely to hand, much like the AR15. They are well positioned for easy reach and rapid use if you are right-handed. For lefties, the safety is awkward and the magazine release is usable but not as easy. The grip feels good and the forearm is better shaped for the hand. The AR10 uses a carrying handle on top, and the bolt-cocking piece looks like a spare trigger. It can be cocked by either hand and easily pulled even with mittens. No bolt-closing device exists. The safety's position is the same as on the AR15; easy to use and convenient. The middle position is the safe position. You push forward for full-auto and to the rear for semi-auto. This helps distinguish between the two. Despite the straight-line stock and what feels like a very low recoil impulse, the AR10 is uncontrollable in hand-held auto firing. When firing full-auto, the first round hit, the next went wild. When firing semi-auto, I was able to rapidly place twenty hits on target.

M1907 SWEDISH

Caliber: 9mm Browning Long   **Manufacturer:** Husqvarna   **Typical Use:** Military and self-defense

 The M1907 Swedish self-loading pistol was a licensed copy of the Model 1903 Browning. It was one of the first semi-auto pistols commonly adopted for military purposes and was available in the 9mm Browning Long cartridge, a unique cartridge not commonly found today. Many of these pistols were converted to fire .380 cartridges when they were imported to the United States in the 1950s. The ninety-year-old model I tested was in mint condition. This weapon has an internal hammer and thumb and separate grip safety. But the thumb safety is flat, and difficult to disengage quickly. You must push in with your thumb to get it off. The magazine has an inefficient butt release, although pulling out the magazine does not cause the slide to close, so speeds reloading. The weapon is flat, has a rounded rear sight, and is free of projections, so can be carried and withdrawn easily. The Model 1907 has a single-column magazine chambered for ammo less powerful than the 9mm Parabellum cartridge. Light recoil permits fast repeat shots. The grip is slightly smaller than on the Colt Government Model. The front sight is narrow and short but was visible in dim light. The slight undercutting on the front sight throws light on the sight, which helps indexing. Group sizes ran just under five inches, twice the average group-size of the M19, but the weapon performed well on the cinema range.

This 9mm pistol was a standard service weapon in Sweden and Finland. It was designed for the Finnish climate and has an accelerator in it that allows the bolt to work even in low temperatures, which can sometimes cause malfunctions in lesser weapons. This weapon is quite heavy and similar to a Luger pistol, except that it is butt-release only, with a safety which is easier and quicker to disengage. By pushing the safety between the thumb, first knuckle, and web of your hand, you can disengage and reengage it rapidly it with your hand on the weapon in a firing position. The magazine is hard to load. It really needs a loading tool to push with after three or four rounds, particularly in winter while wearing mittens. The high front sight mounted on the small diameter allows easy indexing but the rear sight is too small and low. The back of this pistol is cluttered with several mechanisms, which I found distracting when I fired it. Accuracy was very disappointing with or without a stock. Group sizes ran about 3¾ inches, compared with the 2½ inches in groups with a Model 19. The weapon had a shoulder stock lug and I fitted it with a stock. When you are tired or hurt, using a stock is advantageous. The rear sight is U-shaped, and it is hard to hold proper windage in formal target work. It is also quite shallow. Because of the heavy weight of the weapon, recoil is light and it feels solid in my hand.

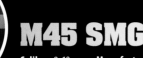

M45 SMG

Caliber: 9x19mm   **Manufacturer:** Husqvarna   **Typical Use:** Military and police

During World War II, Sweden needed to develop and produce its own SMG. Because the Swedes were already familiar with many SMGs, they were able to develop an SMG that incorporated several excellent elements. Swedish designers used the easily-manufactured receiver from the Sten gun, the idea of a folding stock from the MP40, and developed a reliable double-column, double-feed magazine based on the M38 Beretta. By 1945, the Swedes adopted the 9x19mm cartridge, although they frequently used a special loading with greater penetration and velocity. The front sight of the M45 is a post protected by massive stamped wings so the sight stays in alignment. The rear sight is a three-position U-flip-type graduated for a sensible one hundred, two hundred, and three hundred yards. The U-shaped rear blade can be difficult to use. The barrel is covered with a fairly short, light shroud, which provides a place to mount a bayonet. To put the bolt on safely, you must pull the bolt to the rear and carefully rotate the bolt handle into the safety notch. The bolt can be locked in the closed position, thereby avoiding inertia-induced discharges. The location of the bolt handle makes it hard to operate well with either hand, although the centrally-located magazine release is handy. The weapon is not selective fire in most examples, but with the cyclic rate of six hundred rpm, a properly trained shooter should be able to fire rounds in a semi-auto mode by merely pulling the trigger and quickly releasing it. The cyclic rate also results in a very controllable SMG. The stock is a side-folding tubular unit. You must depress the catch and then swing the stock out and away to extend it. Such tube-type stocks are uncomfortable to use. The M45 is a fine if uninspired SMG. It is reliable, fairly short overall, and easy to control, though it is heavy.

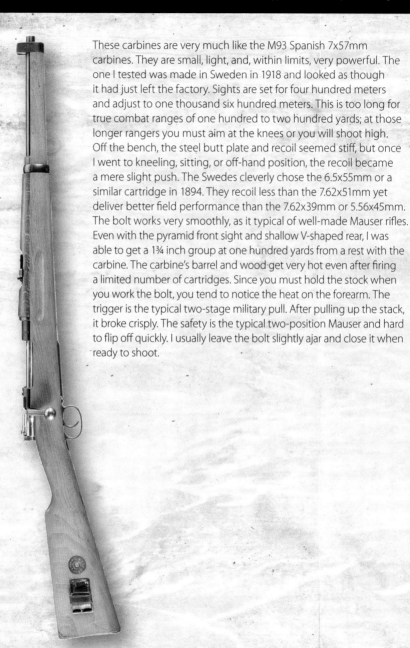

These carbines are very much like the M93 Spanish 7x57mm carbines. They are small, light, and, within limits, very powerful. The one I tested was made in Sweden in 1918 and looked as though it had just left the factory. Sights are set for four hundred meters and adjust to one thousand six hundred meters. This is too long for true combat ranges of one hundred to two hundred yards; at those longer rangers you must aim at the knees or you will shoot high. Off the bench, the steel butt plate and recoil seemed stiff, but once I went to kneeling, sitting, or off-hand position, the recoil became a mere slight push. The Swedes cleverly chose the 6.5x55mm or a similar cartridge in 1894. They recoil less than the 7.62x51mm yet deliver better field performance than the 7.62x39mm or 5.56x45mm. The bolt works very smoothly, as it typical of well-made Mauser rifles. Even with the pyramid front sight and shallow V-shaped rear, I was able to get a 1¾ inch group at one hundred yards from a rest with the carbine. The carbine's barrel and wood get very hot even after firing a limited number of cartridges. Since you must hold the stock when you work the bolt, you tend to notice the heat on the forearm. The trigger is the typical two-stage military pull. After pulling up the stack, it broke crisply. The safety is the typical two-position Mauser and hard to flip off quickly. I usually leave the bolt slightly ajar and close it when ready to shoot.

M1906/29 LUGER

Caliber: 7.65mm (.30 Luger) **Manufacturer:** Luger **Typical Use:** Military and self-defense

The Swiss were the first to adopt the Luger pistol in 1901, even before the German Navy. The Swiss bought the guns from Germany and then bought licenses to make them in Switzerland. In 1929, they modernized the design to make it easier to use and cheaper. The Swiss are excellent craftsmen and interested in maintaining equipment. The militia's purpose is to defend their neighborhoods, a great incentive for keeping equipment in good order. As they only intended to fight in Switzerland, they did not worry about adverse conditions, like those in jungles or deserts. Still, the Swiss-designed Luger has the same problems as its German cousin. The safety is hard to disengage and impossible to reengage without breaking your grip. One could carry with the safety off and rely only on the grip safety, but this is dangerous with any striker-fired weapon. The sights are the barleycorn front and inverted V-shaped rear—a bad combination. But the 1½ inch group produced at fifty feet shows that the weapon can be accurate. The 7.65mm Luger round requires a locking system due to pressure, yet has poor stopping power. By the time this weapon was produced, technology had rendered the Luger design obsolete. Perhaps the Swiss kept using them because they were used to them, and had the factory set up. The Swiss finally changed to the SIG P210 9x19mm in the late 1940s.

SIG P210

Caliber: 9mm Parabellum   **Manufacturer:** Schweizerische Industrie-Gesellschaft   **Typical Use:** Military and self-defense

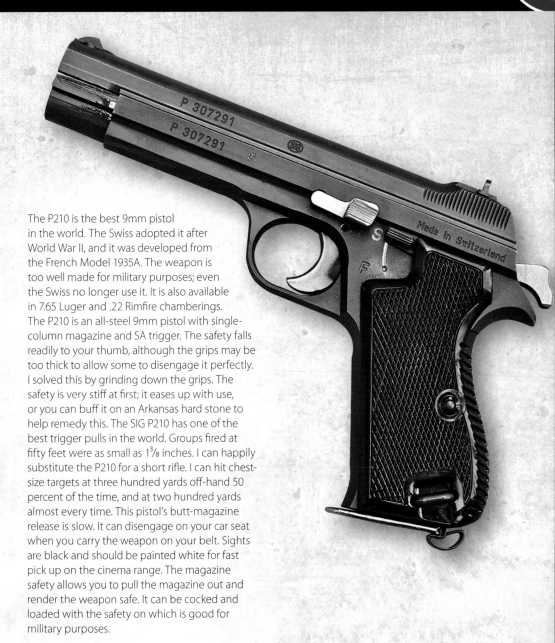

The P210 is the best 9mm pistol in the world. The Swiss adopted it after World War II, and it was developed from the French Model 1935A. The weapon is too well made for military purposes; even the Swiss no longer use it. It is also available in 7.65 Luger and .22 Rimfire chamberings. The P210 is an all-steel 9mm pistol with single-column magazine and SA trigger. The safety falls readily to your thumb, although the grips may be too thick to allow some to disengage it perfectly. I solved this by grinding down the grips. The safety is very stiff at first; it eases up with use, or you can buff it on an Arkansas hard stone to help remedy this. The SIG P210 has one of the best trigger pulls in the world. Groups fired at fifty feet were as small as 1⅜ inches. I can happily substitute the P210 for a short rifle. I can hit chest-size targets at three hundred yards off-hand 50 percent of the time, and at two hundred yards almost every time. This pistol's butt-magazine release is slow. It can disengage on your car seat when you carry the weapon on your belt. Sights are black and should be painted white for fast pick up on the cinema range. The magazine safety allows you to pull the magazine out and render the weapon safe. It can be cocked and loaded with the safety on which is good for military purposes.

SIG P210-7 (.22 RF)

Caliber: 7.65 (9mm, .22 Rimfire) **Manufacturer:** Swiss Arms AG (fka SIG Arms) **Typical Use:** Military and self-defense

The SIG P210 is likely the finest pistol made in 7.65 or 9mm. It is also available in .22 Rimfire either as a complete weapon or as a conversion kit assembled on your centerfire pistol frame. As such, it makes a very fine .22 Rimfire pistol every bit as good as its centerfire counterpart. A straight blowback pistol, it is as accurate as the centerfire pistol with good ammo. This means that although it is a duty-style of weapon, it recoils near match-level accuracy. An X-ring on a fifty-yard target is 1.3 inches in diameter. A .22 SIG P220 with good ammo may not be capable of putting all the rounds into that X-ring at fifty yards as some of the higher-level match pistols can do, but it can put them all into 2½ inches at that distance, which makes it substantially better than almost any other duty-style .22 pistol. As with any other SIG P210, the trigger pull is great, the action incredibly smooth, and the weapon is not likely (in .22 Rimfire) to ever wear out. The safety is difficult to operate until well broken in and the heel-butt-mounted magazine release slow to operate. Anyone who has a centerfire SIG P210 should have a .22 version as well. Anyone who buys a .22 SIG P210 is unlikely to ever sell it for something better.

SIG-SAUER P75

Caliber: 9mm Parabellum **Manufacturer:** Schweizerische Industrie-Gesellschaft **Typical Use:** Military and self-defense

This SIG-Sauer P220 in 9x19mm—known in Switzerland as the P75—is the service weapon in both Switzerland and Japan, and used by some French Army units. The P220 was designed to replace the expensive SIG P210. The standard weapon is 9mm, but it is available in .45 ACP, 7.65 Luger, .22 Rimfire, and .38 Super. The P220 is impressive. My groups were so accurate that I re-tested and got the same results. I placed five shots into little more than two inches; four of those into roughly 1¼ inches. By comparison, my groups with the standard Model 19 Smith & Wessson were 2½ inches. There is no manual safety, only a decocking lever. Thus you must drop the hammer after the first shots or move with it cocked and no safety on, which are both bad choices. There is no magazine safety. The wide white front sight and rear sight allow good indexing in poor light. The DA pull is smooth. The trigger goes too far forward in DA mode for perfection, but is easy to adjust to. The decocking lever falls easily in the hand. The aluminum frame makes this a very lightweight weapon. The heel-mount magazine release on the early P220 and Swiss Military slows reloading. The P220 is now available with the side-button magazine release. The P220 is reliable, accurate, quick to get action, and has good sights.

M41 SMG

Caliber: 9x19mm   **Manufacturer:** Swiss Government Weapon Factory Bern, Switzerland
Typical Use: Military and police

The M41 is almost unheard of outside of Switzerland. The test example was made during World War II at the Swiss government weapon factory at Bern. It features a toggle-action system modeled on the Luger pistol placed on its side. The weapon is well balanced despite its side-mounted magazine. The pistol grip felt good and the aluminum forward pistol grip was handy to use. The safety is located on the top-side just like the LMG25. But the SMG is meant to be an immediate close-range weapon. Even carrying it safety off, on semi mode, bolt closed, will not yield fast results due to the location of the cocking handle. You cannot retract the bolt when the safety is on, which is a good feature. Of course, many SMGs of the period were equally slow. The M41 fired from an open-bolt method. It required powerful ammo for certain functioning. Firing the M41 is quite enjoyable. It has a low cyclic rate and is smooth enough that two-shot groups were easy to achieve. It lacks the heavy mainspring found on some open-bolt weapons, so functions more smoothly at fifty yards on semi than many SMGs. Using the toggle system, you also miss the bolt bottoming out of the rear of the receiver, hitting it a sight-disturbing blow with each shot. The M41 is a fine, well-made SMG. It handles nicely and is quite controllable. It feels lively in the hands and the controls are equivalent to other weapons of that time. Many SMGs existed that were better and cheaper, and it is hard to understand why the Swiss went to the trouble and expense to produce the M41.

SCHMIDT RUBIN M11

Caliber: 7.5mm Swiss **Manufacturer:** W. F. Bern **Typical Use:** Military

When you first pick up an M11 rifle, you may think it feels very long because of its long action and barrel. You must fire it to appreciate what a wonderful weapon it is. The long barrel keeps the muzzle blast of the 7.5mm Swiss round (equivalent to a .30-06) to a minimum and reduces muzzle whip. The rifle's weight and distribution coupled with the stock design keeps recoil low for the caliber used. The Schmidt Rubin has never been tested in war. The front sight is a blade. The rear notch is easy to pick up because the blade allows a good strip of light to be exposed. The safety is applied by turning the round-cocking indicator to the side. Doing so also locks the bolt. This work is slow but certain, and you can tell at a glance if the weapon is ready to fire. The large ring in the indicator should allow the heavily-gloved soldier to handle it. The trigger guard is small for mittens. The trigger pull is a typical two-stage process with the second stage leading up to a fine, crisp pull. The detachable magazine holds six rounds. Such magazines allow unloading the rifle without running ammo through it (always a dangerous practice)and offers the opportunity to develop twenty–twenty five-shot magazines for the rifle. The straight pull action may be a problem when withdrawing oversized or dirty ammo. The best thing about the M11 is its bolt action. The bolt can be pulled back while the weapon is in recoil and pushed forward to lower and realign the weapon. The Schmidt Rubin M11 only needs two strokes to withdraw an empty and load a new round, compared to a typical bolt action which needs four.

This was the last and no doubt best Swiss bolt-action service rifle. It is shorter because the locking lugs are at the front of the bolt rather than the rear, and the bolt is shorter. As with the M11, I found this a very fast rifle to shoot. I was often able to extract an empty and load a fresh cartridge while the empty was still in the air. With some extra effort, I got two empties in the air while firing the third shot! It is very smooth to shoot and probably the finest bolt-action rifle that I tested. The rear ramp-style sight features a U-shape that is too narrow and difficult to use. The front sight has a good blade design and it well protected by sturdy ears. The front sight has slot-cutting to allow for windage. The trigger is good and surprisingly crisp for a military rifle, although it has the typical military two-stage trigger. The stock is the proper length for my five-foot-nine-inch frame, although the pistol grip on the stock is slightly large for comfort. The rifle does not have a butt trap or a cleaning rod under the barrel. The felt recoil is heavy, but the K31 is still pleasant to shoot. Perhaps the shorter barrel on the K31 makes the muzzle blast more noticeable. These Swiss service bolt-action rifles are very fine weapons, underappreciated because of their scarcity.

After World War II, the Swiss wanted a new rifle. They had huge stocks of 7.5mm ammo and decided to design the rifle for that cartridge. The resulting Stg 57 is long and heavy at 13½ pounds, but extremely well made and reliable. Because of the demands of the Swiss shooters, the Stg 57 has excellent, fully-adjustable rear sights. It is not very good for quick, instinctive firing due to the stock's shape, the height of the sight, the weapon's weight, and the design of the safety, the safety lever is on the left side, difficult to operate for left-handed shooters and not quick for right-handed shooters. The lever is very tightly fitted, long, and lacks any real leverage to allow the thumb to flip it off rapidly. You must take your right hand off the grip and push the safety off or use your left hand. The Stg 57 has a heavy metal barrel jacket covering the barrel. It keeps the shooter's fingers off the barrel but adds too much weight. The weight helps keep recoil under control. Although designed as an infantry rifle, the Stg 57 is closer to a machine rifle. As a machine rifle, the weapon lacks a quick-change barrel, has a cyclic rate that is too high to be effective, and excessive weight. Fired on quick semi-auto, the Stg 57 fares better and that is how the Stg 57 was meant to be used.

After extensive testing in the 1990s, the Swiss military adopted the SIG 550, also known as the Stg 90. It met all their requirements and is the finest rifle of its type in the world. The Stg 90 has a standard blade front sight that is well protected and can be used with a radioactive element to glow in the dark by merely flipping it up. The rugged rear sight is a peep unit that can be adjusted for shooting out to four hundred meters. The bolt handle on the Stg 90 is on the right side. It passes through a rubber seal, keeping dirt and debris out of the weapon. The pistol grip feels pleasant in the hand. The trigger guard swings to the side to allow shooting with mittened hands. The magazine release is centrally located, convenient for either hand. Magazines come with twenty- or thirty-round capacity and are transparent plastic so the shooter can easily see how many rounds remain. They are rugged, self-lubricating, and designed to clip together to allow the shooter to carry two or more on the weapon for a speedier reload. The Stg 90's folding stock is as rigid as a wood stock when fixed, yet folds and unfolds easily by pushing a button. The stock has a rubber butt plate to keep the weapon in position. The two-sling swivel position allows for traditional carry and over-the-shoulder carry. The pistol grip contains a hollow, which is convenient for storing cleaning equipment. The safety/selector can be easily flipped with either hand because of its length and precise fitting. Trigger pull is almost up to bolt-action standards. The upper receiver is held to the lower by captive pins, so pushing them out allows the weapons to be quickly disassembled. The forearm is plastic but has a heat shield installed in it. Despite firing eight magazines quickly, the Stg 90 never got as hot as an M16. The forearm is comfortable to hold. The Stg 90 is equipped with a flash hider that functions satisfactorily. The rifle will also fire rifle grenades. Weighing about 8½ pounds, it is not as light as the early M16. The Stg 90 has an adjustable gas system, which is helpful if the shooter is trained to use it. The Stg 90 has a selective-fire capability, but as with any such rifle, it should be used in semi-auto mode unless a true close-range emergency arises. The light recoil of the weapon, excellent trigger pull, and good sights all help produce excellent accuracy.

SIG 552

Caliber: 5.56x45mm   **Manufacturer:** S.I.G Arms   **Typical Use:** Military

The SIG 552 is the mini-version of the excellent SIG Stg 90. The 5.56mm weapon can engage a target at 300 yards whereas a 9x19mm is likely to do so at 150 yards, which helps make the 552 a favorite of hostage/raid teams. The 552 from the front of the receiver rearwards is exactly the same as any standard Stg 90 rifle. The front sight is the same, but appears bigger as it is closer to the rear and the same thickness. Since the velocity from the shorter barrel is slower than that found in a twenty-inch barrel, the rear sight adjustments will be off, especially beyond three hundred yards. All the good points with the SIG Stg 90 appear on the 552: it has a handy safety, excellent easy-to-open/close folding butt which is solid and comfortable in all weather, well located, centrally-mounted magazine release, and a trigger guard which folds out of the way in different directions whether you are left- or right-handed. The night sight front sight option is the same on both rifles. The barrel on the SIG 552 is eight inches and is equipped with an open four-prong flash hider. Without a flash hider, firing standard military 5.56x45mm ammo results in a large fireball. Noise level is higher, especially when fired inside or undercover. A large gas/flame pattern comes out of the flash hider and did scorch a rug I was using, so use caution. If you need a short-barrel 5.56x45mm weapon, you certainly cannot go wrong with a SIG552. While it is harder to control on full-auto and has a lot more blast than a 9x19mm SMG, when used in semi and selecting the proper ammo, it is so far superior to 9x19mm SMG as to make 9mm SMG tactically obsolete.

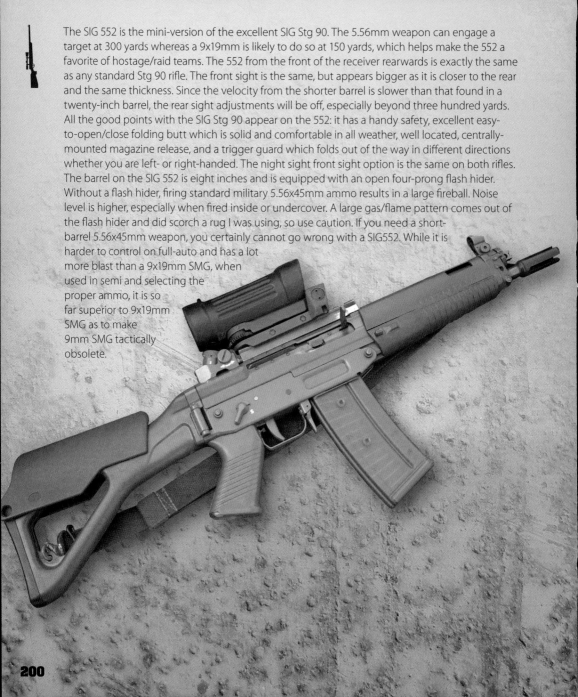

LMG 25

Caliber: 7.5 Swiss   **Manufacturer:** Swiss Weapon Factory, Bern, Switzerland   **Typical Use:** Military

The LMG25 was the standard light machine gun in Switzerland. Since it is rarely seen elsewhere, I traveled to Switzerland to test this weapon. This weapon has a toggle-action much like the Luger pistol turned on its side. When the bolt is pulled to the rear, the side of the action flips open to allow the action to function. This is a long weapon and built of heavy, carefully-machined materials. Both front and rear sights on the weapon are like the service rifle except the front sight has a notch cut into it, so using radium paint would give a rudimentary night sight. In addition to the standard sights, the bipod quickly detaches and a set of anti-aircraft sights can be attached. The LMG25 can be mounted on a tank, and a tripod can be attached to the weapon for long-range defense. The weapon fires, from a single-column feed, a thirty-round detachable magazine that opens along the sides to accept the necessary loading tool to depress the spring once you get more than ten rounds in it. Two people were assigned the weapon—the shooter and the loader. The shooter carried the weapon and two pouches containing three thirty-round magazines. His assistant carried extra ammo. The safety selector is mounted on top. You need a lot of pressure to flip it; you cannot do it quickly. The weapon fired from an open-bolt position and offers both semi- and full-auto fire. Single shots were very easy, recoil minimal due to the weight. The trigger pull was heavy, but workable; the trigger guard is quite small. A switch exists under the weapon to add extra impulse to the action to permit it to function better when dirty or very cold. When the last shot is fired, the bolt does not lock back. The LMG25 is a fine weapon, but many other weapons, such as the BAR and FN30, exist which offer superior designs and are easier to make.

This rifle was Heckler & Koch's original attempt to compete with the Colt M16 series. Heckler & Koch scaled down its very successful G3 rifle chambered in 7.62x51NATO to fit and fire the 5.56x45mm round. The HK 33/93 has the typically poor Heckler & Koch-style sights which make good shooting difficult. The trigger pull is heavy, stiff, and gritty. The safety is difficult to disengage and reapply without breaking your grip. The safety is not ambidextrous, and the trigger guard does not fold down to make winter use easier. The magazine release on the semi-auto version HK 93 is a push-button that is best used by right-handed shooters. The HK 33 selective-fire version offers a button plus a centrally mounted flipper, which is quicker to use. You need to exert a great amount of pressure to pull the bolt to the rear to cock the rifle. The rifle tested had the "tropical forearm," which is larger and does not heat up as quickly as do slimmer ones. But it is broader on the bottom so more difficult for the shooter to grasp firmly. Attaching a bipod exacerbates the problem. The bipod rattles and is noisy when extended. The bipod can be deployed quickly by pushing the legs out and it is sturdy when extended. When the bipod is extended, you can't use the forty-round magazine as it hits the ground. All Heckler & Koch rifles are inherently accurate, but not user-friendly. The HK 33 should not be used in full-auto mode because of control problems with the design of its stock, its high cyclic rate, and its heavy felt recoil.

NAGANT MODEL 95

Caliber: 7.62mm   **Manufacturer:** State arsenals   **Typical Use:** Military and self-defense

The Czarist Russian Army used the Model 95 Nagant revolver as their standard service weapon during World War I, and the Soviet Army used it throughout World War II. I tested one manufactured in 1937. The Model 95 has only one good feature: the high front sight permits rapid indexing on a combat range. Reloading is slow; cases have their necks flared by a gas-seal system. Ejection is slow and a one-at-a-time procedure. The weapon holds seven rounds, but the load of 7.62 Nagant medium-velocity with a full-metal-jacket is not a guaranteed stopper. Recoil is light but the Fiocchi ammo produced a lot of flash on the cinema range. The trigger pull was heavy on SA and DA. The sights were small, dark, and hard to see on formal target work. The gas-seal system on this Nagant Model 95 creates a lot of complications with very little benefit. Upon the final cocking of the action, the cylinder must be pushed forward by what would be the bushing in a normal Smith & Wesson revolver. This forces the cylinder over the barrel thus removing the usual gap. This gives you a heavy trigger pull. It was supposed to improve performance of a load, but tests by *American Rifleman* showed it did not do much. On the cinema and formal range, the heavy trigger pull and the poor sights contributed to a terrible performance in my tests; groups were twice as big as normal.

TT M1933

Caliber: 7.62mm **Manufacturer:** State arsenals **Typical Use:** Military and self-defense

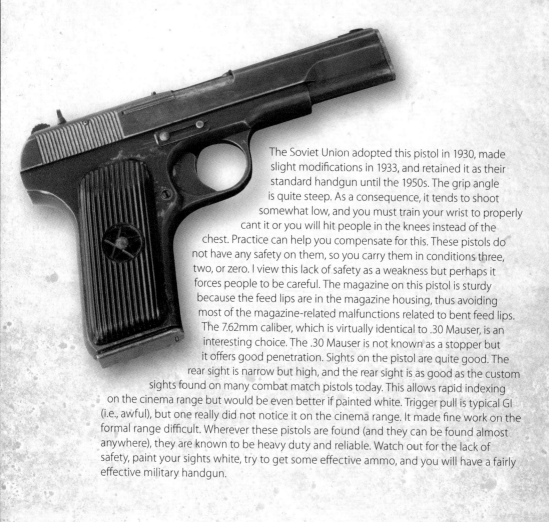

The Soviet Union adopted this pistol in 1930, made slight modifications in 1933, and retained it as their standard handgun until the 1950s. The grip angle is quite steep. As a consequence, it tends to shoot somewhat low, and you must train your wrist to properly cant it or you will hit people in the knees instead of the chest. Practice can help you compensate for this. These pistols do not have any safety on them, so you carry them in conditions three, two, or zero. I view this lack of safety as a weakness but perhaps it forces people to be careful. The magazine on this pistol is sturdy because the feed lips are in the magazine housing, thus avoiding most of the magazine-related malfunctions related to bent feed lips. The 7.62mm caliber, which is virtually identical to .30 Mauser, is an interesting choice. The .30 Mauser is not known as a stopper but it offers good penetration. Sights on the pistol are quite good. The rear sight is narrow but high, and the rear sight is as good as the custom sights found on many combat match pistols today. This allows rapid indexing on the cinema range but would be even better if painted white. Trigger pull is typical GI (i.e., awful), but one really did not notice it on the cinema range. It made fine work on the formal range difficult. Wherever these pistols are found (and they can be found almost anywhere), they are known to be heavy duty and reliable. Watch out for the lack of safety, paint your sights white, try to get some effective ammo, and you will have a fairly effective military handgun.

MAKAROV

Caliber: 9mm   **Manufacturer:** State arsenals   **Typical Use:** Military and self-defense

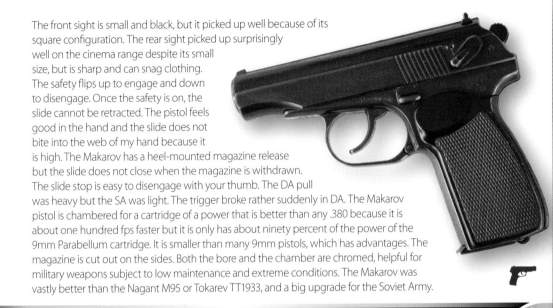

The front sight is small and black, but it picked up well because of its square configuration. The rear sight picked up surprisingly well on the cinema range despite its small size, but is sharp and can snag clothing. The safety flips up to engage and down to disengage. Once the safety is on, the slide cannot be retracted. The pistol feels good in the hand and the slide does not bite into the web of my hand because it is high. The Makarov has a heel-mounted magazine release but the slide does not close when the magazine is withdrawn. The slide stop is easy to disengage with your thumb. The DA pull was heavy but the SA was light. The trigger broke rather suddenly in DA. The Makarov pistol is chambered for a cartridge of a power that is better than any .380 because it is about one hundred fps faster but it is only has about ninety percent of the power of the 9mm Parabellum cartridge. It is smaller than many 9mm pistols, which has advantages. The magazine is cut out on the sides. Both the bore and the chamber are chromed, helpful for military weapons subject to low maintenance and extreme conditions. The Makarov was vastly better than the Nagant M95 or Tokarev TT1933, and a big upgrade for the Soviet Army.

PSM

Caliber: 5.45 PSM   **Manufacturer:** State arsenals   **Typical Use:** Military and self-defense

The original PSM pistol had thin alloy grips whereas this model has equally thin plastic grips. They are slightly longer in the rear, giving the pistol a somewhat fuller grip. Otherwise, this version, which I call the Mk II, is the same. It functions in the same fashion. The sights are the same. Like its senior, it is handy, easy to use, has low recoil, and a pretty good trigger pull. The magazines are identical. I am rather taken with the PSM pistol whether equipped with the original, all-metal grip model or the newer model with the fuller grip. It is quite accurate, has good practical sights, is flat and lightweight, has low recoil and report, yet will punch through soft-body armor likely to be encountered on the street. The PSM pistol is not a full-size battle pistol like a Glock 17 or similar weapon, but for a person who is encumbered with a shoulder weapon along with spare magazines and web gear, it fulfills a need. The PSM carried in a breast pocket makes an excellent addition to the gear normally carried.

PPSH-41

Caliber: 7.62x25mm   **Manufacturer:** Various Soviet arsenals   **Typical Use:** Military and police

The Soviets made more than five million PPSh-41s during World War II. It was cheap to make and easy to maintain. I tested a late-war model, which had a good two-position peep rear sight that was well protected by wings. Earlier examples had open sights with tangent leaf sights calibrated to very long ranges, when most usage occurs at two hundred meters or less. The front sight is a good-sized pin or shaft protected by a sturdy cover. The safety/selector system is handy, as it is in the trigger guard. You can flip it off without breaking the shooting grip. The PPSh-41 has a selective-fire capability which, given its rate of fire, is a good feature. The magazine release is small and not a simple push-and-dump type. The trigger guard is small for mittened use. These weapons typically use seventy one round capacity drums, but they must be carefully matched to the weapon to ensure reliable feeding. Available thirty five round magazines weigh less and make less noise. The cyclic rate of the weapon on full-auto is fast, so it is easy to shoot excessive bursts. Most usage should be on semi-auto. The wood stock and weight give the weapon a solid feel. As the weight is between the hands, the balance doesn't feel heavy or awkward. The weapon is simple to maintain. Pulling the cap at the end of the receiver allows you to tip the entire receiver forward. The bolt is easily removed. The barrel is accessible from the rear. Because it does not use a gas system, the bore can be simply wiped out and the weapon put back into action rapidly. The PPSh-41 is as good as anything made in the Unites States, Britain, or Germany during the same time period.

Developed in 1942 at the height of Germany's siege of Leningrad, the prototype of the PPS-43 was rushed to the front. After some slight changes, the design was standardized and more than a million were made. The PPS-43 is made entirely of metal, except for the grip panels. The stock is a folding design. The struts get very cold or hot depending on weather and hit your cheekbones, which affects your shooting. The PPS-43 uses a thirty five round magazine, not a drum. The magazine is well made with sturdy sides. The trigger guard is a good size. The safety is fast to operate, can be used with either hand with gross motor skills, and can be felt in the dark. The PPS-43 lacks a forward handgrip and gets hot when you rapidly fire more than two magazines; it's easy to burn your hand. When you hold it in the area in front of the magazine, take care that your hand is not struck by the bolt handle. The PPS-43 has a rather crude muzzle brake, which may or may not work. I have never shot one without it, but it certainly makes the weapon loud. The front sight and rear sights are simple cylindrical posts well protected by wings. Cyclic rate is high, mainly a result of a lightweight bolt and high-intensity cartridge. It fires full-auto only, but it is possible to get off single shots with a little practice despite the lack of a selector. Using the tip of your finger on the bottom of the trigger helps you shoot singles. The PPS-43 is every bit as good as the finest Thompson.

STECHKIN

Caliber: 9x18mm Makarov   **Manufacturer:** Soviet state factories   **Typical Use:** Military, police, and self defense

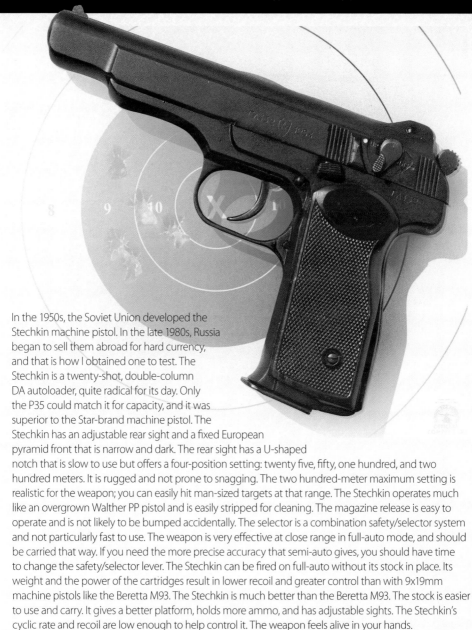

In the 1950s, the Soviet Union developed the Stechkin machine pistol. In the late 1980s, Russia began to sell them abroad for hard currency, and that is how I obtained one to test. The Stechkin is a twenty-shot, double-column DA autoloader, quite radical for its day. Only the P35 could match it for capacity, and it was superior to the Star-brand machine pistol. The Stechkin has an adjustable rear sight and a fixed European pyramid front that is narrow and dark. The rear sight has a U-shaped notch that is slow to use but offers a four-position setting: twenty five, fifty, one hundred, and two hundred meters. It is rugged and not prone to snagging. The two hundred-meter maximum setting is realistic for the weapon; you can easily hit man-sized targets at that range. The Stechkin operates much like an overgrown Walther PP pistol and is easily stripped for cleaning. The magazine release is easy to operate and is not likely to be bumped accidentally. The selector is a combination safety/selector system and not particularly fast to use. The weapon is very effective at close range in full-auto mode, and should be carried that way. If you need the more precise accuracy that semi-auto gives, you should have time to change the safety/selector lever. The Stechkin can be fired on full-auto without its stock in place. Its weight and the power of the cartridges result in lower recoil and greater control than with 9x19mm machine pistols like the Beretta M93. The Stechkin is much better than the Beretta M93. The stock is easier to use and carry. It gives a better platform, holds more ammo, and has adjustable sights. The Stechkin's cyclic rate and recoil are low enough to help control it. The weapon feels alive in your hands.

TOKAREV M40

The M40 is an improvement over the earlier M38. It never displaced the bolt-action M91/30 Mosin-Nagant in the Soviet Armies because it had many problems. It used rimmed cartridges, which are not reliable for box-magazine-fed auto-loading weapons. The firing pins also tend to break because of a large cut in the rifles. Worst, the gas system tends to clog up when using corrosive ammo, and maintenance was marginal. These factors, plus the widespread availability of the PPsH 41 7.62x25mm SMG, meant the Tokarev rifles were issued in limited quantities. The M40's sights are like those on the AK47 and SKS rifles. They are hard to see because they are too dark and the rear notch is too shallow. The safety, a lever behind the trigger to block it, is acceptable. You can easily use it with bare hands, but it would be difficult with gloves or mittens, which the Soviets should have considered essential due to their climate. The weapon has a muzzle brake installed, which increases the noise level. Given the weight and barrel length of the weapon, this brake seems unnecessary. The M40 does feel well balanced. The trigger pull is hard and has a lot of creep. Off-hand shooting performance suffers, although in the firmer kneeling/sitting positions, it is not as big a problem. The magazine is removable but the weapon is not designed to be used with rapidly-detachable magazines. The box merely holds the cartridges and the shooter feeds strips rounds through the top into the weapon. Removing the magazine is slow and awkward.

MOSIN-NAGANT M91/30 SNIPER

Caliber: 7.62 x 54R **Manufacturer:** Soviet state factories **Typical Use:** Military

The M91/30 sniper rifle is like the standard rifle except for the bolt handle, which is bent down, and the addition of a scope. The test weapon was made in the Soviet Union during World War II; the scope was made in 1967, but similar to those used in the war. In my test, the standard M91/30 rifle with iron sights shot a smaller group than this sniper's unit. Trigger pulls are the same. The scope blocks access to the stripper clips, making them unusable, so you must load the rounds one at a time. Because the rifles use a rimmed cartridge, you must put the rims in the notch provided or they will not feed properly, which is a slow process. The bolt handle is bent down and this slows reloading. The handle is so close to the stock that you have to grab it with your fingers and bring it up first, which is slower than being able to hit it with your palm. The scope position also made it very difficult to apply the safety. You need to leave the bolt handle slightly up for safety. The rifle weighs almost twelve pounds loaded. The long barrel makes recoil light and muzzle blast low. Firing the rifle off-hand is difficult because of its weight and length; sitting and kneeling positions were not much better. The telescopic sight is of lower power (2.8X) and has a small field of view. The mount and scope look rugged but they are heavy. The scope does not offer much light-gathering capability, and is adjusted for bullet impact from one hundred to one thousand two hundred meters, too far to be realistic.

The Mosin-Nagant pattern of rifle was obsolete by the start of World War I, yet it persisted throughout World War II and beyond. The test example was in new condition, made in 1954 in Romania. The rear sight is somewhat practical: it is graduated from one hundred to one thousand meters, reasonable distances. The front sight is a cylindrical post and is well protected. The rear blade is a shallow U-notch, difficult to use rapidly or in dim light. The rifle was a military weapon yet the bolt has a high polish, which is odd because it reflects light. The bayonet is meant to be permanently attached, and is a sticker, not a slasher. The weight of the rifle and design of the bayonet allow good penetration. With the shorter barrel and light weight, the recoil and blast are greater than with a full-length rifle. Neither was oppressive nor impeded the quick operation of the weapon. Design flaws, not the recoil, make the action slow to operate. The M44 carbine has no effective safety. The rifle does not have a butt trap but it does have a cleaning rod. The M44 is a handy piece of equipment. It is slightly muzzle heavy for off-hand and kneeling shooting, because of the weight of the bayonet. Its short length helps in handling it. Thus handling it around buildings and vehicles is not as clumsy as it is with the M91 rifle. It is limited by poor sights, sticking action, and lack of safety. It is a definite improvement over the M91 rifle.

SKS

Caliber: 7.62x39mm   **Manufacturer:** Soviet state factories   **Typical Use:** Military, police, and hunting

The SKS was developed as the standard Soviet Infantry rifle in the post–World War II era. The AK47 later displaced it. The Chinese built copies of the SKS and gave them to the North Vietnamese. My sources show more than two million SKS rifles had been brought into the Unites States from China by 1994. The SKS is a good rifle: it is lightweight, shoots an adequate cartridge, and has light recoil due to its cartridge and being a semi-auto. The front sight on the SKS is like the AK47 in terms of shape and adjustment. A large ring, cut open at the top to admit both light and sight adjustment tools, protects the sight. The rear sight is U-shaped and works on a tangent. This combination is hard to use. The gas system in the SKS has proved extremely reliable. The bore on this rifle is chrome lined, excellent when using corrosive ammo. Trigger pull on the SKS is never great, because the heavy bolt slams as it goes back and forth. Its pull is about six–eight pounds. The safety will strike the finger when applied, so alerts the shooter. It cannot simply be flipped off, but it is much faster to than the AK47. The SKS loads with a ten-shot stripper clip using an integral ten-shot magazine, which is not optimal. The stock on the SKS is either wood or plastic. Both are of good length, although some long-armed people find them too short. The butt plate on the SKS is metal and contains cleaning gear for maintenance. Many SKS rifles have a knife bayonet; some carry a spike unit. Soldiers frequently remove them as they add weight and rattle.

The Soviets took the standard AK47 action and modified it to fire the longer 7.62x54R cartridge, which is rimmed, and called it the Dragunov. This is an attempt to develop a self-loading sniping rifle. The semi-auto sniper rifle offers one advantage over a bolt-action rifle: the shooter does not have to move to reload the rifle, and sometimes it is the sniper's movement, more than noise, that gives him away. The trigger system is the main problem with semi-autos. Because the trigger must not double (fire a second round without pulling the trigger), the trigger pull will be much heavier than on a bolt-action rifle. Also, the bolt's movement will affect the scope and its mountings. The Dragunov's trigger pull is little better than that found on the AKM rifle. The rear sight is an open V-notch unit, similar to AK47 rifles, and the front sight is nearly identical to the AK47. The safety is the standard AK47-style safety: slow to disengage, and noisy when moved. Its position forces you to move your shooting hand, and it's almost impossible for a left-handed shooter to use it. The barrel is long and surprisingly light in weight. The flash and report are equal to those of an M91 Mosin-Nagant. The long barrel coupled with the long receiver necessary for the 7.62x54R cartridge makes the weapon unwieldy. The action uses the two-piece stock, and the front handguard strikes the barrel so strongly that it might throw off some shots. When using a sling, the barrel's weight and the handguard set up will shift the impact area. The scope and mount are heavy. The optics are not as good as commercial scopes made in the mid-1980s in the United States, and the power is too low for effective use at ranges more than eight hundred meters.

Early in the Soviet invasion of Afghanistan, rumors circulated about an AK-type rifle that fired a smaller .22-caliber round rather than the standard 7.62x39mm ammo. The Soviets wanted the flat trajectory, light weight, and low recoil of the 5.56x45mm round, and designed their new round based on the old one to minimize development time and costs. Although the 5.45x39mm is not exactly a 7.62x39mm necked down, it is close enough that much of the equipment used by the Soviets could be used for that caliber also. The rifle is the same as the AK47 except the angle of the cartridges permitted the magazine to be straighter. Controls and sights are identical, so the AK74 has the same deficiencies in these areas as its larger-caliber brother. There are no night sights on the AK74. The rifles are equipped with a muzzle brake, which makes the rifles more controllable in full-auto fire. The muzzle brake seems to blow part of the blast backward so the noise level is high. The AK74, like the AK47, comes in both fixed-stock and folding-stock model. The fixed stock is always preferable for serious shooting. The fixed stock is the same as the AK47 but the folder is much better on the AK74. On both weapons, the folder wobbles when the locking point is worn. The shape of the butt plate is not optimal to accept rifle recoil and, with a magazine in the weapon, very little clearance is available on the AK47 folder. On the AK74, the folder is a much stronger design with less potential for wobble, and the strut is gentler on the cheek. The trajectory of the 5.45x39mm is lower than that of the 7.62x39mm but if you accept the fact that infantry rifles are meant to be used within three hundred meters, it becomes a nonissue.

AKSU

Caliber: 5.45x39mm   **Manufacturer:** Soviet state factories   **Typical Use:** Military, police, and self-defense

The AKSU, often mistakenly called a Krinkov, is a Soviet-made variant of the AK74 rifle. The AKSU uses the metal folding stock of the AK47 and has a shorter barrel. It has a cone-shaped flash hider unit which may boost muzzle pressure to assure proper functioning. Unlike the AK74, the top cover is not removable; it folds up and provides the location for the rear sight. The cover does not loosen and is stable. The sight radius is shorter than an AK74. The weapon is easy to shoot and it's well balanced with a good trigger pull. While the 5.45x39mm cartridge is less powerful than the 5.56x45mm cartridge, it is clearly more powerful than the 9x19mm. The AKSU handles more quickly, shoots more accurately, and has a longer effective range than any SMG in 9x19mm. You can readily hit chest-sized plates off-hand at 200 yards and even at three hundred yards from the kneeling/ sitting positions. The weapon carries well and is handy. The sling swivels tend to cause the sling to hit your hands, which is uncomfortable. The AKSU is a fine, practical weapon.

DEGTYAREV DP & DPM LMG

Caliber: 7.62x54R   **Manufacturer:** Soviet arsenals   **Typical Use:** Military

This is the famous World War II pan-style magazine Soviet LMG. Communist China and other countries copied it after the war. I tested a Chinese-manufactured DPM gun, which they called the Type 53 LMG. Unlike the original DP, the DPM, made since 1944, has the recoil springs in the butt rather than surrounding the barrels. The Soviet forces fired such long, constant bursts that the springs would overheat, and relocating them to the butt eliminated this problem. The safety on the DPM is a bar that blocks the trigger. The sights on the DPM consist of a post that adjusts for elevation and a tangent rear with V opening. You adjust the windage by loosening the screw on the front sight and moving it to either side. Both sights are well protected by wings. The weapon has a bipod attached. Because of the weapon's weight, it is useful when firing prone or from the kneeling position. It is too heavy and ill balanced to be used off-hand. The weapon has a three-position gas regulation system which helps keep the weapon clean when firing different quality ammo in varying climates. At six hundred rpm, the cyclic rate is not slow, but I found that I could fire single shots without difficulty, and three-shot bursts were a breeze. The weapon is not a selective-fire LMG. The DPM's length and balance are a problem. The major problem is its drum loading system. It is almost impossible for one person to load these pan magazines; even two find it difficult to do quickly.

This excellent squad automatic weapon was possibly the most common found in the hands of the North Vietnamese Army during the Vietnam War. Given the low velocity of the 7.62x39mm cartridge, the high trajectory, and the general difficulty of estimating ranges, six hundred meters is its effective range, even though catalogs state eight hundred meters. Most LMGs are too heavy and have too much recoil to be effective. The RPD weighs only sixteen pounds and its recoil is light. Although the weapon fires only in the full-auto mode, firing single shots is not difficult, and three- to five-round bursts are easy. The weapon lacks a quick-change barrel but it fires from an open bolt which allows you to avoid cook-offs. The handguard covers both the top and bottom of the barrel so the shooter can avoid accidentally burning his hand. The front sight is protected by a strong circle of metal. Sight adjustments are made for both windage and elevation on the front. Once the sight is zeroed, you use the rear tangent to get different elevations. It takes time to get it sighted properly at one hundred yards, but it is well worth it. The weapon has a safety but, as with all open-bolt guns, ignore it. The bolt handle is on the right, not easy for the left-handed shooter to use. The pistol grip is really too straight for comfort; a slightly greater angle to it would make it much more instinctive. The weapon is light and handy enough to allow you to cradle the weapon much like a rifle when walking. The heavy drum hanging below makes the balance less than ideal for off-hand work. The drums are interchangeable among guns because they do not fit into the feed mechanism, unlike many Soviet designs. Loading the belts by hand is difficult, but there are loading machines that handle this quickly.

The PKM machine gun chambered for the traditional 7.62x54R cartridge is the Russian counterpart to the western army's M60, MG3, and M240/MAG58 light machine guns. The PKM is a bit lighter than those and feels more nimble in my hands than its western counterparts. It uses the non-disintegrating link belts. The ammunition can containing the belt attaches to the side of the weapon so one person can move forward with ammo at the ready. The barrel can be rapidly detached and each barrel can be individually zeroed off the front sight so when a new barrel is installed, you are still on target. The weapon can take a variety of telescopic and night-vision scopes and has a bipod to permit shooting it prone. It's better to install it on its lightweight alloy tripod, though you should weight the legs with sandbags or something to keep movement to a minimum.

These first became available in the United States after the dissolution of the Soviet Union in the mid-1990s. The late Kent Lamont, who is regarded as the finest small arms expert of the last forty years, shot these extensively, and made the following observations. The PKM is a good weapon. While not as durable as an MAG58, the PKM is around six pounds lighter and feels nimble in your hands. Kent bought a couple of brand new Hungarian-made models, and broke within sixty thousand rounds each. The trunnions cracked. A test showed the metal was affected by fatigue caused by vibration. This is a poor showing compared to a MAG58, which had fired over one million rounds with no signs of distress.

The RPK was designed to replace the RPD. It is identical to the AKM rifle except for its butt stock and the length and weight of its barrel. It shoots the same cartridge, uses the same action, and has the same sights. The weapon is heavy at eleven pounds, but this makes it more stable in full-auto fire. Like the AK47, the RPK fires from a closed bolt, limiting the ability to fire extended bursts. It lacks a quick-change barrel, which limits its use as an LMG. The RPK is a squad automatic weapon; not a platoon-level LMG. Soldiers who are familiar with the AK47 can use the RPK without retraining. The RPK's cartridge-carrying system is superior to the RPD. The ammo in the RPK drum will rattle a bit but not like that of the RPD drum. The RPK's forty- or thirty-shot magazines avoid that completely. The forty-round magazine causes the weapon to hit the ground when fired in the prone position, so you should fire if off the bipod. The RPK can be easily fired from the shoulder like a conventional rifle because it balances well and fires from a closed bolt. The closed bolt allows greater accuracy than on any open-bolt gun, but limits the ability to fire for extended periods of time. The RPK has no hold-open device for the bolt. The RPK does not lock open once all ammo is used. The standard remedy is to put three tracers in the end of the magazine, so when you see red (or green), it is time to change. The RPK should be used as a rapid-firing semi-auto weapon whose increased weight allows for more rapid recoil recovery and, hence, faster semi-auto fire.

Once the Soviet Union developed the AK74 rifle, it was clear that an RPK version would soon follow. It is not a light machine gun but rather a convenient squad automatic weapon. Like its bigger 7.62x39mm brother, it lacks a quick-change barrel. It takes a longer forty five-shot magazine as well as the standard rifle magazine while the 7.62x39mm version also accepts a drum which rattles when walking. The 5.45x39mm version uses a forty five-round magazine. The weapon is typically carried with the bipod in place. It is difficult to extend and close. After shooting a few magazines, the barrel gets very hot. Its standard AK74-pattern sights are calibrated to an optimistic one thousand meters, (I believe six hundred meters is the high end of realistic), but it does have a windage adjustment on the rear-sight blade, handy for zeroing. Like its larger-caliber counterpart, the RPK74 fires from a closed bolt. It has an interesting anti-bolt-bounce device designed to make certain the bolt is fully in battery before it fires. The RPK74 carries well and the short butt stock rapidly mounts to the shoulder. The bipod makes it muzzle heavy. The forty five-round magazine precludes resting the weapon on the bipod and the butt stock. But the bipod legs are long enough that the weapon clears the magazine if you are shooting prone. I found the RPK74 very controllable. I was able to fire single shots when set on full-auto readily, and fire two-shot bursts effortlessly. The safety is slow to operate, and the sights hard to use. The RPK74 is a good choice for a base of fire weapon to supplement standard infantry rifles.

SINGLE-ACTION ARMY 4¾–5½ INCHES

Caliber: .44 Special as tested; other calibers available, most notably .45 Colt   **Manufacturer:** Colt
Typical Use: Military, hunting, and self-defense

The Colt Single Action Army (SAA) revolver is possibly one of the most famous handguns in the world. It did not spring full-blown in the world, but was a development in a line of revolvers starting with Colt's original Paterson design. The grip of the Colt SAA is identical to that of the M1851 Navy revolver, which many people thought was the best feeling of the Colt percussion line. While it has many design features that trace back several decades prior to its introduction in 1873, even in the early twenty-first century, it is still an effective weapon within the limits of its cartridge capacity. The lock work on the Colt SAA is similar to that found on antique percussion revolvers and might appear to be fragile in this day and age of coil springs but, while the Colt SAA may break more frequently than a typical DA revolver, it can be fixed more readily than almost any other design. The sights on the Colt SAA leave a lot to be desired. They are more in keeping with the sights found on the prior percussion revolvers. Like many people, I have a fond place in my heart for Colt SAA-style weapons. They represent an interesting period in the history of the United States and are themselves fine weapons for hunting or trips far afield, where the weapon's mission is not purely combat.

People like the five-shot J frame revolver as a second gun, or as a primary handgun when armed with a rifle. The standard Chief's Special is a fine belt gun. But considering the ideal use for a two-inch J frame .38 Special revolver, you realize you may need to shoot through coat pockets. Pulling your revolver out is preferable but not always possible. Fabric may interfere with the fall of the hammer, and keep the weapon from firing. This potentially deadly flaw is the reason hammerless revolvers were developed. While these revolvers were ideal for shooting through pockets, many people found them difficult to shoot, especially when SA firing was needed. Then the factory developed the Bodyguard model (M38-alloy, M49-steel). It had a visible hammer but the sides of the frame were raised up around it keeping material from tying it up, yet still allowing a thumb to cock it.

The M1895 Colt was the first swing-out cylinder, DA revolver adopted by the US military. At the time it was adopted, it seemed like a major step forward. The M1895 Colt is an early DA revolver and suffers from many of the early-period problems. The sights are hard to see due to size and color, and the rear sight notch is quite small. Quick pick up in dim light is very difficult. The front of the cylinder did not lock up, leaving cylinder lock-up marginal at best. Trigger pull was heavy in DA format and acceptable in SA. The grip is not instinctive and will shift when the weapon is fired rapidly. Finish on the M1895 was standard blue and, as the weapon was soon to get its major-battle test in hot, humid parts of the world, this was to prove to be a bad choice. Of course any blued finish would have suffered equally. Being a swing-out cylinder model, the M1895 was perhaps the fastest weapon to reload adopted by the US military up to that point. Early period articles about the new M1895 spoke highly of the new weapon. It had great accuracy, low report and recoil, and no doubt less smoke than its .45 caliber predecessor. But they had forgotten one thing—the real purpose of a combat handgun, stopping armed assailants typically at close range as rapidly as possible. The reaction to the load's deficiency caused people to immediately condemn the M1895. While it was certainly not as good as later DA revolvers made by Colt, it was not really bad but merely chambered for a weak cartridge.

STEVENS M35

Caliber: .22 Long Rifle **Manufacturer:** Stevens **Typical Use:** Target shooting, hunting, and plinking

The Stevens M35 is a single shot .22 Rimfire pistol. It has good sights and can be accurately zeroed. Its good, crisp trigger allows you to properly place your shots. It is chambered for the long rifle cartridge but can chamber any of the shorter variations as well. As it is a single shot, the noise level is less than that of a revolver or auto-loader. It is not out of its depth when shooting at bullseye targets at fifty yards, something done frequently with Stevens single-shot pistols in the pre–World War I era. They are every bit as accurate today as they were when first produced in the early 1900s.

COLT NEW SERVICE TARGET .44

Caliber: .44 Russian/Special **Manufacturer:** Colt **Typical Use:** Military, police, and self-defense

The Colt New Service is a well-regarded weapon, and when it came out in 1898, it was certainly an improvement over earlier DA Colt pistols. The Colt New Service was rugged, dependable, and chambered for a cartridge with good stopping power. Many find the grip to be large for practical use and do not like the DA trigger pull that tends to be very heavy and subject to stacking. Others are not bothered by it and like the simultaneous extraction offered on the New Service as well as its ability to carry six rounds in comparative safety. Many people find the fixed sights troublesome, especially if concerned about target accuracy. As with the early SA models, the factory offered a version with a heavy, flat top that permitted an adjustable (for windage) rear sight to be installed. This coupled with a screw adjustment (for elevation) front sight, allowed the shooter to adjust his sights. The sights were easier to pick up.

COLT WOODSMAN

Caliber: .22 Rimfire **Manufacturer:** Colt **Typical Use:** Police, military, and self-defense

The Colt .22 auto-loading pistol, later known as the Woodsman, is a breakthrough weapon made in many models and variations. It was the first self-loading pistol chambered for the .22 Rimfire cartridge. It first came out in 1915 and to have a reliable autoloader at a time when ammunition loadings varied so widely, including the use of blackpowder, was remarkable. The early Woodsman pistols were thin, light, and offered both good sights and trigger pull. The ten-shot capacity was greater than a revolver. It was easy to clean. It had a light, consistent, trigger-pull that did not require a thumb to cock the hammer. The weapons were inherently pretty accurate. The Woodsman was popular with target shooters. Due to its small size, it also became popular with campers and fishermen. From its introduction in 1915 through the mid-1960s, the Woodsman was offered in many models and variations. Its popularity waned because it was expensive to produce, and many other weapons worked as well.

COLT M1905 .45

Caliber: .45   **Manufacturer:** Colt   **Typical Use:** Military and self-defense

The M1905 was an early contender to replace the .38 revolver for the US military. The M1905 was similar to the .38 autoloaders. The front sight is small, short, and difficult to see. The rear sight notch is far too small, but is rounded on the edges. The magazine release is located on the butt which is awkward. The grips are nicely shaped and the weapon lacks the grip safety. The M1905 lacks a side safety. The shooter is forced to carry it either with the chamber empty, the chamber full but hammer down, or loaded with the hammer cocked. Trigger pull on the tested M1905 was like a standard Colt Government Model or about six pounds. The slide is thinner, the weight fine, and it feels very lively in the hand. There is some question about its durability. I tested the M1905 using 185-grain target loads as I did not wish to stress the one hundred-plus-year-old weapon. Recoil and blast were fine. The M1905 proved to be a handy pistol and a step forward at the time.

COLT 1903/8

Caliber: 7.65 Browning (.32 ACP), 9x17mm (.380 ACP)   **Manufacturer:** Colt   **Typical Use:** Military and self-defense

The Colt 1903/8 pocket pistols in .32 ACP or .380 caliber have been used by the US military as nonstandard weapons over the years. The sights are too small and the rear sight too narrow for proper sighting. Its front sight is shallow in height, and difficult to pick up rapidly in poor light. The recoil on this weapon is light. The heavy trigger pull, about fifteen pounds, makes it difficult to handle on a formal target range but fine on the cinema range. The safety falls under the thumb for rapid disengagement and reapplication. You need considerable pressure to get it off with certainty. The Colt 1908 can fire if a weapon is dropped with a round in the chamber. A noted gun writer was killed recently when this happened. The magazine is difficult to insert properly because of the small size of the hole at the bottom of the grip. The magazine-release button pressing on the magazine back slows removal as well.

SMITH & WESSON FIRST MODEL HAND EJECTOR (TRIPLE LOCK)

Caliber: .44 Special   **Manufacturer:** Smith & Wesson   **Typical Use:** Military and self-defense

The famous Smith & Wesson Triple Lock revolver was designed for target and defense shooters. Available in .44 Special, (rarely in .44/40, .38/40, and .45 Colt) it was also made in .455 for the British market. In 1914 and 1915, the British bought five thousand of them. The mud in France was the undoing of the design and no doubt a fitter's nightmare. The sights are hard to see on the cinema range; they are dark and the rear notch was low and small. My test groups were disappointingly large, I believe due to the sights. The trigger in the DA-mode is good and allows rapid follow-up shots. With the low recoil of the .455 cartridge for slow fire, the non-Magna grip design was fine, but problematical when a high-powered .44 Special load is fired. Rapid repeat shots with the .455 rounds drove the weapon into the web of the hand and caused shifting. The trigger face was smooth like a modern combat revolver, better for fast DA shooting. This is a large pistol with an N frame and typically six and a half-inch barrel, but the skinny barrel and large holes in the barrel and cylinder keep the weight down. The New Century is a very well-made and well-designed revolver, but better military revolvers were available for the time period.

COLT M1909

Caliber: .45 Long Colt   **Manufacturer:** Colt   **Typical Use:** Military and self-defense

Prior to World War I, the US military wanted a modern semiautomatic pistol in .45 caliber. The call went out. John Browning's M1905 was on the right path but lacked some safety features, and was not very reliable. While Browning ultimately prevailed with his M1911, the US military needed a modern, large-bore handgun, as the .38 caliber revolvers then in use lacked stopping power. The M1909 is a standard Colt New Service 5½-inch-barrel handgun chambered for .45 Colt with military-specified grips and finish. The low, narrow notch in the rear sight makes triangulating difficult. The SA pull is good, but because of the grip size, I find the DA pull heavy. The ejector rod hangs out under the barrel unsupported, which can result in jams, when twigs and debris prevent the cylinder from opening. The ejector rod will bend when striking a human head. The M1909 was short-lived in US military circles, replaced once the .45 ACP cartridge was developed. It saw little use in either World War.

SMITH & WESSON M1917

Caliber: .45 ACP   **Manufacturer:** Smith & Wesson   **Typical Use:** Military and self-defense

This pistol was a disappointment to me. The Model 1917 has a DA pull that must have weighed at least twenty pounds. This weight, coupled with the grip that had no adapter, caused the weapon to shift in my hand with each shot and throw the shots right each time. Accuracy with the pistol is a problem. During rapid firing on the cinema range, the grip configuration caused the weapon to shift in the web of my hand, reducing efficiency considerably. Cases tended to stick in the chamber even though I was using commercial full-metal-jacket and military ball loads. The three-shot half-moon clips were difficult to remove in a hurry. As a result, my groups were about 4⅝ inches, or roughly twice those of the Model 19 Smith & Wesson fired the same day. All in all, the Model 1917 would appear to be a safe military weapon, but one is hard pressed to see that it is as good as many other big-bore revolvers.

COLT M1917

Caliber: .45 ACP   **Manufacturer:** Colt   **Typical Use:** Military and self-defense

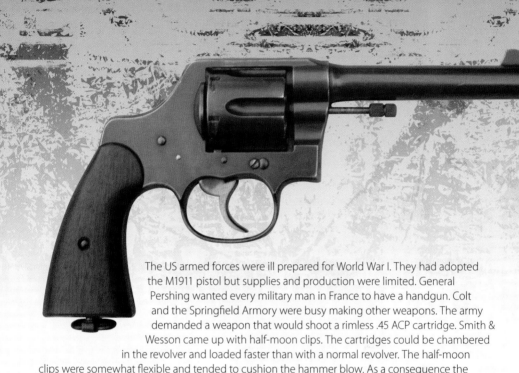

The US armed forces were ill prepared for World War I. They had adopted the M1911 pistol but supplies and production were limited. General Pershing wanted every military man in France to have a handgun. Colt and the Springfield Armory were busy making other weapons. The army demanded a weapon that would shoot a rimless .45 ACP cartridge. Smith & Wesson came up with half-moon clips. The cartridges could be chambered in the revolver and loaded faster than with a normal revolver. The half-moon clips were somewhat flexible and tended to cushion the hammer blow. As a consequence the hammer had to fall harder on a .45 ACP-chambered revolver than on a .45 Colt or other rimmed-caliber revolver, and the trigger pull was generally harder. The M1917 is simply a Colt New Service with a 5½-inch barrel, a rough finish, smooth wooden grips, and a trigger pull that is generally heavier because of the half-moon clip. Like the New Service, the sights are hard to see and the grip too large for many people. Recoil will often make it shift in your hand, slowing follow up shots. In the 1960s, surplus M1917s sold, for as little as $29.95. Most who bought them modified them. Consequently, the few that remain unaltered and in good condition are now worth more than a new N frame Smith & Wesson.

A .44 Special fixed-sight revolver, such as the M1926, which was only made as a special-order item, was the first choice for many knowledgeable shooters in the pre-war era. The grips below are Magna-style but many have non-Magna-style pearl grips. Many people sneer at pearl grips, but I found them good. They allowed the weapon to shift in the hand when a hasty hold was obtained. The pistol featured the pre–World War II long action. It was smooth on the DA and crisp on the SA. The sights were very difficult to use. Having a narrow notch and thick front blade makes it very difficult to get a quick and certain sight picture with the weapon. Due to the large holes in the barrel and cylinder, the M1926 revolver was no heavier than a Colt Government Model. The encased ejector rod kept the ejector rod from being bent and kept the balance forward, helping to mitigate muzzle whip. This pistol is a fine example of a fighting revolver that could be put to good use without hesitation.

Both the Smith & Wesson Heavy Duty and the Outdoorsman were .38 Special revolvers built on the fine N frame receiver. Barrel lengths ranged from four inches to 6½ inches. The Heavy Duty was marketed to the self-defense market and the Outdoorsman to the sportsman. Made before the 1935 arrival of the .357 Magnum, both were designed to allow the hand loader, and even the factory, to load .38 Special cartridges to a high-pressure level like +P or +P+ today. Both models are fitted with tapered barrels and originally the pre–World War II Outdoorsman had no rib. Both weapons are equipped with full integral lug barrels. The sights on the Outdoorsman are easily used. However, pre-war models don't hold adjustments as well as current models do. The Heavy Duty fixed sights are harder to see and use. As with all N frame revolvers, both are heavy and have large grips. The weight makes for low felt recoil, even with high-speed .38 Special ammo. A proper belt and holster combination solves the weight issue. Both the Heavy Duty and Outdoorsman revolvers are excellent weapons. They perform as well today as they did when they left the factory nearly a century ago during the Great Depression.

COLT DETECTIVE SPECIAL

Caliber: .38 Special   **Manufacturer:** Colt   **Typical Use:** Military and self-defense

At one time, this weapon was the standard-issue weapon among US Army Criminal Investigative Command special agents, and this is where I first encountered it as a military-issue weapon. Because it was in the inventory, it also trickled into other units. With the addition of the hammer shroud, which was a common factory part, this weapon was ideal for carry in military parkas and coat pockets. The weapon is rather difficult to shoot because of the stacking of the trigger. However, the Colt has better sights than the standard 2-inch J frame Smith & Wesson and the Colt is smaller than the K frame M10 Smith & Wesson. I find this to be a very good service weapon for the line troops and much more deadly than a bayonet. A short-barrel .38 with proper ammo will allow a soldier to stop five or six enemy soldiers whereas he would be lucky to get one with a bayonet. For those who do carry a rifle, a revolver such as this, tucked in some out-of-the-way place, ready to be grabbed when your rifle is unavailable, is worth its weight in gold.

REMINGTON PA51

Caliber: .380 ACP   **Manufacturer:** Remington   **Typical Use:** Military and self-defense

The Remington P51 was not in common use, but it had one very important fan—General George S. Patton. General Patton was knowledgeable about weapons. From 1916 as a junior officer in Mexico until his death in Germany in 1945, General Patton always carried handguns. He was most famous for his pair of belt guns, a 5½-inch .45 Colt SAA and a 3½-inch .357 Magnum Smith & Wesson, but he also carried a pocket pistol in his waistband. He selected a Remington PA 51 .380, the thinnest pistol of its type in 1944. On the formal range, I found the sights narrow, small, and dark. The rear sight notch was difficult to use, and produced poor groups. On the cinema range, the same problems made it difficult to index rapidly and to triangulate. The pitch of the grip made it quite handy on the range, aiding instinctive work. I found the thinness of the weapon quite charming as well. Although there are clearly superior choices today, in 1934 when the Remington PA 51 was last produced, it had many fine points to recommend it. I would agree with General Patton that, given a choice between the PA 51 and an 08 Colt, the Remington would win every time.

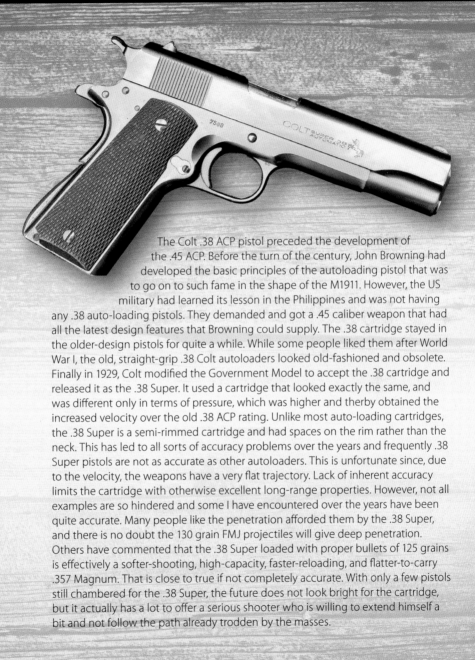

The Colt .38 ACP pistol preceded the development of the .45 ACP. Before the turn of the century, John Browning had developed the basic principles of the autoloading pistol that was to go on to such fame in the shape of the M1911. However, the US military had learned its lesson in the Philippines and was not having any .38 auto-loading pistols. They demanded and got a .45 caliber weapon that had all the latest design features that Browning could supply. The .38 cartridge stayed in the older-design pistols for quite a while. While some people liked them after World War I, the old, straight-grip .38 Colt autoloaders looked old-fashioned and obsolete. Finally in 1929, Colt modified the Government Model to accept the .38 cartridge and released it as the .38 Super. It used a cartridge that looked exactly the same, and was different only in terms of pressure, which was higher and therby obtained the increased velocity over the old .38 ACP rating. Unlike most auto-loading cartridges, the .38 Super is a semi-rimmed cartridge and had spaces on the rim rather than the neck. This has led to all sorts of accuracy problems over the years and frequently .38 Super pistols are not as accurate as other autoloaders. This is unfortunate since, due to the velocity, the weapons have a very flat trajectory. Lack of inherent accuracy limits the cartridge with otherwise excellent long-range properties. However, not all examples are so hindered and some I have encountered over the years have been quite accurate. Many people like the penetration afforded them by the .38 Super, and there is no doubt the 130 grain FMJ projectiles will give deep penetration. Others have commented that the .38 Super loaded with proper bullets of 125 grains is effectively a softer-shooting, high-capacity, faster-reloading, and flatter-to-carry .357 Magnum. That is close to true if not completely accurate. With only a few pistols still chambered for the .38 Super, the future does not look bright for the cartridge, but it actually has a lot to offer a serious shooter who is willing to extend himself a bit and not follow the path already trodden by the masses.

The Colt Government Model .45 pistol, introduced in 1911, was immediately popular. People liked the design, but soon wanted a weapon that was cheaper to shoot, made less noise, and had less felt recoil. The call went out for a .22 version of the Government Model but, for various reasons, the early versions were all slow and quite unsatisfactory. Colt developed the Ace pistol in the early 1930s. It was almost identical in size to a Government Model except a tad shorter in barrel and slide length. The slide was hollowed out to allow it to function with .22 Rimfire ammo, now more powerful and clean shooting than in the past. The magazine held ten rounds, instead of the seven rounds of the Government Model. The Ace pistol used the lightweight slide to function with a straight-blow-back system. Colt developed the Service Ace and conversion a few years later which allowed a shooter to use his standard Government Model, or more likely a "bring back" from the war, to change his .45 to a .22 version. These used Williams's "floating chamber" to get positive functioning and similar recoil. My Ace pictured here was made in 1937 and functions well. Accuracy is fine, and it duplicates the Government Model, but with less felt recoil, noise, and expense.

Colt produced the pre-war National Match .45 pistol from 1932–1941. Based on a standard Government Model and hand built, it had a carefully-fitted barrel and slide and a better trigger pull. It was expensive, especially for the Depression. Men who wanted the best .45 auto available from the factory purchased it. Still, it cost much less than buying from a custom gunsmith, was available instantly, and had a well known company backing it. The pistol was available in nickel and blue finish, with adjustable or fixed sights. Ivory and pearl grips could be fitted, carved if desired, and factory engraving was available. A review of the records of original owners lists many serious gunmen. When you load a pre-war National Match and rack the slide to chamber a round, you cannot help but notice the smooth action. When you pull the trigger and compare that to a standard model, you will appreciate the work of the master craftsmen who made it. This weapon gives fine accuracy, is reliable, and fires a dependable cartridge. I highly recommend this fine pistol.

The pre-war Registered .357 Magnum is quite possibly the most collectible Smith & Wesson handgun today. Over five thousand were made from 1935–1941, and it was never a military weapon. I have authored a book devoted to this weapon, titled *Magnum*. If given a choice between a pre-war .357 Magnum and an M1926 Target model in .44 Special, I would rather take the latter. But I find the pre-war Magnum very interesting. The Magnum was a well-made piece since the factory put its best fitter on the project. The weapons were never cheap and were frequently ordered with interesting alternatives in sights, sighting distances, or other alternatives by serious gunmen. These weapons represent a real breakthrough by the factory for the power level of the cartridge. The pre-war Magnum thus tends to serve as a time machine for many of us. When we see one, put our hands on it, work the action, or shoot it on the range, we are immediately transported to another time and place.

FITZ COLTS

Caliber: .45 (.38 Special)   **Manufacturer:** Colt   **Typical Use:** Military and self-defense

J. Henry FitzGerald was a salesman and shooting demonstrator for the Colt Firearms Company between 1919 and 1940. A big, jovial Irishman, "Fitz" attended pistol matches representing the company and visited many police agencies promoting Colt products. His book *Shooting*, published in 1930, is still a useful, practical work on defense shooting. Fitz is best remembered for his signature item. He devised the cut-away trigger guard, known as a "Fitz" trigger guard. Even today people who have no idea who he was call a weapon with the trigger guard missing a "Fitz gun." There is some debate as to how practical these are, and they take some getting used to. Your use would determine whether you would want this modification on your weapon, but as collectibles, such factory-modified Colt weapons are highly desirable. "Fitz" trigger guards are found on many types of revolvers available during Fitz's time, including the Detective Special, Official Police (or Army Special), and the New Service revolver. Semi-auto Government Model-type pistols in .45 or .38 Super can be found with this modification.

LIBERATOR .45 ACP

Caliber: .45 ACP   **Manufacturer:** Guide Lamp Corp. of GM   **Typical Use:** Military and self-defense

The Liberator cost $1.72 in 1942 and was designed to be flown into occupied countries to arm underground fighters. That's a good concept, but a Sten Gun cost $10.00 then and was a far superior weapon. The Liberator is a fairly large pistol. The sights are rudimentary, a pyramid-style point on the front grip strap and a notch between the cocking knob. Trigger pull is hard and heavy. To load, you pull the knob rearward and to the side. The slide stop-like piece is then pulled upwards, a round inserted, and the stop slides downward holding the round in place. The knob is turned back to the center position. Recoil is brisk. The barrel is a smooth-bore piece of thick tubing. Due to its internal size, pressure is quite low. The cases fell out by merely tipping the weapon up. It was not the most comfortable weapon to fire, but it is not in any way hazardous. I fired the weapon about twelve times at twenty five feet—a reasonable distance assuming it was to be used for taking out a sentry. I shot a six-inch group. Still, the Liberator no doubt could easily perform its intended job.

Famous border patrolman Bill Jordan introduced this weapon in 1956 on the TV show "You Asked For It." He called it "the answer to a peace officer's dream." It is a six-shot K frame revolver chambered for the .357 Magnum cartridge. It has a straight profile barrel and encased ejector rod to lend weight to the front, aiding instinctive pointing. It was designed to use lower-power .38 Special rounds for practice, then full-power Magnums for serious defense. Many ignored this, and early revolvers often broke down due to the overuse of Magnum ammo. In 2013, over fifty years after it came out, the factory finally altered the design and the currently-manufactured weapon can take the Magnum cartridge in virtually unlimited quantities without damage. In the late 1960s, a 2½-inch model with a rounded butt was offered, and many plainclothes officers considered this "the weapon." I prefer the three- or four-inch model as it has a full-length ejector rod, which the 2½-inch-barrel version lacks. This presents a problem with sticking high pressure cases left in the change hole of the cylinder. A round butt four-inch Combat Mangum is an ideal service revolver if worn on a belt. They are accurate, can be quickly and consistently zeroed for a given load, and, with proper ammo, will hold up very well. They are small enough to be readily concealed yet big enough to be effective.

The Colt Agent is an alloy-framed version of the famed Detective Special but with a shortened butt. The sights, caliber, trigger system, and capacity are all the same. Both Smith & Wesson and Colt make two-inch-barrel revolvers of steel and alloy. The Smith & Wessons hold five shots and have a narrower cylinder while the butt on the Colts is shorter. The Colt has better sights than any but the current line of J frame Smith & Wesson revolvers. The sights pick up quickly in poor light. You have to buy and install the accessory hammer shroud on the Colt, whereas specific factory designs of the Smith & Wesson, the Bodyguard and Centennial, have one. Some people prefer the six-shot Colts to the five-shot Smith & Wesson. I prefer the shorter butt; two-inch-barreled .38 Special revolvers are pocket pistols, so the shorter butt allows easier carry and concealment in a pocket. Accuracy is typical for a lightweight, two-inch barrel revolver and is aided by the broader front sight. SA pull is crisp while DA is stiff and subject to stacking. The Colt trigger is grooved and narrow, thus bites into the finger. The cylinder release is problematic. On Colts, you pull it to the rear rather than pushing it forward with your thumb as on a Smith & Wesson. But there should be few situations where you need to reload a pocket pistol.

SMITH & WESSON M60

Caliber: .38 Special　　**Manufacturer:** Smith & Wesson　　**Typical Use:** Military and self-defense

This was "the pistol" during the Vietnam War, not because of its caliber, design, or quality of construction, but rather its material. Announced in 1965, the M60 was the first handgun made entirely out of stainless steel. Everybody who knew anything about handguns and anticipated going to Vietnam wanted one. Small pocket pistols are typically carried close to the body and are subject to heat and humidity extremes. For years, blue-finished handguns had been turning brown on people. In Vietnam, they often turned brown literally overnight. Nickel-plated guns were fine as long as the nickel was intact, but as soon as it chipped or flaked, the whole finish was under attack. Stainless steel altered this whole equation. People who never would have accepted a bright pistol before flocked to the M60. The M60 suffers from the same drawback of all J frame Smith & Wesson revolvers: the sights. The front sights are too narrow (except in the most recently released models that finally have gone for one-eighth-inch sights), and the rear-sight notch is narrow and shallow. The short-barrel magnifies any sighting error, making it difficult to get good groups on a formal range. The trigger pull on SA is not bad, but the coil springs and short hammer fall usually produce a very heavy, stiff DA pull. The weapon is light and hence recoils a bit; the barrel is short so muzzle blast is high; the grips are small allowing the weapon to shift in the hand. I cannot shoot one accurately without a grip adapter installed because the weapon shifts excessively in my hand.

Smith & Wesson released this model with the new short action after World War II. It is available in .44 Special, .45 ACP, and .45 Colt. Equipped with a tapered four-inch barrel, it is light enough to be carried as a belt gun all day long without strain. A nickel-plated four-inch M1950 Target in .45 ACP is an excellent police service revolver. It can be quickly reloaded with half-moon clips and is an accurate weapon with adequate power for self-defense loads. Recoil is not too aggressive and it is wonderfully accurate. When the M29 .44 Magnum came out in 1956, many people switched to that revolver, but it is four ounces heavier. Originally they thought they needed the extra power, but often went back to the M1950 for everyday purposes. The advent of really fine .45 autos effectively caused shooters who previously shot revolvers in handgun matches to switch to the easier-to-shoot, in rapid fire at least, .45 Auto from the M1950 Target. The demand for the weapon in .45 ACP declined after this. The M1950 Target is the gun for those who wanted a practical, accurate and fairly-powerful weapon for their belt gun needs. For this elite group of users, the M1950 Target with the barrel trimmed to four inches was near perfection.

The Colt Commander, aka the Lightweight Commander, was introduced in 1950 as a possible replacement for the M1911A1 pistol in the US military. The barrel is 4¼ inches instead of five inches. The frame is aluminum rather than steel, making the weapon weigh twenty six ounces rather than thirty nine ounces. All other aspects are similar to the standard Government Model. This fine fighting weapon is available in 9mm Luger, .38 Super, and .45 ACP. They are nimble in the hands, convenient to carry on the belt, and more than practically accurate. Trigger pulls and sights need a bit of help, but modifying will not be a major project. Picking chamberings is interesting; the 9mm ones are pleasant to shoot, but you would be better off with a Browning P35 Hi-Power if you are going to accept 9mm. The .38 Super is fine if you are going places that mandate that chambering, but the best Commanders are in .45 ACP. They have more felt recoil than a standard Government Model. With a good two-hand hold, neither this, nor recovery, is an issue. I carried a .45 Commander both in the army and as a federal law enforcement agent and found it to be an excellent weapon.

COLT NEW FRONTIER

Caliber: 44 Special   **Manufacturer:** Colt   **Typical Use:** Military and self-defense

The New Frontier has a strong, heavy top strap, into which is machined an adjustable rear sight that is a great aid when firing. The front sight is a well-designed ramp sight, which is tall enough to allow the shooter to effectively utilize the weapon at long range. The trigger action on the New Frontier was equivalent to other SA weapons of the period. Unlike an SA autoloader, you have no concern about jarring off the hammer, so it can have a much lighter pull. The New Frontier, as any other Colt SA, is slow to load, and can be safely carried with only five rounds. But you can load it on the run without emptying the weapon or taking it out of service, as is the case with a Smith & Wesson, Colt, Webley, or similar DA-revolver. As with all Colt SAs, the grip feels good. The grip design minimizes recoil in the hand for most people although some find it more painful than an Smith & Wesson-style grip. The finish on the New Frontier is a combination of case-hardened frame and blued-barrel cylinder, ejector rod and grip straps. This is not a durable finish—look at any old Colt SA—but it is attractive even if maintenance intensive. This is the revolver that Elmer Keith wanted in the mid-1920s when he and Harold Croft did so much experimentation with the Colt Single Action.

COLT PYTHON .357 MAGNUM

Caliber: .357 Magnum   **Manufacturer:** Colt   **Typical Use:** Military and self-defense

The Colt Python comes from the old-style revolver system with a leaf spring lock, which first saw the light of day when Spaniards ruled Cuba. In the 1950s, Colt added a ventilated rib and heavy under-lug to make a very stylish pistol. It not only looked good, but it shot well due to three features: The rifling rate was pitched at a rate that many feel is better for wadcutter bullets than the one-in-twelve rate found in Smith & Wesson revolvers. The lock-up system, which only fully locked up the cylinder at the last instant, did lock it up very tightly. The trigger pull, finally, is both light and very smooth. Due to the design of the trigger action, a trigger pull of 1½ pounds on SA and as low as six pounds on DA could be achieved and still allow full detonation of Magnum primers. The Python also has very nice, easily-adjustable rear sights, and a good ramp front so a person can plant bullets perfectly. The weapon has a heavy forward balance point which minimizes muzzle whip on one hand and aided instinctive pointing on the other. The weapon is light enough to be worn on the belt all day without difficulty, and the grip was small enough that any average-sized hand could handle it without difficulty. While it held only six shots in a day when autoloaders in police work were almost unheard of, it made no difference. Many people like the look of the Colt ventilated rib and it certainly does give a distinctive look to the weapon, showing off machining talent and lightening up the weapon while still projecting the balance point forward. I find it rather odd looking. Also, it just makes the weapon that much more difficult and time-consuming to clean properly. If you are going to have only one revolver and wear your weapon on an external belt, a well-modified Python is a fine personal defense handgun.

SMITH & WESSON M46

Caliber: .22 Long Rifle   **Manufacturer:** Smith & Wesson   **Typical Use:** Target shooting

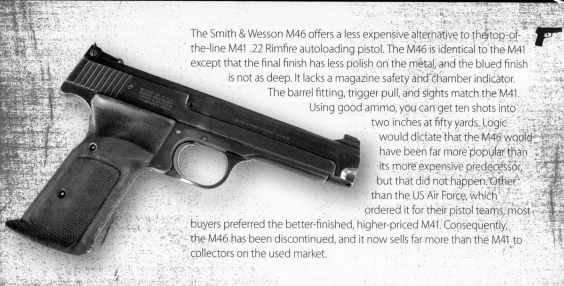

The Smith & Wesson M46 offers a less expensive alternative to the top-of-the-line M41 .22 Rimfire autoloading pistol. The M46 is identical to the M41 except that the final finish has less polish on the metal, and the blued finish is not as deep. It lacks a magazine safety and chamber indicator. The barrel fitting, trigger pull, and sights match the M41. Using good ammo, you can get ten shots into two inches at fifty yards. Logic would dictate that the M46 would have been far more popular than its more expensive predecessor, but that did not happen. Other than the US Air Force, which ordered it for their pistol teams, most buyers preferred the better-finished, higher-priced M41. Consequently, the M46 has been discontinued, and it now sells far more than the M41 to collectors on the used market.

SMITH & WESSON M52

Caliber: .38 Special   **Manufacturer:** Smith & Wesson   **Typical Use:** Military and self-defense

The Smith & Wesson M52 is truly a specialty handgun, useful for very few shooters. It holds only five rounds in the magazine. It shoots only target power .38 Special ammo, and only that when loaded with flush seated wadcutters. The safety is slow to disengage. It is made of conventional steel with a highly-polished blue finish. It is fairly big and fairly heavy. That said, this pistol is incredibly accurate and easy to shoot well. The sights are excellent and easily adjustable to get a perfect zero. The trigger pull breaks like a glass rod and overtravel is simply not there. The barrel is carefully fitted, as is the slide, and the whole package works like the door on a fine safe does as it swings to close. All this, coupled with mild-mannered loading that has light recoil, low blast, and non-existent flash, makes shooting a pleasure. All of this fitting produces a highly-accurate weapon. With good ammo, the M52 will put every round into a two-inch circle at fifty yards. This gun makes you want to achieve that goal.

SMITH & WESSON K22

Caliber: .22 Rimfire   **Manufacturer:** Smith & Wesson   **Typical Use:** Military and self-defense

The K22 was the standard target rimfire revolver until pushed aside by the self-loading pistol. From its beginning in the late 1930s, it offered excellent accuracy along with good sights and fine trigger pull. Post-war guns had a rib on the top of the barrel that could be adjusted in width so that a .22 target revolver weighed the same as a similarly-loaded .38 target revolver, making training for a .38 revolver inexpensive. It even maintained the exact same balance, which is especially helpful when the revolver is shot off-hand with one hand only. If one truly wants to learn to shoot a pistol, the K22 revolver, named the M17 after 1957, should be the first or perhaps second weapon purchased. It is accurate, has good sights and an excellent trigger, and is quite well balanced. The ammo is .22 Rimfire, is widely available, and is usually very accurate and inexpensive. One can develop good skills in six months with a K22 revolver and a double case (ten thousand rounds) of Rimfire ammo. The experienced shooter can likewise keep his skills up with little cost.

HI-STANDARD FLITE KING .22 SHORT

Caliber: .22 Short   **Manufacturer:** High Standard   **Typical Use:** Target shooting

The High Standard Flite King series of .22 autoloaders were designed to be plinking pistols. High Standard made many fine target .22 autoloaders with excellent sights and great accuracy for handgun match shooting on the highest level. The Flite King line was not among those pistols. Still, the Flite King brought with it the High Standard tradition of good accuracy, reliable functioning, and good triggers. While not up to match grade by any means, it is clear that it will shoot better than probably 90 percent of the people who will ever shoot it. Having said this, why include it here among our 365 guns that you should shoot? The answer is its chambering. Most plinkers are chambered for the more common .22 long rifle. This pistol is chambered for the .22 short. As a consequence, it has a very low noise level, almost to the stage of a fair suppressor design. This will allow you to shoot it a wide variety of places that otherwise might not be acceptable. While by no means a toy, you can use the .22 short where a more powerful loading would be excluded.

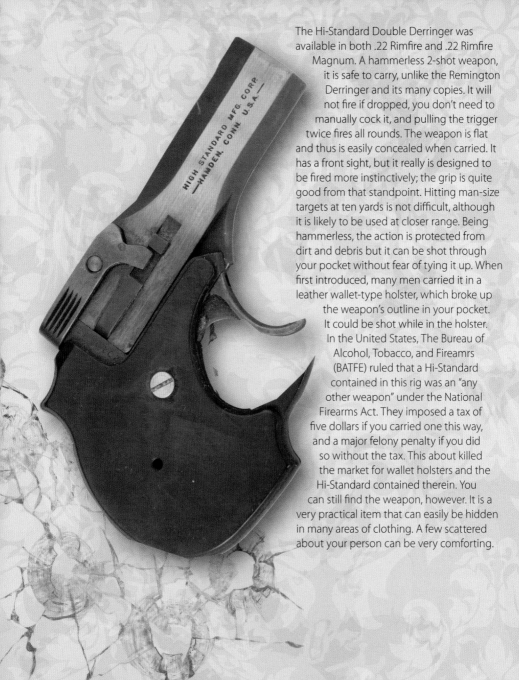

The Hi-Standard Double Derringer was available in both .22 Rimfire and .22 Rimfire Magnum. A hammerless 2-shot weapon, it is safe to carry, unlike the Remington Derringer and its many copies. It will not fire if dropped, you don't need to manually cock it, and pulling the trigger twice fires all rounds. The weapon is flat and thus is easily concealed when carried. It has a front sight, but it really is designed to be fired more instinctively; the grip is quite good from that standpoint. Hitting man-size targets at ten yards is not difficult, although it is likely to be used at closer range. Being hammerless, the action is protected from dirt and debris but it can be shot through your pocket without fear of tying it up. When first introduced, many men carried it in a leather wallet-type holster, which broke up the weapon's outline in your pocket. It could be shot while in the holster. In the United States, The Bureau of Alcohol, Tobacco, and Fireamrs (BATFE) ruled that a Hi-Standard contained in this rig was an "any other weapon" under the National Firearms Act. They imposed a tax of five dollars if you carried one this way, and a major felony penalty if you did so without the tax. This about killed the market for wallet holsters and the Hi-Standard contained therein. You can still find the weapon, however. It is a very practical item that can easily be hidden in many areas of clothing. A few scattered about your person can be very comforting.

The M13 was the last official revolver adopted by the FBI. They adopted the round-butt, three-inch-barrel mode although the weapon is available in square butt with a four-inch barrel. The M13 is a carbon steel weapon; the same weapon in stainless steel is called the M65. The M13s were sighted for the FBI's standard load for .38 Special—Winchester +P 158 grain lead hollow-point. All FBI-issued guns had a pinned front sight. At the academy, armors were on hand to fit different heights of front sights to the individual shooter, giving the agent a perfectly sighted weapon for its load. At this time, the FBI issued +P .38 Special to the field agents but had Magnum ammo at the field office level "in case the need arose for more power." This seemed odd as the agents would have no experience with that ammo and would have to go to the office to get it. The M13 has a wide front sight and an integral rear sight that is square in appearance. The FBI chose a three-inch barrel believing it was easier to conceal, but actually the four-inch locks into the waistband better. The three-inch gives less velocity and is not as good for instinctive pointing. The round-butt K frame fits most people. The FBI's M13 had the SA hammer notch and the spur on it. As using the weapon at long-range is unlikely, the DA SA notch is an invitation to a lawsuit. Since the agents carried their weapons concealed, the spur is not needed to lock the weapon in a holster, and is likely to snag on a coat lining while being drawn.

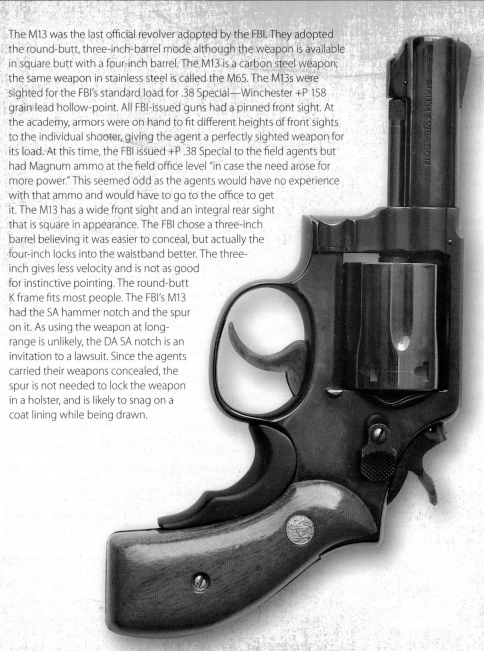

The .41 Magnum cartridge was introduced in 1964, meant for use in two loads and two revolvers. For the outdoorsman, there was 210 grain load of 1,400 fps, a serious hunting load. The revolver would have the enclosed ejector rod and adjustable sights. Retailing for $140, most would be in the six-inch barrel or longer. The other model, costing $90, was a fixed-sight revolver. It had a four-inch barrel, blue or nickel, and the ejector rod was not enclosed. It looked like a slightly overgrown M10HB .38 Special. The loads were a soft lead bullet of 210 grains going around 850 fps. This weapon cartridge combination was aimed at law enforcement; serious self-defense shooters would also appreciate its qualities. Although adopted by some law enforcement agencies, the M58 was never widely used—around twenty thousand were sold. The fact that it is a heavy N frame revolver using a new, expensive specialty round limited its desirability. Still, those who bought the M58 liked it. With the big, heavy four-inch barrel, the weapon had a good forward balance to help with instinctive shooting. The weapon is heavy, over three pounds fully loaded, but a good holster and belt combination will help avoid problems. This same weight will quickly reduce the felt recoil of the so-called duty rounds of 210 grains at 850 fps. The N frame is big and can be difficult for those with small hands. Based on the N frame action, the M58 is a reliable, long-lasting weapon. It is a great combat revolver that has inherent drawbacks for people with small hands.

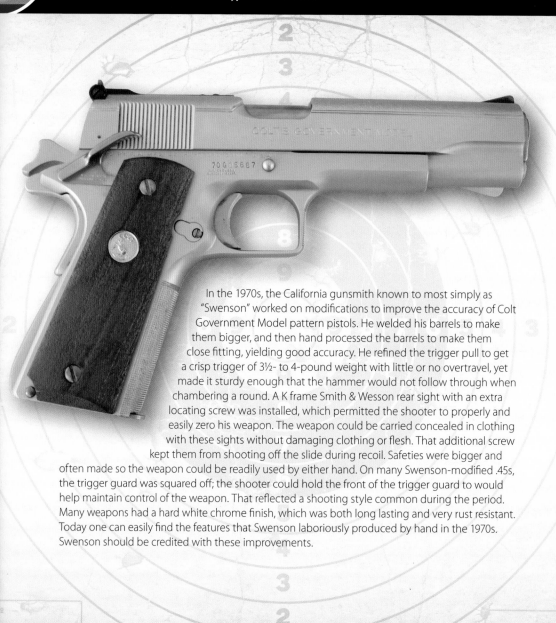

In the 1970s, the California gunsmith known to most simply as "Swenson" worked on modifications to improve the accuracy of Colt Government Model pattern pistols. He welded his barrels to make them bigger, and then hand processed the barrels to make them close fitting, yielding good accuracy. He refined the trigger pull to get a crisp trigger of 3½- to 4-pound weight with little or no overtravel, yet made it sturdy enough that the hammer would not follow through when chambering a round. A K frame Smith & Wesson rear sight with an extra locating screw was installed, which permitted the shooter to properly and easily zero his weapon. The weapon could be carried concealed in clothing with these sights without damaging clothing or flesh. That additional screw kept them from shooting off the slide during recoil. Safeties were bigger and often made so the weapon could be readily used by either hand. On many Swenson-modified .45s, the trigger guard was squared off; the shooter could hold the front of the trigger guard to would help maintain control of the weapon. That reflected a shooting style common during the period. Many weapons had a hard white chrome finish, which was both long lasting and very rust resistant. Today one can easily find the features that Swenson laboriously produced by hand in the 1970s. Swenson should be credited with these improvements.

Jeff Cooper was the foremost advocate for the Government Model, or M1911/A1 pistol, in the last half of the twentieth century. He believed you needed only a few modifications to make the pistol an excellent self-defense weapon. Cooper, at his world-famous training facility in Arizona called "Gunsite," began offering a modification package called the Gunsite Service Pistol. This superior model was of unquestionable quality. Cooper thought a good, crisp trigger of 3½ to 4 pounds was correct. He wanted sights that were regulated correctly; so smooth as to not snag, but quick to pick up in dim light. They did not have to glow in the dark, and he liked black-on-black sights. For those who needed it due to using a high thumb position, he advocated pining off the grip safety. The entire weapon should be smooth all over, like a bar of soap. If the weapon was not stainless steel, it needed a good finish to avoid rust. For small-handed people, slimming down the frame was a helpful feature. This modification also helped women shooters and men with small hands. Cooper found left-handed people needed a safety on that side, but saw no need for dual safeties generally. A slightly larger safety was useful and not bulky. The Gunsite GSP package, reflecting Cooper's theories, makes a very nice belt gun for general use. As he said, "Everything you need and nothing you don't."

For many years, the New York Police Department wanted a weapon that was cheap, as officers had to buy their own weapons, and safe for those who were not well trained. They also hoped this weapon would help minimize some common litigation problems. The NYPD required the weapons fire only in the self-cocking mode to avoid claims for accidental discharge from cocked revolvers. The hammer spurs were cut off, as they were not needed to stabilize the revolver in the holster. Triggers were smooth faced to improve control. The M64 bull barrel adds four ounces to the weapon but gives it much better instinctive feel. The sights are a good-size front sight coupled with a fixed integral rear. The revolvers also were both extremely accurate—one of the pair I tested shot two-inch groups at fifty yards and the other 2¼ inches. The trigger pull on both examples was quite smooth and broke cleanly, contributing to accuracy. The ejector rod is full length, allowing complete extraction of the empties. The grip frame whether square or round butt, is good for small and average sized hands. The M64 HB NYPD-style .38 Special revolver is probably the best designed combat revolver made in that caliber for police service. It can easily be carried by plainclothes as well as uniformed officers. The cartridge is not the most powerful but it is cheap, readily available, and with proper loads has a good track record.

BERETTA M92

Caliber: 9mm Parabellum **Manufacturer:** Pietro Beretta SpA **Typical Use:** Military, police, and self-defense

In 1982, the US military adopted the M92 Beretta, its first new handgun for general use since World War II. Some US police forces have since chosen the Beretta. As a military handgun for infantry troops, the Beretta M9 leaves a lot to be desired. The sights are easy to use on both the formal and cinema ranges and have contrasting color. The pistol weighs as much and is as big as and thicker than the Colt Government Model it replaced. The DA trigger mechanism is not selectable, creating a safety issue as many will run with them cocked and no safety during a shooting incident. The grip size is bigger and the DA trigger system makes it harder for smaller people, like women, to handle than the SA-trigger-style of the Colt Government Model. The M92 has a light recoil, normal for a pistol that weighs forty ounces and shoots only 9x19mm cartridges. The Beretta uses the Walther-type lock, which makes for a wide pistol. These locking blocks tend to break without warning, tying up your weapon. Early on the Beretta M9/M10 had such a problem with slides breaking that the military instructed they be replaced every one thousand rounds. This was traced to the poor steel quality, and has been corrected. The weapon lacks a magazine safety but does offer a loaded-cartridge indictor. In short, the M92 is an acceptable handgun. It is accurate, easy to shoot, and surprisingly nimble despite its size. The problem of the locking blocks breaking without warning is a serious drawback.

COLT POCKETLITE .380

Caliber: .380   **Manufacturer:** Colt   **Typical Use:** Military and self-defense

When I first saw the Pocketlite announced, I thought it was very interesting as it was a lot like the Star DK 380, which I had always liked. One of the first things you note when comparing them with the DK is that the weapon is thicker and wider through the receiver. The Star DK looks like a race horse and the Colt like a plow horse. The trigger pull on the test example was acceptable but the rear sight was too narrow, too sharp on the edges, and the notch needed to be deeper. The front sight was also gray in color which I find difficult to see in poor light but a dab of white paint would help. I thought the side safety was too easy to brush off in your pocket and any real pocket pistol should have a butt-release magazine release instead of a side button which can be depressed by pressure against your leg, allowing the magazine to drop out of place. The weapon also lacks a magazine safety which is a real safety benefit on personal defense weapon. Does the weapon have any viable place in the world today? I really like the Star DK .380 and while the Pocketlite Colt is similar in many aspects to the DK, I am forced to conclude that time marches on and actually neither the DK nor the Pocketlite do anything today that cannot be done better by other pistols.

The term "Kit Gun" comes from a time when campers and fisherman had "kits" to take on their trips. This kit often included a .22 revolver. It could be used to shoot snakes, fishing lines hooked on limbs, and most likely just to have fun plinking away at tin cans, pine cones, and other targets. The ammo was cheap and light, and noise was low enough not to be bothersome. Originally produced on the I frame, the Kit Gun changed over to J frame used on the .38 Special revolver in the 1950s. These had good adjustable sights, fine triggers, and good fitting so that high accuracy was possible. They were light and the grip somewhat small, but Smith & Wesson produced them with the same care as their other target-grade revolvers. Barrel lengths were available from two inches to 6 inches in both steel (both standard and stainless) and alloy. Finishes were standard blue or nickel plate. While typically available in .22 Long Rifle, you can find a .22 Rimfire Magnum version. Some models offer two separate cylinders chambered for both cartridges thus allowing you to use both. The two-inch models are fun to shoot and excellent training tools for those using J frame .38 revolvers for defense. I have shot incredibly well with the six-inch model (494 out of 500 on a standard twenty five yard target), which is surprising given its light weight and size.

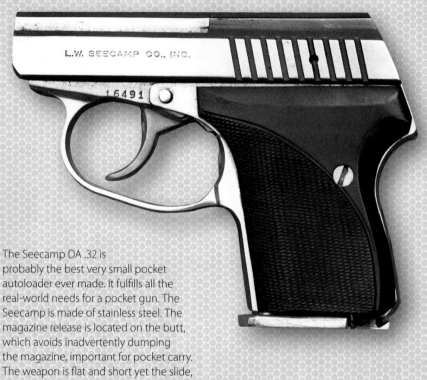

The Seecamp DA .32 is probably the best very small pocket autoloader ever made. It fulfills all the real-world needs for a pocket gun. The Seecamp is made of stainless steel. The magazine release is located on the butt, which avoids inadvertently dumping the magazine, important for pocket carry. The weapon is flat and short yet the slide, riding high on the receiver, will not slice your hand. The Seecamp is trigger cocking (commonly but mistakenly called 'double action') and hammer fired. This helps prevent accidental discharge in your pocket. But it is not meant to be fired in the pocket, for it can get tied up in the cloth. The pistol is fitted with a magazine safety, which disables the weapon, a good feature for a gun likely to be dumped on your desk when you're at home. The Seecamp has no sights. This disturbs many people, but Larry Seecamp apparently believes sights would encourage people to use this pistol for purposes for which it was not intended. The Seecamp is quite light. The recoil is manageable; it is just sharper than what one might expect for .32 ACP self-loaders. Most small pocket pistols are either SA trigger designs or .22/25 caliber weapons. Only the Seecamp gives you the power level of the .32 ACP with good stopping power ammo, and it is smaller than most .25 ACP self-loaders. Its safety, rust resistance, and practical accuracy make this a fine weapon.

When the first .357 Magnum revolver was sent to Elmer Keith to review in the 1935 *American Rifleman*, he wrote that he wished it were a .44 rather than this smaller-bored revolver. In the period before the factory make this available, Keith used a variety of .44 Special revolvers loaded with his powerful handloads. But Keith put his .44 Special revolvers away in 1956 when Smith & Wesson sent him one of the first .44 Magnum revolvers made. In 1957 when numbers replaced names, this revolver was called the M29. Keith always said he could shoot a squirrel or a buffalo with the M29. And indeed, I have killed a water moccasin at thirty five yards and an American Bison at fifteen yards with this weapon. It is accurate, and fully capable of drilling the 1½-inch X-ring out of a twenty five-yard pistol target. It is powerful enough to shoot through an American Bison, and yet can be loaded to permit rapid DA work for self-defense. As with most N frame Smith & Wessons, the adjustable sights are excellent, maintaining their positions through thousands of rounds. The action is smooth with a good DA pull and fine SA. The weight of this four-inch model is forty three ounces empty, so adding six-loaded rounds make its weight three pounds. A good holster and belt combination allows you to carry it in comfort.

SEMMERLING LM4

Caliber: .45 ACP   **Manufacturer:** Semmerling and American Derringer Co.   **Typical Use:** Self-defense

The Semmerling LM4 is a manually-operated repeating .45 ACP pistol. It is one of the smallest .45 ACP pistols made. It utilizes a forward action to permit short overall length. The action works easily as it has no stiff springs to keep the slide in place. It is very well machined, so the surfaces mesh well, which improves smoothness. The model tested was finished in industrial white chrome, which no doubt improved smoothness as well. In tests, the weapon could be easily flicked open and closed with a thumb. The weapon tested was the thin version, which is the standard version without grips. The slide would pull forward when withdrawing the weapon from the holster. Activating the slide-lock-catch solves this problem. The catch is released by pulling slightly to the rear on the trigger, releasing the trigger, and then completely pulling it to the rear to fire the weapon. You must practice to get used to this. Sights are fixed. Although small, the rear sight is easy to see. The front sight is high and wide enough to be rapidly picked up even in dim light. The magazine holds four rounds inside to keep the grip length to a minimum and one in the chamber, making it a five-shot weapon. The magazine release is in the butt—flanges in the magazine spring out to hold it in place. This is excellent for pocket carry, although removing the magazine to reload is slow. Accuracy is good. Recoil is heavy enough to make your hand sore if shooting more than one hundred rounds. The LM4 has some limitations, but as a backup pistol carried in the front pants pocket, it is possibly the best and biggest-bore weapon available.

The M4506 offered the DA-SA trigger system that so many who wanted a duty .45 autoloader had been seeking for years. Early models had a thin slide and later models the heavier slide necessitated by the 10mm cartridge. The .45 ACP cartridge operating at a much lower pressure range than the 10mm, alloy-framed .45 autoloaders were available. The M4563 was a DA/SA model with slide-mounted safety that coupled a stainless slide and a 4¼-inch barrel with an alloy frame. Before the September 11 attacks, when Smith & Wesson was short on work and hence more flexible about short orders, some friends and I got them to build a special run of M4566 pistols with a dark Mellonite finish, special barrel bushing system to get us three-inch groups for ten shots at fifty yards and, in my case at least, Bo-Mar adjustable sight. Special serial numbers containing the owner's initials were also part of the project. Some other useful and interesting variations on this idea were the constant trigger (DAO) models in either stainless or alloy frame found in the M4586 or M4583. By the time the Third Generation guns came out, stainless steel, at least for slides and barrels, was the expected construction material but some were made of conventional steel both on the receiver and slide, and assigned the model number M4505 to reflect that material. At least one of those was subsequently factory engraved and gold plated, making for a very interesting collectible for the years ahead.

The M39 came out in 1954, and was the first double-action autolader available in 9x19mm since the Walther P38. The M39 gave US police forces a semi-auto pistol that could be carried without concern for safety manipulation. Many liked the M39's light weight, flat shape, and trigger system. It went through many design improvements. The barrel feed ramp was changed to accommodate hollow-point ammunition. The one piece extractor broke easily and was hard to adjust, so it was replaced by a smaller, more reliable unit. The barrel bushings would break, tying up the weapon, and those were strengthened. The Warrick, Rhode Island, force was the first to adopt it in 1961, followed by the prestigious Illinois State Police. Soon its use was widespread in the United States. The M39, representing a rather high tech weapon, also attracted the attention of many who liked self-loading pistols but found the SA, all steel .45 M1911A1-type pistols rather old fashioned. The US Navy, never really big on handguns, bought a few for their SEAL teams. This in turn led, via a couple of twists and turns, to the development of the high-capacity M39 or what we know as the M59. The M59 gave you the same cartridge capacity (or more) as the P35 and yet offered the DA trigger system. Jeff Cooper condemned it as an answer to an unasked question, but for many chiefs of police or department supervisors who were rarely "gun guys," it did not seem so. The success of this variation of the M39 along with the US military desire for a high capacity 9x19mm DA led to all the "wonder nines" which truly changed the police scene. In the mid-1980s, the auto-loading pistol was a rare alternative to the revolver in US police and self-defense circles. By the first decade of the twenty-first century, the revolver on police hips was very unusual.

SMITH & WESSON M5943

Caliber: 9x19mm   **Manufacturer:** Smith & Wesson   **Typical Use:** Police and self-defense

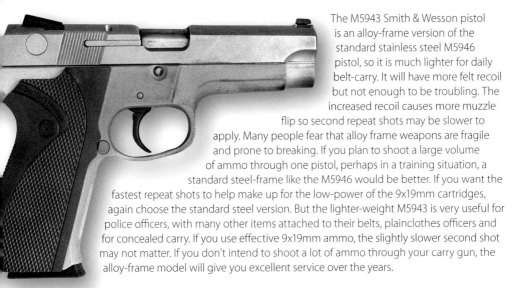

The M5943 Smith & Wesson pistol is an alloy-frame version of the standard stainless steel M5946 pistol, so it is much lighter for daily belt-carry. It will have more felt recoil but not enough to be troubling. The increased recoil causes more muzzle flip so second repeat shots may be slower to apply. Many people fear that alloy frame weapons are fragile and prone to breaking. If you plan to shoot a large volume of ammo through one pistol, perhaps in a training situation, a standard steel-frame like the M5946 would be better. If you want the fastest repeat shots to help make up for the low-power of the 9x19mm cartridges, again choose the standard steel version. But the lighter-weight M5943 is very useful for police officers, with many other items attached to their belts, plainclothes officers and for concealed carry. If you use effective 9x19mm ammo, the slightly slower second shot may not matter. If you don't intend to shoot a lot of ammo through your carry gun, the alloy-frame model will give you excellent service over the years.

BROWNING BDM

Caliber: 9x19mm Parabellum   **Manufacturer:** Browning Arms   **Typical Use:** Police and self-defense

The Browning BDM was not extensively produced as it was much different than most self-loading pistols. It was made of steel at a time when polymer was preferred. The trigger action and thinness make this pistol both interesting and almost unique. The trigger action can operate like a typical DA first shot, SA thereafter. No great development there. But by turning the selector on the slide, it can be converted to a pistol that fires like a standard DA revolver, but unlike all other DAO autoloaders, it can be cocked for fire in SA mode. The shooter can choose the easier-to-shoot SA trigger yet the normal trigger will be the consistent DA pull, a much better design and system. The very thin slide and slender grip were wonderful features. Sadly, the BDM was not successful. When released, DAO pistols were popular, and the SA capability was being removed from DA revolvers to prevent negligent discharge. The market didn't want an autoloading pistol that was like a traditional DA revolver, and its thinness and nimble feeling did not save it. Another issue was the safety on the BDM. It was fast and practical but different enough that many found it hard to get used to, as it worked in the reverse of a normal Government Model safety. Since it was a DA auto really, you could ignore it as you can with many such weapons but it threw people off. Lastly while the BDM was practically accurate, usually four to five inches at twenty five yards, many other autoloaders were better.

The M657 is the stainless steel version of the old tool steel M57. It does not have a pinned barrel or rebated cylinder probably, which are not really necessary for strength or accuracy. The stainless steel finish is far superior to nickel. The trigger pull on the tested example was very good. No doubt it will improve with shooting as the surfaces wear until they give the glass-rod-like effect Smith & Wesson shooters love. The .41 Magnum itself weighs more than a .44 Magnum but the bullet is lighter, so the felt recoil is about 10 percent less. The adjustable sights are excellent. The red ramp front and white outline rear make a good combination especially for an outdoor gun. Surprisingly for an outdoor gun, it has no lanyard ring. The factory target grips are too large and are built backwards. They get bigger at the bottom which weakens your grip, causing greater felt recoil and slow repeat shots. For a real outdoor gun, the M657 four-inch is hard to beat.

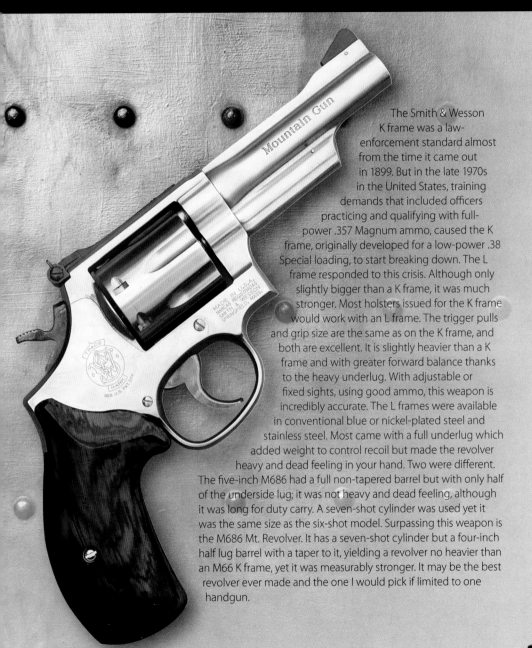

The Smith & Wesson K frame was a law-enforcement standard almost from the time it came out in 1899. But in the late 1970s in the United States, training demands that included officers practicing and qualifying with full-power .357 Magnum ammo, caused the K frame, originally developed for a low-power .38 Special loading, to start breaking down. The L frame responded to this crisis. Although only slightly bigger than a K frame, it was much stronger. Most holsters issued for the K frame would work with an L frame. The trigger pulls and grip size are the same as on the K frame, and both are excellent. It is slightly heavier than a K frame and with greater forward balance thanks to the heavy underlug. With adjustable or fixed sights, using good ammo, this weapon is incredibly accurate. The L frames were available in conventional blue or nickel-plated steel and stainless steel. Most came with a full underlug which added weight to control recoil but made the revolver heavy and dead feeling in your hand. Two were different. The five-inch M686 had a full non-tapered barrel but with only half of the underside lug; it was not heavy and dead feeling, although it was long for duty carry. A seven-shot cylinder was used yet it was the same size as the six-shot model. Surpassing this weapon is the M686 Mt. Revolver. It has a seven-shot cylinder but a four-inch half lug barrel with a taper to it, yielding a revolver no heavier than an M66 K frame, yet it was measurably stronger. It may be the best revolver ever made and the one I would pick if limited to one handgun.

The M317 offers many good features. Weighing eight to nine ounces and with fixed sights, it is easy to carry in the pocket. The M317 takes eight rounds of .22 Rimfire ammo, almost as good as many autoloaders. When I first saw the M317, I was impressed. It is lightweight and clever. The grip straps have been ground to reduce weight. An integral lanyard allows the weapon to be carried attached to the neck or belt, which would be convenient for joggers, bikers, or those working on water. The M317 has all the latest J-frame improvements including cylinder release and a good, wide, front sight. The weapon is made of alloy and stainless parts so will not rust. The frame and cylinder are aluminum as is the barrel except for a small diameter stainless steel liner. The hammer spur does not snag pockets. Trigger pull on SA is heavy but acceptable, while the double pull was fourteen pounds. The engineer at the Smith & Wesson SHOT Show booth explained this was needed to assure reliable ignition in the notoriously-difficult-to-fire rimfire cartridge. The factory-fitted grips are boot-grip style in wood or a rubber material. Both felt good in the hand. Accuracy at fifty feet is good but not exceptional, so not suitable as a survival pistol. Compare the M327 to an M642 and it is clear that you have a lighter weapon with eight shots, but I don't think that makes it superior. Who, then, is its audience? Smith & Wesson seems to have designed it for women who want a very lightweight, low-recoiling weapon to carry for self-defense, but its heavy DA pull may make this a problem. The M317 is a better choice than a .25 or .32 ACP pistol.

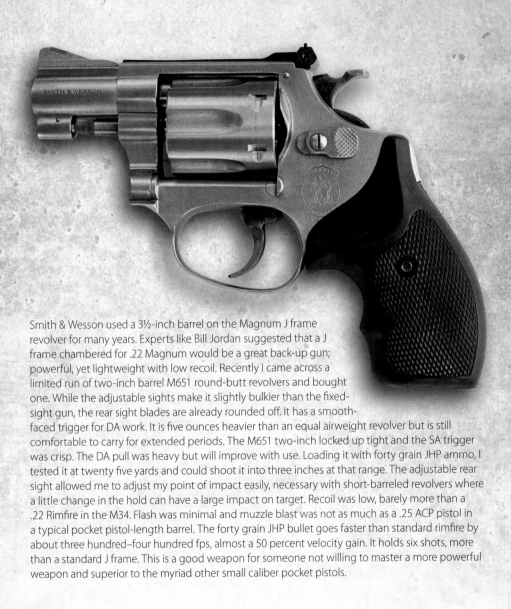

Smith & Wesson used a 3½-inch barrel on the Magnum J frame revolver for many years. Experts like Bill Jordan suggested that a J frame chambered for .22 Magnum would be a great back-up gun; powerful, yet lightweight with low recoil. Recently I came across a limited run of two-inch barrel M651 round-butt revolvers and bought one. While the adjustable sights make it slightly bulkier than the fixed-sight gun, the rear sight blades are already rounded off. It has a smooth-faced trigger for DA work. It is five ounces heavier than an equal airweight revolver but is still comfortable to carry for extended periods. The M651 two-inch locked up tight and the SA trigger was crisp. The DA pull was heavy but will improve with use. Loading it with forty grain JHP ammo, I tested it at twenty five yards and could shoot it into three inches at that range. The adjustable rear sight allowed me to adjust my point of impact easily, necessary with short-barreled revolvers where a little change in the hold can have a large impact on target. Recoil was low, barely more than a .22 Rimfire in the M34. Flash was minimal and muzzle blast was not as much as a .25 ACP pistol in a typical pocket pistol-length barrel. The forty grain JHP bullet goes faster than standard rimfire by about three hundred–four hundred fps, almost a 50 percent velocity gain. It holds six shots, more than a standard J frame. This is a good weapon for someone not willing to master a more powerful weapon and superior to the myriad other small caliber pocket pistols.

SMITH & WESSON M3953

Caliber: 9x19mm   **Manufacturer:** Smith & Wesson   **Typical Use:** Police and self-defense

The Smith & Wesson M39 9x19mm self-loader, introduced in 1954, spawned many variations. The original M39 has become thicker (the M59), made out of better materials such as stainless steel, been equipped with adjustable sights, and converted to DA-only format. The M3953 is the best variation. It is smaller than the original M39 and has the DAO trigger style Smith & Wesson developed to compete against the Glock. The M3953 is highly rust resistant, having a stainless slide and barrel and a bright finish alloy receiver. It holds as many shots as the M39 due to the clever alternation of the magazine follower. The grip, made of synthetic material, is thinner so that the trigger reach is shorter than the initial M39, making it easier to handle for small-to-average-size hands. Accuracy on the initial M39 pistols was often a "sometimes" thing but the shorter M3953 seems properly fitted at the muzzle and accuracy is quite good. The front sight is good with an excellent white dot to allow rapid pick up while the rear is the Novak style. The M3953 typically has a magazine safety, but can be found without one. Trigger pull is heavy but smooth, allowing good target accuracy at fifty feet. Recoil was snappy, but did not pound my palm. The shorter barrel made the blast greater than with a longer barrel, but it was not excessive.

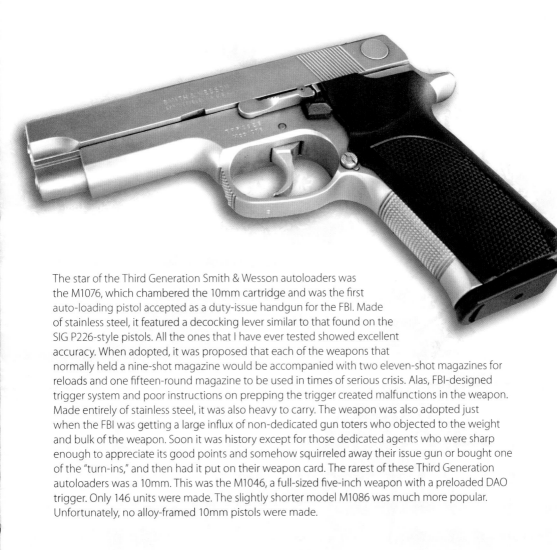

The star of the Third Generation Smith & Wesson autoloaders was the M1076, which chambered the 10mm cartridge and was the first auto-loading pistol accepted as a duty-issue handgun for the FBI. Made of stainless steel, it featured a decocking lever similar to that found on the SIG P226-style pistols. All the ones that I have ever tested showed excellent accuracy. When adopted, it was proposed that each of the weapons that normally held a nine-shot magazine would be accompanied with two eleven-shot magazines for reloads and one fifteen-round magazine to be used in times of serious crisis. Alas, FBI-designed trigger system and poor instructions on prepping the trigger created malfunctions in the weapon. Made entirely of stainless steel, it was also heavy to carry. The weapon was also adopted just when the FBI was getting a large influx of non-dedicated gun toters who objected to the weight and bulk of the weapon. Soon it was history except for those dedicated agents who were sharp enough to appreciate its good points and somehow squirreled away their issue gun or bought one of the "turn-ins," and then had it put on their weapon card. The rarest of these Third Generation autoloaders was a 10mm. This was the M1046, a full-sized five-inch weapon with a preloaded DAO trigger. Only 146 units were made. The slightly shorter model M1086 was much more popular. Unfortunately, no alloy-framed 10mm pistols were made.

The M4506 was developed from the M645 pistol, which was good but not very reliable. The M4506 I own has never malfunctioned. The M4506 weighs the same as the standard Colt Government Model. The M4506 has three safeties. A firing pin safety keeps the weapon from firing unless the trigger is pulled. A magazine safety renders the weapon safe by merely withdrawing the magazine. This is useful for those who have their weapons within reach of children and inexperienced adults. Last, the slide safety on the Smith & Wesson M4506 is not particularly fast or convenient to use. Bumping it with the thumb when drawing is the technique that works best. Many people simply use the slide safety as a decocking lever. The SA pull is gritty and has much overtravel. The DA pull is heavy but constant. The more you shoot DA the better the pull becomes. Sights are nice and quick to pick up, offering a white dot on the front and two dots on the edge of the sight. The M4506 was designed for the person who wishes to have a very effective defense pistol in a caliber that delivers the goods. It is small and light enough to be carried totally concealed.

SMITH & WESSON M&P AUTO

Caliber: .45 ACP, .40 STW, .357 526, 9x19mm   **Manufacturer:** Smith & Wesson   **Typical Use:** Military and self-defense

Smith & Wesson designed the Military & Police (M&P) Auto to compete with the Glock pistol as a police and self-defense weapon. The Glock pistol is recognized as the world's best military pistol and the world's most reliable pistol. How, then, can the M&P best the Glock? Glock is, as a rule, unwilling to modify or change their pistol, believing it is perfect. Smith & Wesson will modify pistols to improve them. The Smith offers different size grips, fitting small to large hands. It is available with or without a magazine safety and you can get a manual safety. (Glock currently will not add a manual safety.) The slides on the Smith are more tapered and thinner, making holstering easier. Both share excellent metal finishes and are about the same weight. The Smith offers a superior field-stripping system; it does not have to be snapped before it can be stripped. This avoids negligent shootings for you cannot strip the Smith without the magazine out and the slide back. Also, if the shooter wants a .45 ACP weapon, the Smith has a thinner slide and grip, so suitable for the average hand. It holds only ten rounds (thirteen for the Glock), but extension magazines of fourteen rounds are available. Due to the cotton tampon that must be inserted into the trigger spring to avoid breakage from vibration and metal fatigue, the M&P is not as reliable as the Glock. This tampon will get wet, causing the spring to rust and break. You can avoid this issue by paying attention to it. If you tend to be careless about maintenance, a Glock is a better choice.

SMITH & WESSON M351

Caliber: .22 Rimfire Magnum   **Manufacturer:** Smith & Wesson   **Typical Use:** Military and self-defense

The M351 is a two-inch J-frame revolver with fixed sights. Made of scandium with an alloy cylinder resulting in an extremely light revolver at ten ounces, it is a rarity in that it is chambered for the .22 Rimfire Magnum cartridge, holding seven rounds in its cylinder. The M351 loaded stays light due to the lightweight cartridges, unlike other lightweight weapons. The M351 utilizies the Rimfire Magnum cartridge; while it is loud and has some muzzle flash, it produces very little felt recoil, so is pleasant to shoot. The cartridge delivers stopping power well in excess of what its diminutive size and weight suggest. You may need to return the M351 to get it properly zeroed, as I did. Once this is done, the revolver hits to point at twenty five yards with a good, wide ramp front sight and a wide enough rear notch to allow good work in dim light. I could get six-inch groups for ten shots at twenty five yards with mine, which I believe establishes that this is a serious weapon. It is a DA/SA trigger weapon. Due to the issues with reliable ignition with rimfire ammo, the trigger pull will be heavier than desirable, but as long as it is smooth with little overtravel, it is worth it. The M351 in a good side-pocket holster is, I believe, about the best jacket side-pocket revolver. One caveat: it is so light you may forget to take it out of your jacket.

ROCKY MOUNTAIN ARMS MINI REVOLVER

Caliber: .22 Rimfire   **Manufacturer:** Rocky Mountain Arms   **Typical Use:** Self-defense

The Rocky Mountain Arms Mini Revolver is a small five-shot .22 Rimfire revolver that works in SA mode only. Extremely small in size and lightweight despite its stainless steel construction, it is simply "cute." Men will buy them for their ladies for that reason, and the fact that they are small enough to fit in a small purse. Small .22 revolvers are not new—Sears catalogs from the late-1890s feature similar weapons, although not as well made. Shooting one is quite surprising. Because they are so small it is quite easy to get your hand in front of the muzzle. This is exacerbated by a lack of leverage. This and a heavy mainspring make cocking the hammer difficult. As a result the muzzle tends to move a lot. Once cocked the trigger pull is crisp and short. Recoil is remarkably high even when held in a firm grip. While the weapon has a front sight and can be aligned properly, it is not zeroed accurately, thus holding off is needed. Instinctive shooting is best. Repeat shots are slow due to pistol movement in the grip and the heavy cocking effort needed. This is clearly not a serious defense weapon.

AMERICAN DERRINGER PEN GUN

Caliber: .25 ACP, .22 Rimfire   **Manufacturer:** American Derringer Company   **Typical Use:** Self-defense

Per US federal law, weapons that look like pens or pencils can only be sold in the United States by paying a $5 transfer tax, awaiting the government to issue a "permission slip," and then subjecting them to NFA restrictions. As a consequence, the American Derringer Company designed a single-shot weapon, available in both .25 ACP and .22 Rimfire, that looks like a pen gun subject to the tax, but it is not. The design is such that it must be twisted and a portion of the weapon bent downward. A spur trigger is exposed which can be depressed to fire while your hand grabs the downward projecting part of the weapon. Once fired it can again be twisted and returned to its cylindrical pen-gun shape. It is very clever, but slow to operate, single shot, and small caliber; a pretty marginal weapon. Recoil is surprisingly high and, since it lacks sights, you are reduced to instinctive pointing. At three yards it is not particularly accurate, at least at hitting a small target, and worthless beyond 10 yards. One assumes it is intended for close range use only.

COLT DELTA 10MM

Caliber: 10mm **Manufacturer:** Colt **Typical Use:** Military and self-defense

The 10mm cartridge was developed around 1980 and originally made for the Bren 10 pistol, but that weapon died on the vine. Colt saved the cartridge when they chambered their famous Government Model for it. Some slight design changes resulted in a very fine pistol in 10mm. The 10mm cartridge is a much higher pressure cartridge than the .45 ACP and yields more power than the .45 ACP. Not all 10mm cartridges are the full-power loads (within 10 percent of .41 Magnum power levels) but the Colt pistol will accept those as well as the lower-power subsonic loads. The 180 grain subsonic or FBI loads are pleasant to shoot and the full-power loads are clearly more pleasant to shoot than similar level .41 Magnum loads. After Ed Brown modified my Colt Delta to include good Bo-Mar sights and Bar-Sto barrel, I found the 10mm cartridge to be inherently accurate. The Series 80 safety system will start malfunctioning when it gets dirty from powder and lead residue. Replacing it with the parts kits Brownell sells to modify Series 80 weapons to Series 70 or standard-style weapons solves the problem. With high-power loads, whether the Corbin 135 JHP load, the 175 grain Silver tips, or the two hundred grain full-power load, at 1200 fps, the muzzle flip is a bit aggressive. With practice, one can control this and get a second shot off more quickly than with similar power level revolvers.

This fourth-generation Smith & Wesson is unique and useful. It is designed to be carried in a pocket or on the ankle and offers good stopping power against human assailants. It is superior to the J frame in many ways. It holds eight rounds, including a round in the chamber, of 9x19mm ammo. It has greater stopping power, is easier to use, and more pleasant to shoot than a J frame. The magazine release is a side-mounted system; the shooter must pinch the indented area to relieve the tension and remove the magazine. While too slow for a holster weapon, this is ideal for a pocket pistol. The trigger system is DAO, safe for pocket carry. There are no external manual safeties, so nothing to forget or to have accidentally applied as it rides in your pocket. The weapon is narrow which helps it fit into traditional trouser pockets and lay flat. The slide, no thicker than the frame, makes it somewhat harder to rack. The stiff spring of the blowback action requires will ease up with use. The sights on the pistol are a simple groove in the rear of the slide coupled with a low bump on the front. They were difficult to see on the indoor range. Worse, the weapon was sighted to fire very low, and it was hard to keep the sights centered at twenty five yards. However, most uses of this weapon would not require the sights. When tested at seven yards, I could place five rounds of Federal 115 grain +P+ ammo into a group the size of a half dollar, but could barely keep the rounds on a man-sized target at twenty five yards. The heavy trigger pull made it difficult to get the same position at discharge every time and poor sights made it difficult to ascertain small sighting errors. As a pocket carry and, to an extent, ankle carry self-loading pistol, there are few serious competitors to the Smith & Wesson 9mm.

KAHR 9MM

Caliber: 9mm   **Manufacturer:** Kahr Arms, Worcester, MA   **Typical Use:** Military and self-defense

New in 1995, the KAHR 9mm looks like a Glock 17 that has shrunk by about 20 percent. It has a steel frame and weighs twenty five ounces, one ounce heavier than a Glock 17. The Kahr has a single-column magazine capacity of eight rounds instead of a double-column magazine. Grips are made of a rubber-like substance that feels good in the hand. Due to the heavy recoil spring fitted to the weapon, pulling the slide rearward is difficult. Felt recoil is high. Trigger pull on the Kahr 9, again like the Glock 17, is good and becomes lighter and smoother with use. The sights also looked like Glock 17 sights and were good in dim light. They were quick on pick up and accuracy was quite acceptable at twenty five yards. The magazine release is conveniently placed, but the magazine itself appears to be weak. The plastic floorplate broke at the five hundred–round mark, causing the spring to be launched and never found. Is there any place for the Kahr 9? It is smaller and thinner than the Glock 17, but heavier and recoils more. It is too heavy for an ankle holster and too large to conceal in a pocket. It is a decent weapon, but without much to make one choose it over the Glock 17.

Les Baer manufactures versions of the Colt Government Model. Les Baer pistols are well known for accuracy. The Premiere II is equipped with Bo-Mar-style adjustable sights to allow proper zeroing. This is a practical self-defense carry weapon. With a good trigger pull of around 3½ to four pounds, it is an accurate weapon capable of groups of 3 inches or so at fifty yards with good ammo. Most are chambered for the .45 ACP cartridge but are also found in .38 Super, 9x19mm, and rarely 9x23mm. The plain finish Premiere II is a rare 9x23mm model. It is a 1½-inch model: Les Baer certifies that it will shoot into 1½-inches at fifty yards, impressive. With its smaller bore, it is heavier than a .45 ACP model but the 9x23mm produces less felt recoil. It gives a shooter a ten-shot, full .357 Magnum power level weapon with low recoil, quick reloading, and wonderful accuracy. The Thunder Ranch model of Les Baer .45 Auto is similar to the Gunsight Service Pistol (GSP). This one sports a hard chrome version. It has good sights and trigger pull, with a slightly bigger safety and good accuracy. This is a fine belt gun for self-defense. The last Les Baer model combines the Les Baer top half and workmanship with a wide, double-column steel frame made by Para Ordnance. Created to fit the specs of the FBI Hostage Rescue Team, this is a highly accurate pistol suitable for precision shots, and has the high capacity desired. The inherent design issues with the Para Ordnance frames and the magazines create some issues. As long as they are maintained and working properly, they are excellent weapons although heavier and not as nimble as desired in a fighting pistol.

I own a number of Government Model-patterned .45 Auto pistols. But the ones I shoot most are my Springfield Armory Operators. The Springfield Operators illustrated here were from a group I ordered a few years back made to specifications. One of those specifications was that they had to group ten shots of Federal 230 grain Hydroshock ammo in three inches at fifty yards. Any pistol that will do that means that you should be able to get every round into the X ring of a standard twenty five yard bullseye target at that range. Anything outside it is you, the shooter, not the weapon or ammo. Fifty thousand rounds have gone through each of the pair I bought. I recently shot ten shots in two inches at twenty five yards, seven in the X ring off hand. Pretty fair shooting I would say. The Operator differs from the standard model in having a rail on the dust cover to mount lights, lasers, or other gee-whiz-type stuff on it. Good triggers are essential to good results in shooting and they are here, as well as good Bo-Mar adjustable sight, which I like since I find different loads and different range lighting conditions can shift the point of impact. A smooth finish was specified so all sharp edges are gone. A dual safety was specified so I could use the weapon with either hand, for I believe it important to know how and to practice shooting with both hands. Not as pretty as some of my .45s, not nearly as valuable, yet these Operators are likely the ones I shoot the most today.

GROVER'S NO. 5

Caliber: .44 Magnum   **Manufacturer:** Bill Grover   **Typical Use:** Self-defense

In the 1920s, Elmer Keith and others attempted to modify the Colt Single Action Army to make it a more useful, effective weapon. The result was the No. 5 made famous in Keith's article "The Last Word" in the 1927 *American Rifleman*. Many have made No. 5-type handguns since then, including the Ruger factory. Their version was called the Bisley model and was inexpensive. It was somewhat different but not better than Keith's model. Bill Grover was the Texas gun maker who specialized in western-style six-guns. In his Texas shop, he made many fine weapons in the Colt Single Action style. Bill admired Keith, and decided to make his improved version of the No.5. It was slightly bigger and stronger, chambered for the .44 Magnum cartridge. This makes it heavier and less nimble feeling. But more critically, he decided that the weapon should remain in the firing hand when being reloaded. You cannot do this with a typical Colt Single Action. With the Grover model, the loading gate and ejector rod housing are located on the left side, so everything needed to reload can be done with the weapon still firmly in the right hand. This is an excellent idea but difficult to get used to. It is an important modification and perhaps Keith would have approved, as his interest was to make the best weapon possible.

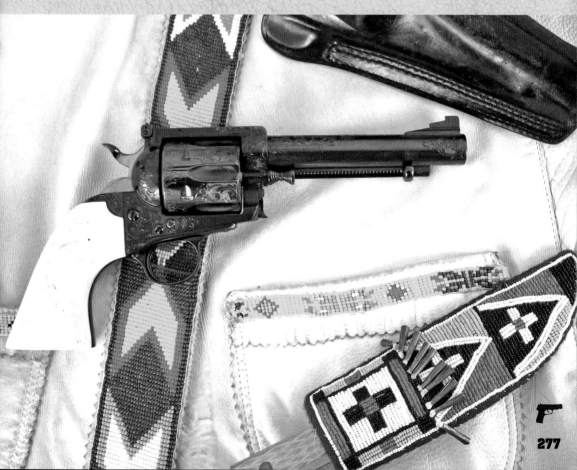

RUGER .475 LINEBAUGH

Caliber: .475/500 Linebaugh   **Manufacturer:** John Linebaugh, Cody, Wyoming modified Ruger Bisley
Typical Use: Protection from dangerous wild animals and hunting

John Linebaugh developed the .475 and .500 Linebaugh cartridges and the Magnum version of both loads. While the .44 Magnum properly loaded has killed every big game animal on the planet, it is still a bit light for some game and circumstances. Handgun hunters who recognize this tend to use large, single-shot handguns firing rifle length cartridges to overcome the issue. John Linebaugh believes your handgun should be accessible 24/7. He developed his loads knowing that penetration is essential, so basing power on weight and size will get you greater power on target consistently. A .475 Linebaugh with its 375-grain bullet at 1,200 fps is far superior to a .44 Magnum round with a 250 grain .429 bullet at the same velocity. This extra power generates strong recoil, but using the Bisley grip frame will moderate it. The cartridges are bigger than a .44 Magnum, so the cylinder now will contain only five rounds but that should be sufficient for most confrontations. A Ruger Bisley revolver rechambered for the .475 Linebaugh cartridge is not a beginner's weapon. Nor is it intended for target shooting or self-defense. The Ruger Bisley is meant to be worn on the belt for weeks on end as you hunt large game.

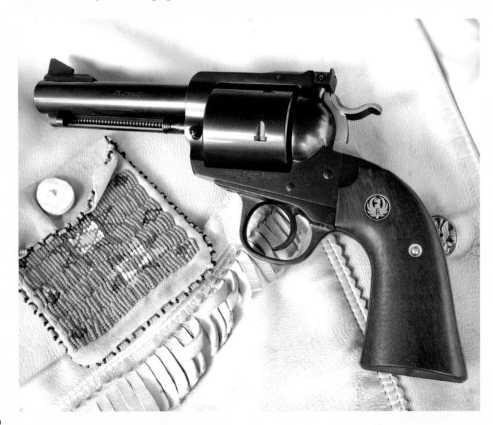

THOMPSON CONTENDER

Caliber: Multiple Chamberings, tested in .22RF **Manufacturer:** Thompson/Center Arms **Typical Use:** Sporting

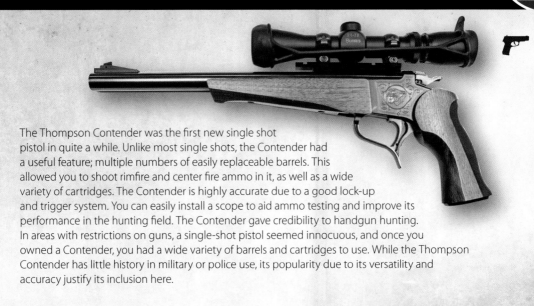

The Thompson Contender was the first new single shot pistol in quite a while. Unlike most single shots, the Contender had a useful feature; multiple numbers of easily replaceable barrels. This allowed you to shoot rimfire and center fire ammo in it, as well as a wide variety of cartridges. The Contender is highly accurate due to a good lock-up and trigger system. You can easily install a scope to aid ammo testing and improve its performance in the hunting field. The Contender gave credibility to handgun hunting. In areas with restrictions on guns, a single-shot pistol seemed innocuous, and once you owned a Contender, you had a wide variety of barrels and cartridges to use. While the Thompson Contender has little history in military or police use, its popularity due to its versatility and accuracy justify its inclusion here.

SMITH & WESSON M500 "ROSS 500"

Caliber: 500 S&W **Manufacturer:** Smith & Wesson **Typical Use:** Hunting and self-defense

When Smith & Wesson announced a new X-frame revolver chambered for the 500 S&W Magnum cartridge, my good friend, John Ross, was excited. He likes big-bore revolvers and shooting heavy bullets at high velocity. John bought a few of the first M500 revolvers and started load development. He discovered it really would not take the really heavy, 750 grain bullets he liked—too slow in the twist. I complained about the weight and appearance. Together we decided that with a few modifications, it would be a lot better as a practical revolver. John put his money where his mouth was; Smith & Wesson agreed to make the modifications if he ordered five hundred of them. So the order went in and resulted in the best M500 ever made. The Ross M500 is a much more practical, nimble feeling weapon. The main differences are: 1. Five-inch barrel and only half lug—no bulky heavy underlug; 2. No ugly loud compensator; 3. Barrel twist suitable for heavy bullets up to 750 grains; 4. Black finish on barrel and frame on 250 of the 500 purchased for variety.

The SIG P290RS is a single-column magazine, DA only, 9x19mm pistol. It offers excellent accuracy, good sights, and is small enough to carry in a pants-pocket holster. This makes a great combination. Most pistols this size are only .380 in power. For these reasons it is far superior to other weapons of this type. The SIG P290RS, with its hammer-fired DA pull, can be safely carried in the pants pocket, holstering it while your thumb holds the hammer down, which prevents snagging it. A DAO trigger means you need not worry about disengaging the safety prior to firing. With a thin, flat profile, it will fit flush into the pocket, and hold six rounds. It won't shoot through your pocket like a hammerless revolver but unless you need that, the SIG P290RS is a superior choice. In the last twenty or so years, the autoloading pistol has effectively replaced the revolver as a duty weapon in law enforcement and to a great degree in the self-defense sector. As a backup weapon, the small, DA .38 Special is still popular. The SIG P290RS solved almost all problems found in the snub-nosed .38 Special. It is so superior that it may in fact replace the revolver in the future except for use in ankle and coat-pocket carry.

The SIG 516P exists because the US law imposes a serious tax on weapons designed to be fired from the shoulder when the barrel, if rifled, is under sixteen inches. The SIG 516P is based on an AR15 action and thus, has a buffer tube. This buffer tube offers an advantage as it can be used to help support the weapon upon firing. But, most critically, the SIG 516P is not designed to be shot off the shoulder. Due to the low recoil of the weapon, you can shoot from the shoulder, and it helps to maintain sight index alignment. When you shorten the barrel on the typical AR15 rifle, the direct gas impingement system impairs functioning. With a piston system, you avoid this problem. The 516P also offers different gas ports so you can adjust the weapon to the level of gas found in different ammunition. The SIG 516P is offered in two barrel lengths and I prefer the 7½-inch model. Coupled with a good white light to illuminate targets, an Aimpoint red dot scope, and one of the new sixty- or one hundred-round Surefire magazines, it makes for a very handy, practical home defense handgun. It is comparable to short barrel rifle versions of the same design, and you do not have to pay the tax.

DOUBLE TAP DERRINGER

Caliber: .45 ACP; 9x19mm   **Manufacturer:** Helzer Arms   **Typical Use:** Self-defense

The Double Tap Derringer is a weapon that has no value or purpose. Chambered for either the .45 ACP or 9x19mm cartridge, the weapon holds two rounds and weighs more than an alloy J-frame Smith & Wesson revolver. It can be shot through your pocket without fear of tying it up, but so can certain Smith & Wesson or Colt revolvers. While the .45 ACP cartridge offers greater stopping power, the five-shot Smith & Wesson with good loads will equal or better it. The sights on the Double Tap are almost impossible to see. While you would not use sights if shooting through your pocket, you would need them in many situations. Trigger pull with the weapon is both heavy and long, and the pull varies from one shot to the next. The two barrels each strike a substantially different point on a target. It seems the manufacturer made no attempt to align the barrels. The grip is terrible with a major bump at the rear, which painfully pounds the palm of your hand each time you fire.

The first Seecamp pistol effectively rendered single-action autoloaders obsolete as pocket guns. Seecamp pistols were expensive and hard to find, though, and the market responded with the Kel Tec P.32 and P.380, later. The Kel Tec was slighter larger than the Seecamp but lighter thanks to its polymer-shell construction. The pistol uses belt clips to help station itself on various positions of your clothing, and can be attached from either side. The Seecamp has no sights. The Kel Tec has sights, and they are small enough to avoid snagging. It has a side-button release. Some like this, but it can lead to dumped magazines. The hammer is visible and lends weight to the firing pin strike. The trigger guard is a bit small for people with large hands. The butt is short, but given the power of the cartridge, controlling the pistol is no big challenge. Pistols of this type are to be shot in magazine-capacity burst. With practice, you can match the effectiveness of a single load of twelve-gauge buckshot. Accuracy, both inherent and practical, is good. Recoil on the .32 version is reasonable while the .380 is clearly greater. While I normally prefer larger calibers, here I believe the .32 ACP is the better choice.

The Thompson is easily the most recognized SMG shape in the world. The Thompson SMG comes in a variety of models made by several manufacturers, and quality varies. The earliest models, the M1921 and M1921/8, were beautifully made in 1920 and 1921 by the Colt Firearms Company. The M1921 and the M1921/8 are the same except for cyclic rate: the M1921 shoots at 850 to 950 rpm; the later model shoots about 200 rpm less. They both come with or without a Cutts Compensator. While this device may not be worthwhile, it adds a distinctive look to a Thompson. The butt stock is wood but is readily detachable. This causes some wobbling and, the drop in the stock is much greater than it should be for best results on full-auto fire. The rear grip on the Thompson is quick, handy, and because it is wood, comfortable even in very cold weather. The Thompson's safety, selector system, and magazine release are all set up for the right-handed shooter. The early versions of the Thompson—the M1921, M1921/8, and M1928—all accept fifty- and one hundred-round drums. These drums were awkward to carry, noisy, and soon disappeared. Early stick magazines were only twenty-shots, which proved too few. The standard soon became the thirty-round magazine. The Thompson comes with two types of forearms and two styles of barrels. Early weapons had the vertical foregrip with a pistol-style grip and a finned barrel, with or without a Cutts Compensator. Such grips tend to break easily. The horizontal forearm was designed to avoid this issue. The caliber and weight of the Thompson SMG are drawbacks. The ammo is heavy and lacks penetration. All Thompsons are heavy; loaded, you have a ten-pound-plus weapon. It is simply too much weight for too little benefit. Still they are neat and every red-blooded American boy wants a Tommy gun, don't they?

In the early days of World War II, when US forces were critically short of weapons of all types, the Reising SMG appeared. It did not have totally interchangeable parts. If you did not get your weapon's exact parts back, it might not work. The Reising M50, as well as its folding-stock brother the M55, fires from a closed bolt, although it is a retarded blowback-locking-system weapon, which makes it easier to shoot accurately. Unfortunately to cock the weapon, you must insert a finger into the groove in the bottom of the stock and pull the action bar to the rear, a slow and uncertain process. The safety selector is at the rear of the receiver area and the shooter must move his hand from the firing position to shift it, a slow and unreliable procedure. The stock is one piece, solid wood, and feels good while shooting. The rear peep sight is good if not very well protected. The front sight is hard to see and not protected from damage. The barrel has unnecessary cooling fins on it. Twelve-shot and twenty-shot magazines were furnished. The twelve-shot was totally unsatisfactory and the twenty-shot was not much better. The Reising went out of use in the military as soon as more dependable SMGs were available, although they were seen in police arsenals for the next fifty years.

Looking at it from today's vantage point, we can see that the submachine gun was a technological dead end. But in early 1941, that was not obvious. What was obvious was that the Thompson SMG was too expensive to make efficiently and too long and heavy for combat use. When you hold a loaded M3 in your hand, it feels quite heavy and rather dead. The sights on the M3 consist of a fixed ramp-style front, which is integral with the receiver, and a fixed peep rear. To load the weapon, you insert the magazine in the small, non-flared magazine well. This is slow. The magazines are a serious problem because they are single feed, a design that by its very nature is subject to malfunctions. The magazine is difficult to load beyond fifteen or so rounds without a loading tool. Like most SMGs, the M3 fires from an open bolt. The dust cover operates as a safety on the M3 and M3A1. With the dust cover closed, the projection on it prevents the rearward movement of the bolt. Opening the dust cover allows you to cock the weapon. The M3 has a cocking handle on the right side. On the simpler M3A1, you pull it firmly to the rear with your finger. The stock on the M3/M3A1 is a simple wire unit and not very stable. The M3/M3A1 is made entirely of metal. You are supposed to hold on to the magazine housing when shooting with the M3/M3A1. Be sure to hold the housing, not the magazine. The barrel on the M3/M3A1 screws out easily, allowing full access to the weapon and bolt system for cleaning those parts and the barrel. Perhaps its best feature is its low cyclic rate. Because of its very heavy bolt, the cyclic rate with typical .45 ACP, standard 230-grain, full-metal-jacket ammo is between 350 and 450 rpm. This allows the shooter to fire single shots easily even though there is no selector on the weapon. More critically, it allows you to fire a long, very accurate burst. Except for its low cyclic rate aiding control, the M3/M3A1 really does nothing better than any other weapon of similar blowback design.

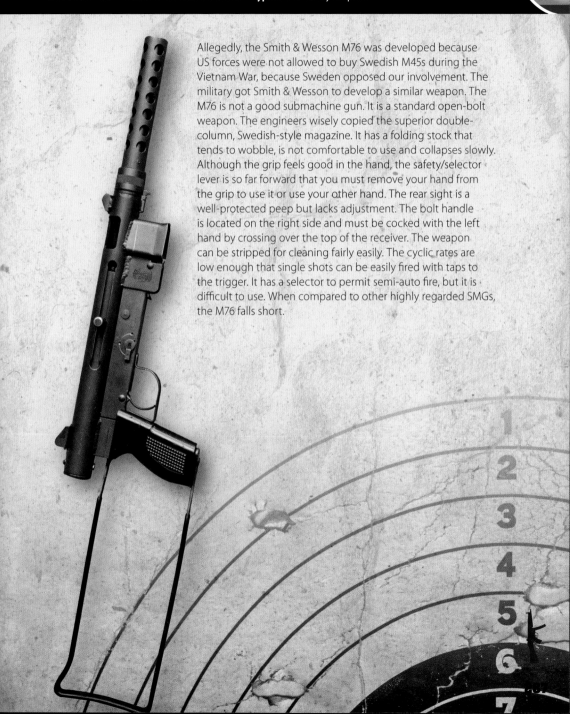

SMITH & WESSON M76

Caliber: 9x19mm   **Manufacturer:** Smith & Wesson   **Typical Use:** Military and police

Allegedly, the Smith & Wesson M76 was developed because US forces were not allowed to buy Swedish M45s during the Vietnam War, because Sweden opposed our involvement. The military got Smith & Wesson to develop a similar weapon. The M76 is not a good submachine gun. It is a standard open-bolt weapon. The engineers wisely copied the superior double-column, Swedish-style magazine. It has a folding stock that tends to wobble, is not comfortable to use and collapses slowly. Although the grip feels good in the hand, the safety/selector lever is so far forward that you must remove your hand from the grip to use it or use your other hand. The rear sight is a well-protected peep but lacks adjustment. The bolt handle is located on the right side and must be cocked with the left hand by crossing over the top of the receiver. The weapon can be stripped for cleaning fairly easily. The cyclic rates are low enough that single shots can be easily fired with taps to the trigger. It has a selector to permit semi-auto fire, but it is difficult to use. When compared to other highly regarded SMGs, the M76 falls short.

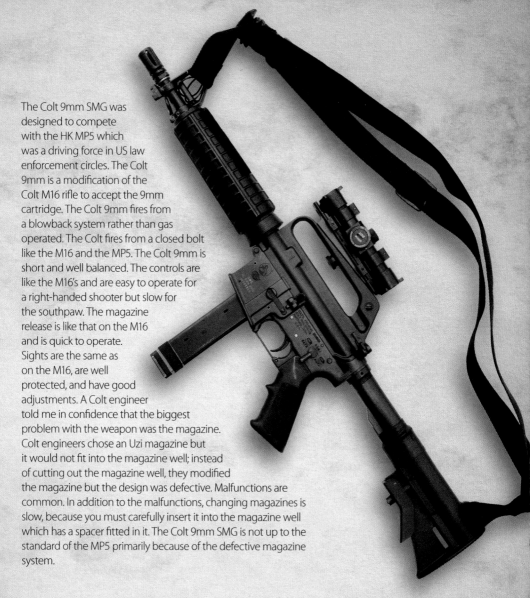

The Colt 9mm SMG was designed to compete with the HK MP5 which was a driving force in US law enforcement circles. The Colt 9mm is a modification of the Colt M16 rifle to accept the 9mm cartridge. The Colt 9mm fires from a blowback system rather than gas operated. The Colt fires from a closed bolt like the M16 and the MP5. The Colt 9mm is short and well balanced. The controls are like the M16's and are easy to operate for a right-handed shooter but slow for the southpaw. The magazine release is like that on the M16 and is quick to operate. Sights are the same as on the M16, are well protected, and have good adjustments. A Colt engineer told me in confidence that the biggest problem with the weapon was the magazine. Colt engineers chose an Uzi magazine but it would not fit into the magazine well; instead of cutting out the magazine well, they modified the magazine but the design was defective. Malfunctions are common. In addition to the malfunctions, changing magazines is slow, because you must carefully insert it into the magazine well which has a spacer fitted in it. The Colt 9mm SMG is not up to the standard of the MP5 primarily because of the defective magazine system.

The Winchester M97 repeating shotgun was the weapon that made the ten-gauge shotgun obsolete as a combat weapon. During World War I, the M97 was militarized by putting a ventilated handguard that incorporated a bayonet lug on it. Both were good ideas for trench warfare.

The M97 has a bead front sight and mere receiver groove as the rear, adequate for short ranges. The only safety on the M97 is the half-cock notch. Additionally, to lower the hammer, you pull the trigger and carefully lower the hammer. To fire it, you must cock it manually and then pull the trigger. This is a method destined to cause accidental discharges, especially with wet or cold hands. The M97 also lacks a disconnector. If you hold back the trigger and rack the action, the weapon will fire as the slide is closed. The trigger guard is small, making it difficult to put a gloved finger through it. The stock angle is low, which allows a greater felt recoil impulse and slows repeat shots. All buckshot-loaded shotguns lack effective range and penetration. A shotgun should be able to place a load of buckshot on a man-target up to thirty five yards in a twelve-gauge with current ammo. At seventy five yards, even with 00 buck, the loads have very little penetration. Even acknowledging the design drawbacks, the M97 is an effective combat shotgun.

M12 WINCHESTER 12-GAUGE

Caliber: 12-gauge   **Manufacturer:** Winchester   **Typical Use:** Military, police, self-defense and hunting

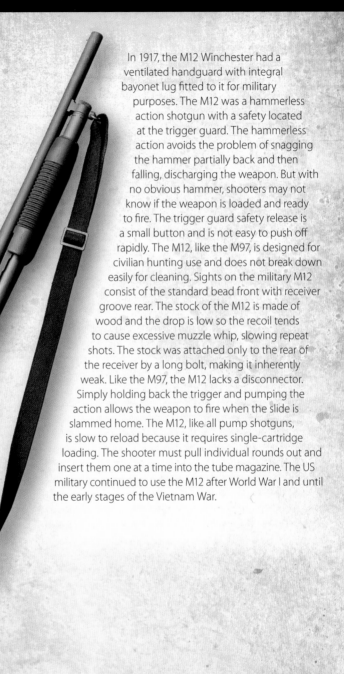

In 1917, the M12 Winchester had a ventilated handguard with integral bayonet lug fitted to it for military purposes. The M12 was a hammerless action shotgun with a safety located at the trigger guard. The hammerless action avoids the problem of snagging the hammer partially back and then falling, discharging the weapon. But with no obvious hammer, shooters may not know if the weapon is loaded and ready to fire. The trigger guard safety release is a small button and is not easy to push off rapidly. The M12, like the M97, is designed for civilian hunting use and does not break down easily for cleaning. Sights on the military M12 consist of the standard bead front with receiver groove rear. The stock of the M12 is made of wood and the drop is low so the recoil tends to cause excessive muzzle whip, slowing repeat shots. The stock was attached only to the rear of the receiver by a long bolt, making it inherently weak. Like the M97, the M12 lacks a disconnector. Simply holding back the trigger and pumping the action allows the weapon to fire when the slide is slammed home. The M12, like all pump shotguns, is slow to reload because it requires single-cartridge loading. The shooter must pull individual rounds out and insert them one at a time into the tube magazine. The US military continued to use the M12 after World War I and until the early stages of the Vietnam War.

The Ithaca Auto Burglar is a double-barrel, small-frame, twenty-gauge shotgun with the barrels trimmed to ten to twelve inches (depending on the model) and equipped with a saw-handle pistol grip. A well-made weapon, it is hammerless. It has the typical top-lever release and safety system. Front sight consists of a small bead typical of the period but easily replaced with a larger "glo-worm type" that allows quicker pick up. Recoil is not excessive. Most models have double triggers but a single trigger could be fitted. The Auto Burglar was designed at a time when cars had become common, yet the roads were still dark and dangerous for the traveler before the 1934 National Firearms Act. This act taxed such weapons, and the tax was often ten times the value of the weapon, which put it out of reach for most people. In that brief, golden period, the weapon was often carried on the steering column so you were ready if attacked. You hold these weapons with both hands and fire from the high-hip position or thrust the weapon forward at the chin level, focusing on the throat. They are quite devastating at close range but limited, as reloading after two shots is quite time consuming.

ITHACA M37 13½-INCH 20-GAUGE

Caliber: 20-gauge   **Manufacturer:** Ithaca   **Typical Use:** Police, self-defense, hunting, and sporting

The combat shotgun should have the shortest barrel possible to make it more convenient inside buildings or cars. Due to the magazine tube system on most shotguns, you cannot make the barrel shorter than the muzzle tube. This, coupled with the US law which imposes tax and registration on barrel lengths less than eighteen inches, means that most combat shotguns will have eighteen-inch barrels. A thirteen- or fourteen-inch barrel, the length of a standard four-shot tube magazine, is preferable; twenty-gauge is better than twelve-gauge; twenty-gauge shotguns are more nimble to use and the shotgun cartridge gets its power and usefulness from the size and number of pellets not by the gauge. A twenty-gauge shoots pellets the same size and velocity as a twelve-gauge, only it shoots fewer of them. The only effect is to reduce the range by 5 yards. The M37 Ithaca shotgun is a fairly lightweight, reliable weapon. It loads from the bottom, making it easier to use with either hand. The safety is somewhat small. If carried in "cruiser ready" position (magazine tube loaded, chamber empty), you can operate it fairly quickly and you get four certain rounds of No. 3 buckshot. Such loads are effective up to twenty five yards. The action on the M37 is quick and the light recoil of the twenty-gauge allows rapid work.

REMINGTON .22 SMOOTH-BORE SHOTGUN

Caliber: .22 Rimfire   **Manufacturer:** Remington   **Typical Use:** Sporting

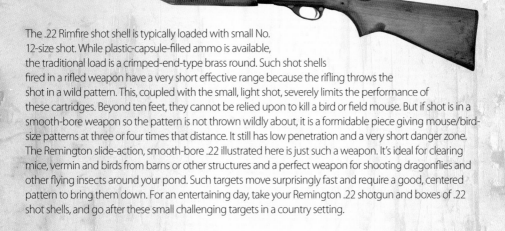

The .22 Rimfire shot shell is typically loaded with small No. 12-size shot. While plastic-capsule-filled ammo is available, the traditional load is a crimped-end-type brass round. Such shot shells fired in a rifled weapon have a very short effective range because the rifling throws the shot in a wild pattern. This, coupled with the small, light shot, severely limits the performance of these cartridges. Beyond ten feet, they cannot be relied upon to kill a bird or field mouse. But if shot is in a smooth-bore weapon so the pattern is not thrown wildly about, it is a formidable piece giving mouse/bird-size patterns at three or four times that distance. It still has low penetration and a very short danger zone. The Remington slide-action, smooth-bore .22 illustrated here is just such a weapon. It's ideal for clearing mice, vermin and birds from barns or other structures and a perfect weapon for shooting dragonflies and other flying insects around your pond. Such targets move surprisingly fast and require a good, centered pattern to bring them down. For an entertaining day, take your Remington .22 shotgun and boxes of .22 shot shells, and go after these small challenging targets in a country setting.

HI-STANDARD MODEL 10B

Caliber: 12 gauge   **Manufacturer:** Hi Standard   **Typical Use:** Police and self defense

The Hi-Standard M10B is based on the civilian auto-loading shotgun but it has been placed in a synthetic bullpup-style stock which makes the weapon much more suitable for police use. It is impossible to shoot it from the left shoulder. The M10B developed from the 10A, which had the flashlight in the handle of the shotgun. The M10B keeps the height of the weapon to a minimum. A flashlight can be screwed into place for illumination. The M10A and B both used a pistol grip with a push-button safety, convenient to both apply and disengage. The weapon is cocked by pulling the cocking handle to the rear, and it is awkwardly placed. The standard M10A and B models have a four-shot tube magazine. Sights on the M10A and B are rather rudimentary. The rear butt plate was a piece of coated metal which swiveled. The design allowed you to place the brace sideways on your arm and shoot it. Very uncomfortable. The M10A and especially the M10B reflect a real attempt to address the needs of a serious fighting shotgun.

293

USAS 12-GAUGE

Caliber: 12-gauge   **Manufacturer:** Daewoo   **Typical Use:** Police

The USAS 12-gauge was made specifically for the police rather than developed from an existing sporting weapon. It is a selective-fire shotgun that looks a lot like an M16 rifle. The pistol grip, safety/selector, and magazine release are identical. The USAS 12-gauge uses either ten-shot magazine or a drum magazine that holds twenty rounds. The ten-shot magazine is more comfortable to use and carry. The sights are not sophisticated, consisting of a post front and an adjustable peep rear. The cocking handle is located on the front left side. The USAS 12 appears to be very reliable selective-fire shotgun. The recoil is light due to its straight-line stock and weight. The light recoil and low cyclic rate meant that I could fire two-shot bursts by trigger manipulation only. But I could only make the first round hit the man-target. Using a USAS 12 on semi-auto only would provide better results and little loss in speed. The USAS 12 is so large I found it very awkward to use. It does not mount rapidly so tracking a target is difficult.

The single-shot M1873 has proven itself rugged and has sufficient power to disable an attacker. Years of developing loads and sights gave this weapon good accuracy. The M1873 Springfield rifle was designed for foot troops and the carbine for cavalrymen. The carbine shot a load of a 405-grain bullet and 55 grains of powder; the rifle shot the 500-grain bullet backed by 70 grains of black powder. The front sight on both is difficult to see except in excellent light. The rear sight is a very involved unit that allows the shooter to use the rifle at extremely long ranges. Both rifle and carbine lack a top handguard. The stocks on both weapons are good, solid wood and have thick wrists, helpful in avoiding repairs. Both rifles have solid, smooth-finished butt plates, which hold up well, but do allow more felt recoil. The distinguishing characteristic of the M1873 is the action. To load, cock the hammer to the half-cocked position, flip the catch, and the action will open like a door. Chamber a cartridge, slam the action closed, finish cocking the hammer, and pull the trigger to fire. The trigger pull is heavy and the hammer falls long and hard. The recoil is heavier than today's weapons, and if black powder is used, there is a big ball of smoke each time the weapon is fired.

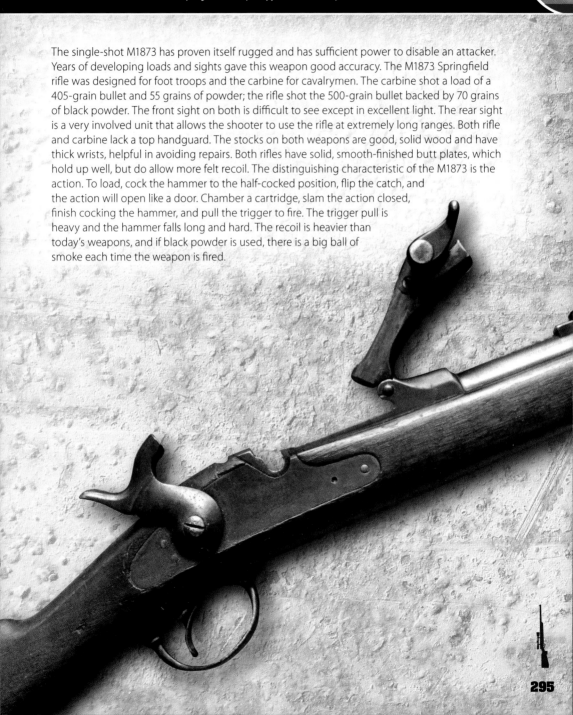

M94 WINCHESTER

Caliber: .30/30 (.38/55, .25/35, .32)   **Manufacturer:** Winchester   **Typical Use:** Sporting

The M94 Winchester is the iconic deer rifle in the United States. It is often called the "Thurty-Thurty" rather than by the actual model number. The .30 WCF (or .30/30) is the most popular chambering, but is available in other chamberings, and perhaps the best are .38/55 and .25/35. But the .32 caliber model is not bad if you insist on reloading with black powder. It is lightweight (at least the carbine version is) and well balanced, so carrying it while traveling over land is not major burden. It does not pretend to be a match rifle, although it is good enough for three- or four-inch groups at one hundred yards. Nor does it claim to be overly powerful, although many are the deer, moose, and other animals that have fallen to it. It's not easy to clean, but will still operate under rigorous conditions with little maintenance beyond wiping it off and running a patch down the bore. Most come with open buckhorn-style sights, but the more sophisticated users will typically install a peep unit and a flat-faced front sight. Millions of the weapons have been made in all sorts of variations, from long rifles with heavy barrels to nimble-feeling fourteen-inch short carbines. They are fairly inexpensive. There is good reason this weapon has been popular for over one hundred years.

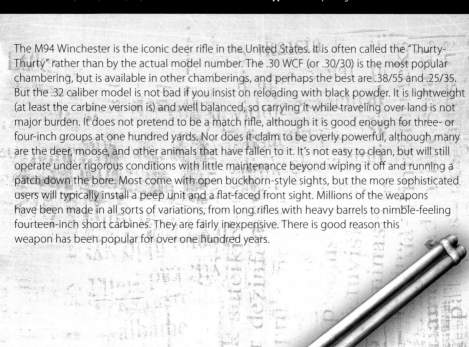

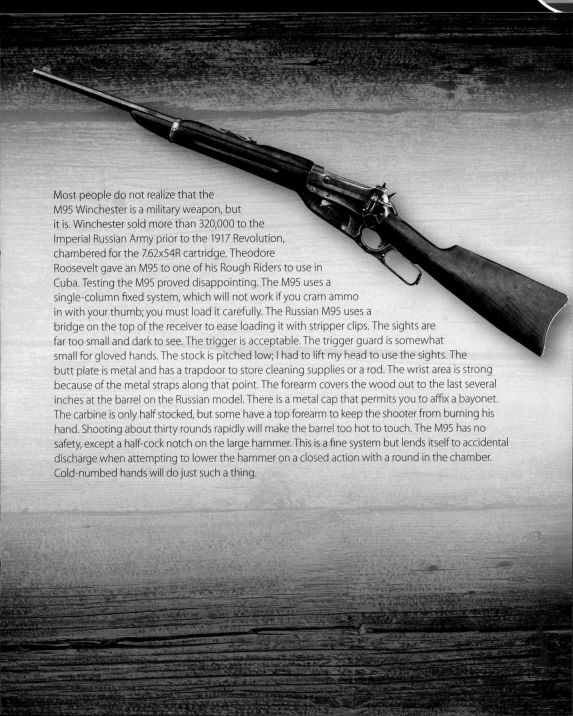

M95 WINCHESTER

Caliber: 7.62x54R, 30/40, 30'06, and others   **Manufacturer:** Winchester   **Typical Use:** Military

Most people do not realize that the M95 Winchester is a military weapon, but it is. Winchester sold more than 320,000 to the Imperial Russian Army prior to the 1917 Revolution, chambered for the 7.62x54R cartridge. Theodore Roosevelt gave an M95 to one of his Rough Riders to use in Cuba. Testing the M95 proved disappointing. The M95 uses a single-column fixed system, which will not work if you cram ammo in with your thumb; you must load it carefully. The Russian M95 uses a bridge on the top of the receiver to ease loading it with stripper clips. The sights are far too small and dark to see. The trigger is acceptable. The trigger guard is somewhat small for gloved hands. The stock is pitched low; I had to lift my head to use the sights. The butt plate is metal and has a trapdoor to store cleaning supplies or a rod. The wrist area is strong because of the metal straps along that point. The forearm covers the wood out to the last several inches at the barrel on the Russian model. There is a metal cap that permits you to affix a bayonet. The carbine is only half stocked, but some have a top forearm to keep the shooter from burning his hand. Shooting about thirty rounds rapidly will make the barrel too hot to touch. The M95 has no safety, except a half-cock notch on the large hammer. This is a fine system but lends itself to accidental discharge when attempting to lower the hammer on a closed action with a round in the chamber. Cold-numbed hands will do just such a thing.

KRAG M96

Caliber: 30/40   **Manufacturer:** Springfield Armory   **Typical Use:** Military and hunting

Around 1890, the US Army selected the Krag as its new magazine-fed rifle. It had two barrel lengths—long for infantry, shorter for cavalry—desirable at that time. The Krag has a slick action and a cartridge that is actually better than a .308 because it can take a 220-grain bullet. The Krag action has only a single-locking lug, so you must not use ammo that fires at the .30-06 level of pressure. The bolt handle is conveniently shaped and set at the proper angle. Its smooth finish is better for rapid work. The Krag uses a big box on the side, which some find bulky. To load, you open the box, place the rounds in one at a time, and then close the box. This allows you to load your rifle with a round still in the chamber. The Krag's action is its selling point; it is so slick, and no other rifle bests it. Even though this rifle was produced over a century ago, it is the standard other rifle actions are judged by. The stock is solid, well-made wood with a wrist area thick enough to keep it from breaking. The trigger is a typical two-stage military pull and not light. The safety is a wing type located on the rear of the bolt and is slow to remove.

M1903 SPRINGFIELD

Caliber: .30-06 **Manufacturer:** Springfield Armory and others **Typical Use:** Military and hunting

Springfield M1903s come in a variety of models from the pre–World War I low-number models, prone to blowing up because of improper heat treatment, through the 1930s-vintage National Match guns, to the last World War II rush-production Remington-made 1903A4 with stamped parts and a two-groove barrel. Despite the variety, they all share certain features. Many people love the M1903 because it had sights that could be adjusted in very small increments for the target shooters and it was the first bolt-action rifle widely available to sportsmen. The trigger is a two-pull military trigger. The front sight on the M1903 is small and thin, protected by a hood. This allows accurate shooting on target bulls-eyes at extended ranges but makes it difficult to shoot the weapon accurately in the field. There is a magazine cutoff that allows the shooter to use the rifle as a single loader while reserving the five rounds in the magazine for an emergency. The safety on the M1903 is certain enough but very slow to disengage or engage. With most M1903s, the standard rear sights are much too difficult to see. The peep portion of the sight is so far forward that it is virtually unusable, and the open part is so fine that it takes too much time aligning it with the rear. The Springfield has a twenty four-inch barrel, which splits the traditional distance between a real carbine version (sixteen to twenty inches) and a rifle length (twenty eight to thirty one inches).

I wanted to test the 03A3 sniper rifle since I knew it did not have poor sights on the standard rifle. The scope, a Weaver unit, had simple crosshairs. Such crosshairs tend to get lost when it is dark. This is a poor choice for military snipers, who hope to gain shooting time at dawn and dusk by using a scope. Eye relief is acceptable, although the field of view is limited. (We must remember that telescopic sights have improved dramatically since 1945.) The 03A3 Sniper rifle has a standard trigger, which limits accuracy at distances. The safety is difficult to operate because the safety lever is too close to the scope tube. I assume most snipers ignore the safety. The rifle is heavy and slightly ill balanced for either off-hand or kneeling shooting. Shooting Federal Premium ammo, I found the groups disappointing; I could only get groups into 1½ inches at one hundred yards. The 03A3 sniper has many negatives, and clearly shows the United States did not lead the way during World War II in terms of good sniper rifles.

REMINGTON M8/81

Caliber: .25, .30, and .35 Remington   **Manufacturer:** Remington   **Typical Use:** Police, self-defense, and sporting

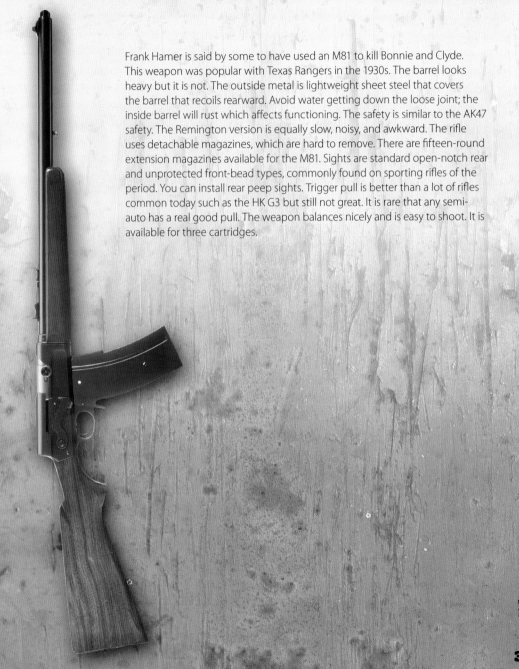

Frank Hamer is said by some to have used an M81 to kill Bonnie and Clyde. This weapon was popular with Texas Rangers in the 1930s. The barrel looks heavy but it is not. The outside metal is lightweight sheet steel that covers the barrel that recoils rearward. Avoid water getting down the loose joint; the inside barrel will rust which affects functioning. The safety is similar to the AK47 safety. The Remington version is equally slow, noisy, and awkward. The rifle uses detachable magazines, which are hard to remove. There are fifteen-round extension magazines available for the M81. Sights are standard open-notch rear and unprotected front-bead types, commonly found on sporting rifles of the period. You can install rear peep sights. Trigger pull is better than a lot of rifles common today such as the HK G3 but still not great. It is rare that any semi-auto has a real good pull. The weapon balances nicely and is easy to shoot. It is available for three cartridges.

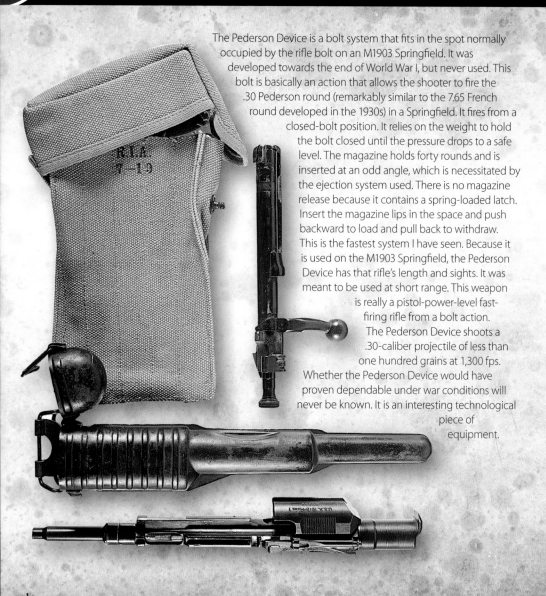

The Pederson Device is a bolt system that fits in the spot normally occupied by the rifle bolt on an M1903 Springfield. It was developed towards the end of World War I, but never used. This bolt is basically an action that allows the shooter to fire the .30 Pederson round (remarkably similar to the 7.65 French round developed in the 1930s) in a Springfield. It fires from a closed-bolt position. It relies on the weight to hold the bolt closed until the pressure drops to a safe level. The magazine holds forty rounds and is inserted at an odd angle, which is necessitated by the ejection system used. There is no magazine release because it contains a spring-loaded latch. Insert the magazine lips in the space and push backward to load and pull back to withdraw. This is the fastest system I have seen. Because it is used on the M1903 Springfield, the Pederson Device has that rifle's length and sights. It was meant to be used at short range. This weapon is really a pistol-power-level fast-firing rifle from a bolt action.

The Pederson Device shoots a .30-caliber projectile of less than one hundred grains at 1,300 fps. Whether the Pederson Device would have proven dependable under war conditions will never be known. It is an interesting technological piece of equipment.

M1 GARAND

Caliber: .30-06   **Manufacturer:** Springfield Armory, Winchester, Beretta, and others   **Typical Use:** Military

During World War II, the United States was the only army with a semi-auto rifle as its standard issue infantry weapon, the M1 Garand. The sights on the M1 Garand are good. The front is a blade, well protected by two heavy wings. The rear sight is an excellent peep sight, again well protected by wings, with plenty of adjustments. This sight is quick to use in poor light or on moving targets. The trigger pull on the M1 Garand is very good for a semi-auto rifle. Accuracy is good. The stock has a nice shape to it and offers a butt trap for cleaning supplies. The weapon can be quickly field stripped and the stock removed to allow maintenance to the action beneath the wood. The safety on the M1 is centrally located so the shooter can quickly disengage it with either hand. The bolt handle is located on the right, which makes it more difficult to cock for the left-handed shooter. The weakest feature of the M1 has always been its eight-shot capacity and the fact that you have to empty the weapon entirely to load it. You can reload quickly with M1 clips, but you still have the dilemma of first needing to empty the weapon. The M1 is heavy, rather ill balanced, and long when compared to an M1903. But it is lighter and more powerful than some M4 rifles used today.

M1 CARBINE (M1A1-M2)

Caliber: .30 Carbine   **Manufacturer:** Winchester, Inland, and others
Typical Use: Military, police, self defense, and hunting

In the early 1940s, the US Army adopted the M1 carbine. The M1 carbine is lightweight, easy to shoot, low in recoil, and reasonably accurate. It was the only weapon-cartridge combination of its day that used noncorrosive ammo, making maintenance easier. The front sight on the carbine is a nice-sized blade protected by sturdy ears. The rear sight is a rugged peep sight. Early models had a push-button safety and a push-button magazine release. Toward the end of the carbine's manufacture, the safety button was replaced by a switch or lever. The M1 carbine and its variants use a wood stock. The M1A1 carbine uses a folding stock and pistol grip. The carbine comes in two variations: the M1A1 and M2. The M1A1 is the standard version inserted in a folding stock developed for airborne use in World War II. Unless size is critica, the standard stock is better. In 1944, the selective-fire version, or M2, came out. The cyclic rate coupled with the recoil impulse and pitch of the stock did not make a very effective weapon. At twenty five yards the first round in the burst was good, the second round would hit the man-target, but the third round was off target. The best modification for the M1 carbine (or M2) is to put it in a folding stock, then chop off the barrel in front of the forearm. You shorten the weapon by six inches. The M1 cartridge lacks stopping power. The 110-grain, .30-caliber, round-hose bullets with thick metal jackets going 1,900 fps are not rifle cartridges. Light and handy, the M1 carbine is a fine piece of equipment, much better than many people are willing to admit.

The M4 carbine uses the standard flash hider and a 14½-inch barrel. It is fitted with the faster one-in-seven twist barrel to allow use of the new SS109 ammo and uses the new heavy barrel diameter in front of the sights, while offering the old M16-style tapered barrel under the fore end. This permits the mounting of the M203 on the M4 carbine. The rifle uses a tube-type sliding stock that can be adjusted to suit each shooter's reach. Otherwise, the M4 carbine is similar to the M16A2 rifle. It uses the same burst-fire mechanism, which makes good semi-auto work difficult, and the same replaceable-handle sighting system. The M4A1 offers semi- and full-auto only, the trigger pull is thus better. The sight radius on the M4 carbine is less than on the standard M16A2, and causes few sighting errors. Installing the Elcan or other optical unit solves any problem. The 5½-inch shorter barrel may cause velocity to suffer, but a good load should solve that. The sliding stock is subject to breakage. Because of the sliding stock, no cleaning rods are attached. The safety/magazine release and bolt device are standard M16 and they are handy and quick to use. The balance it good, but the weapon is slightly muzzle heavy, and does not feel lively.

With its factory-installed sixteen-inch barrel, this variation of the standard Marlin M336 rifle is very nimble. The test example was chambered for the .35 Remington cartridge, which is superior to the standard 30/30 model thanks to a larger and heavier bullet. Using a side-eject action, you can easily mount a scope on it for accuracy. You can mount a good peep sight on them of a style that is clearly click-adjustable and maintains its position, unlike some earlier peep units found on Winchester M94 rifles. No drilling of the receiver is needed either. It is a handy, well-balanced rifle, easy to carry in your hands for long distances. Accuracy has always been good with Marlins, and two- to three-inch, three-shot groups at one hundred yards when equipped with good sights are easy to achieve. Simple to maintain and rugged in construction, these are fine rifles and the Marlin Marauder in .35 Remington is the best variation of them all.

COLT COMMANDO

Caliber: 5.56x45mm   **Manufacturer:** Colt Firearms   **Typical Use:** Military, police, and self-defense

The Colt Commando is a ten-inch barrel version of the M4 rifle. The handguards are shorter and thinner. The butt stock and the sights are the same. As it is 4½ inches shorter than the M4, it is handier in vehicles. The shorter barrel lowers velocity, which is fine at close range since the velocity for the 5.56x45mm cartridge is still high, but past three hundred yards it may be problematic. The Commando's flash is greater, as is its report since more powder burns in the air. This is quite apparent when firing ammo without fire retardant in it. The Commando is a handy and nimble weapon. It balances nicely between my hands and does not seem muzzle heavy, so off-hand and kneeling shooting is easy. Equipped with an optical sight such as the Elcan, one can place shots just as well as with a longer barrel unit. While the noise and flash can be distracting when fired inside, outdoors it should not be an issue.

AR18 (AR-180)

Caliber: 5.56x45mm   **Typical Use:** Military, police, and self-defense
Manufacturer: ArmaLite Company; HOWA machine; and Sterling Arms

After developing the AR15, the ArmaLite Company decided to simplify the manufacture of the weapon and this became the AR18; the AR-180 is a semi-auto version. ArmaLite attempted to correct many of the design flaws of the AR15 and to make it cheaper and easier to manufacturer. They achieved their goals. The AR18 avoids the high sights and carrying handle of the AR15. This allows the shooter to get a faster sight picture. The front sight has a good set of wings to protect it and uses the same type of post found on the AR15. Adjustments are identical. The rear sight is well protected but, due to the knobs available, corrections are easier to make than on the AR15. Unlike the AR15, the AR18 has a traditional cocking handle. The AR18 has a safety/selector system that works from either side. The magazine catch on the AR18 is similar to the AR15. The magazine is the same as on the AR15 except for a small slot in the magazine that engages the catch. Magazines seem to stick in the magazine wall, which slows reloading. The stock is quite rigid when it locks open and can be opened or closed simply. The stock feels much more comfortable than tube-type stocks, and it gives you a more compact package. The handguard is more pleasing to use than the triangular handguards found on early AR15 rifles. The flash hider is similar to early AR15 rifles. The AR18/180 is a nice, light, well-balanced rifle. Original Costa Mesa weapons made by ArmaLite weapons proved to be reliable and accurate.

I don't think the Ruger Mini 14 series is as rugged as a true military weapon or as easy to maintain, but the AC 556K had a number of interesting features. The test example was equipped with a three-shot burst mechanism, in addition to semi- and full-auto. The safety is centrally located on the trigger guard, and the rate of fire is low enough that you can easily control it. Ruger lacks a metal liner to dispel heat in the handguard. The wood forearm gets very hot after rapid shooting of three or four magazines. The action is held in the stock with a barrel-clamping device which makes removal difficult and time consuming. A full cleaning will mean you need to re-sight the weapon. The front sight is poor. The rear sight is a good aperture design and readily adjustable but appears fragile. The magazine release is centrally located. I don't like folding stock rifles, but I found the tube broad enough and the recoil light enough that I did not find it painful to use. It locked up tight and solid. The short barrel on the AC 556K is equipped with a flash hider that seems to be fairly effective. The AC 556K is lightweight, quite handy, and lively feeling compared to other short-barrel 556 rifles tested, like the Galil SAR and HK 53.

AR15 .22 RIMFIRE CONVERSIONS

Caliber: .22 RF Long Rifle   **Manufacturer:** Various in United States   **Typical Use:** Military, police training, self-defense training

Any serious centerfire rifle or handgun should be accompanied by an identical version chambered for .22 Rimfire, in effect, an "understudy" weapon. Using the understudy, you must set up a course of fire for training that will duplicate the course of fire you use with your centerfire weapon. For rifles, you must use reduced-range targets, as the rimfire is more subject to wind effects and the trajectory is steeper. By using reduced-scale targets, you get the practice you need with your rimfire that is immediately transferrable to your centerfire rifle. The weapon illustrated is an understudy to a Colt Commando. It uses a .22 conversion kit to fire the round. With proper ammo, it will shoot into eight inches at two hundred yards so 10x14-inch plates at that distance are reasonable targets. Windy days will soon teach you to analyze the wind in the same way you need to at six hundred yards with your 5.56x45mm weapon. The illustrated weapon has a sound suppressor, so the shooter doesn't need muffs and hears the impacted plates when struck at two hundred or three hundred yards. Using a standard AR15 lower receiver, I get identical trigger pull, safety systems, and balance as my normal Commando. The understudy weapon gives inexpensive practice, which any serious shooter will appreciate.

NORRELL SEAR IN A RUGER 10/22

Caliber: .22   **Manufacturer:** John Norrell Inc.   **Typical Use:** Police, plinking, training

In my experience, everyone likes to fire machine guns. Even people who have never fired a weapon, and may not be "friendly" towards guns, get excited if you offer them the chance to shoot a Thompson or an Uzi. After all, it looks like so much fun on TV and in the movies! The major drawback to shooting machine guns is the price of ammo. Long, continuous bursts at 350–1,500 rpm will get pretty expensive even with the cheapest of surplus military ammo. This is when the John Norrell .22 Sear comes in. This device can be installed on a Ruger 10/22 rifle that will permit it to fire in semi-auto (pulling the trigger partially back)or full-auto mode at around 1,200 rpm (pulling the trigger completely to the rear). Coupling the 10/22 with magazines of twenty five–fifty round capacity, gives the pleasure of full-auto fire at fairly low cost with little noise or recoil. I have found non-shooters get quite a thrill out of firing this weapon. The hard-core tactical shooter will like it enough to try to figure out how he can justify purchasing one.

RUGER M10/77 SUPPRESSED

Caliber: .22 Long Rifle   **Manufacturer:** Ruger   **Typical Use:** Police, plinking, and hunting

The Ruger M10/77 bolt-action rifle is a fairly low-cost weapon, probably designed to meet the demands for an inexpensive plinking-grade rifle since Winchester and Remington abandoned that market. The Ruger Company realized that such rifles, often used for small game hunting, are exposed to hostile weather conditions, so they made the rifle entirely out of stainless steel with a nylon stock. The version modified by the Elite Iron Company from Montana is very interesting. They installed an integral suppressor that looks much like a bull barrel. Since it is not a solid barrel, the weapon remains lightweight. With a sixteen-inch barrel, it is well balanced and nimble. As the bolt-action rifle does not have any moving parts when it fires (unlike a semi-automatic rifle action), it is amazingly quiet. The weapon actually makes more noise when snapping on an empty chamber than it does when it fires an actual round. The lack of noise allows a shooter to fire his weapon in many more places than a louder weapon. You will quickly discover many potential uses, from eliminating urban pests to training beginning shooters who often find the noise disturbing. Nosy neighbors and gun haters will be blissfully ignorant of your actions as you rid your yard of squirrels. A problem avoided is better than a problem solved.

The Cricket .22, the quintessential first gun, is amazingly accurate thanks to the peep sight and fairly decent trigger. Hitting eight-inch plates at ninety yards off-hand is easy for adults, although you do have to squeeze up a bit on the stock due to its short length. The trigger pull is decent but the action is especially good for children. It is a single-shot bolt-action but it will not fire until you pull the cocking knob to the rear. The spring on that knob needs enough strength to almost guarantee that a young shooter will be old enough to understand the safety issues involved. Besides a stock that is suitable for short people, it is lightweight—2½ pounds—and thin enough that a child can hold it without straining or wobbling. Chambered for .22 long rifle, it can shoot everything shorter.

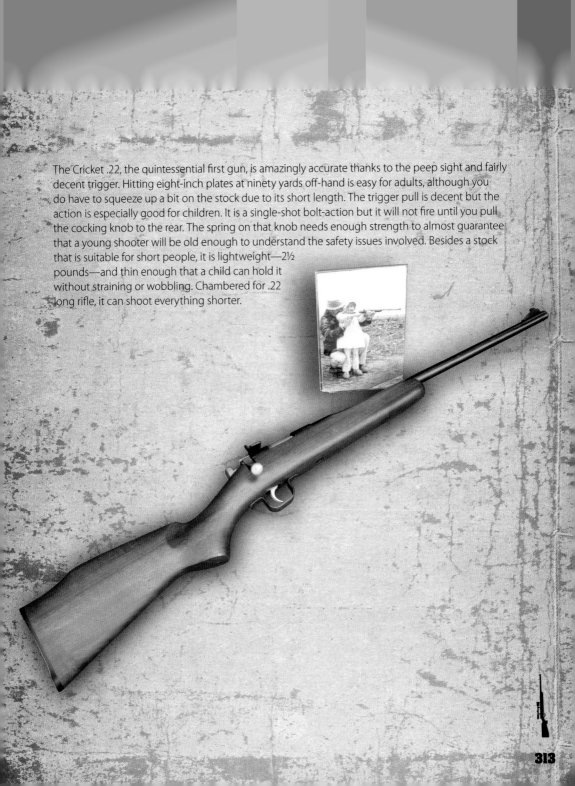

The stock is oddly shaped and difficult to use. The rear peep sight is very complicated; it includes an open-type notch as well as peep, so night use should be easier. The front sight is too dark. Loading the M1909 is a nightmare and gave it bad publicity. Pull the bolt to the rear then insert the stripper clip. The clips will insert in more than one way, but only one way is correct. Once properly loaded, the gun fired without any problems. Once you learn the trick, reloading with stripper clips is very fast. The safety is located on the end of the bolt handle, and it can be put into semi-auto as well as full-auto mode. The safety is easy to work, although you do have to take your hand off the firing position to operate it. The cyclic rate is low enough so that single shots are possible even on the full-auto position, and two- and three-shot bursts are easily accomplished. The weapon's weight and poor balance make it difficult to fire from the kneeling or off-hand position. The barrel gets very hot after firing a strip and a half. The weapon is also ill balanced side-to-side, shifting weight as stripper clips are fired.

The Browning Automatic Rifle (BAR) first appeared in the US armory in 1918. It met the requirements of all true infantrymen: it was reliable and hit a hard blow. The early BARs, with no bipod or monopod, weighed sixteen pounds, about seven pounds heavier than an M1903 or M1917. The BAR fired the same cartridge, had a twenty-shot capacity, much faster reloading, and the capability of firing in either semi-auto or full-auto mode. This represented a big advance at a small price in increased weight. The BAR fired from an open-bolt and the military version is quite long. Because of its weight, length, and open-bolt design, off-hand shooting is difficult. It is not an LMG: its 20-round magazine capacity is too low, and the barrel cannot be exchanged in the field. Later models do not have the semi-auto feature, but rather two rates of fire: the standard 650 rpm and the slower 350 rpm. The slow rate allows very good work. It is gas operated and when used with corrosive primers, common at the time it was introduced, calls for careful cleaning of the weapon. The sights on the BAR are adequate. The front sight is well protected and has a good-sized blade. The rear sight, also well protected, has a nice peep unit. The barrel is heavier than a standard rifle, but heats up rapidly. Firing three magazines quickly can cause burns to the hands if you're not careful. The cocking handle is on the left side, allowing the right-handed shooter to keep his hand on the grip. It is difficult to maintain control in long bursts because of the weapon's light weight in contrast to the cartridge fired. After firing the first round with the .30-06 guns, the peep sights seem to blur and are not helpful.

The Germans developed the light machine gun in the mid-1930s. It was a belt-fed weapon with a barrel that could be rapidly replaced when it got hot so the weapon could stay in action. It was light enough to be carried by one man, and shot off a bipod when utilized by one man or two. It could be installed on a tripod, offering a performance nearly equal to the water-cooled machine guns common at the time such as the Maxium 08, the Vickers, and Colt. The MG34 was the first example and by 1942, the stamped receiver M42 had been released and was even better. The US military had no such weapon. Our LMGs were either the BAR M1918, a box-fed, oversized-automatic rifle capable of full-auto fire, or the M1919 Browning, which was an air-cooled version of the water-cooled M1917. That weapon needed at least three men and a tripod to operate it. The US ordnance people attempted to compete with German weapons by using the M1919A6. This was the standard M1919 with the addition of a bipod on front and a butt stock behind. It is far too heavy and awkward and makes a very uncomfortable load on patrol. It is possible for one person to operate it, but that is rarely done. It offers no competition to the German guns.

COLT MONITOR MACHINE RIFLE

Caliber: .30-06   **Manufacturer:** Colt   **Typical Use:** Military and police

The Monitor was Colt Firearms Company's attempt to modify the Browning Automatic Rifle for police use during the Roaring Twenties. This was a full-auto, open-bolt, .30-06 heavy rifle that was also expensive; few were sold. The Colt Monitor has the same controls of a standard early-model BAR. It fires from an open bolt and fires semi- or full-auto. The safety is difficult to use due to the size of the grip and receiver. The barrel is shorter and lighter on the Monitor so you get greater muzzle blast and it heats up more rapidly than on the military pattern weapon. The Cutts compensator installed is huge, seems to reduce recoil, and gives the weapon its distinctive appearance. The Colt Monitor is heavy enough that firing off-hand is difficult. It does not feel lively in your hands. Sights are a blade front coupled with a peep sight that can easily be adjusted. Firing the Monitor is an interesting experience. But as a serious fighting weapon, it is a failure.

HEAVY MACHINE GUNS

Caliber: 45/70 **Manufacturer:** Richard J. Gatling Co. **Typical Use:** Military

I have heard that George Custer refused to take a Gatling gun with him to the Little Big Horn campaign. If you've never worked with one, you might fault Custer, but if you have, you might not criticize. The Gatling gun tested was a ten-barrel model in 45/70 chambering. Colt made this weapon, equipped with a sturdy wooden tripod and fed off box magazines. When the tripod is firmly placed and the gun locked down on it, the weapon fires just as quickly as you can revolve the crank. It can fire over 600 rpm, and even firing in a leisurely fashion was more than 300 rpm. It is very accurate; I could empty a magazine completely into a man-sized target at one hundred yards. Like real machine guns, the Gatling gun is not meant to be fired at an individual target, but this shows how effective the tripod and weapon mount are. The Gatling gun should be placed on each side of the battle line. The enemy has to cross this line to attack your soldiers. With luck (and a good cartridge like the 45/70), you will strike multiple enemy soldiers with a single round. The test weapon was beautifully made of brass and that, plus the multiple barrels and firing mechanism, made it quite heavy and awkward. The wooden tripod is also heavy. To feed the Gatling takes lots of ammo: on test day, we fired ten thousand rounds. The total weight an army would need to carry allows one to understand why Custer decided against using the Gatling Gun.

.50 BROWNING M2HB

Caliber: .50 Browning **Manufacturer:** Colt, AC Sparkplug, and others **Typical Use:** Military

This weapon defines the term heavy machine gun. Although the Soviet-designed 12.7mm and 14.5mm guns are its equal (or in the case of the 14.5mm, ballistically superior), both of these weapons are heavier and have a much greater muzzle blast and flash than the .50-caliber Browning. Ammo for the .50 BMG is well developed and much cheaper than 20mm ammo, and this has allowed the .50 BMG to persist in inventory since the cartridge first came on line in 1921. Browning machine guns of all types are noted for their reliability, and the .50 BMG stands at the head of the class. Once the .50 BMGs are properly adjusted, they will fire without any serious problems. It is extremely rare to break any part on the .50 BMG. The .50 BMG is a heavy weapon to lug about. The tripod and the ammo are heavy. You do need strength to operate this weapon. A .50 BMG M2HB well dug in, well supplied with ammo, and operated by skilled people is a formidable tool.

M79/M203

Caliber: 40 mm   **Manufacturer:** Colt and others   **Typical Use:** Military

When I was first in the Army, a 40mm grenade launcher was found in each rifle squad in the form of the M79. It was a single-barrel break-open weapon. It is rifled in bore firing a 40mm explosive grenade at low velocity. Felt recoil was about like a twenty-gauge shotgun. The weapon was quite accurate. If you used it with the butt placed firmly on the ground and had an assistant, you could get ten grenades in the air before the first one hit. The major drawback was that the radius for the fragments thrown out was only five meters but you could strike a target much farther away than with a hand grenade. After a while, the M203 came out, and could be attached to your M16 rifle. The M203 is not as easy to shoot accurately as the M79, but you don't lose a rifleman just to get a 40mm grenade launcher as you do with the M79. It is far better to use the M203 than an M79, even though the M203 is not as fast on repeat shots.